SQ

CONNECTING
with our
SPIRITUAL INTELLIGENCE

Danah Zohar & Dr Ian Marshall

BLOOMSBURY

Published by Bloomsbury Publishing, New York and London.
Distributed to the trade by St. Martin's Press

A CIP catalogue record for this book
is available from the Library of Congress

ISBN 1-58234-044-7

First U.S. Edition 2000
10 9 8 7 6 5 4 3 2 1

Typeset by Hewer Text Ltd, Scotland
Printed in the United States of America by
R.R. Donnelley & Sons Company, Harrisonburg, Virginia

Diagrams by Kate Simunek
Ox drawings by Ilaira Bouratinos

ACKNOWLEDGEMENTS

In gratitude, I would like to thank Quentin Baer and Cambridge Management Consultants for their generous contribution to research and writing time for this book.

'Healing' from *The Complete Poems of D.H. Lawrence* by D.H. Lawrence, edited by V. de Sola Pinto, F.W. Roberts, copyright © 1964, 1971 by Angelo Ravagli and C.M. Weekley, Executors of the Estate of Frieda Lawrence Ravagli. Used by permission of Viking Penguin, a division of Penguin Putnam Inc., and Laurence Pollinger Ltd.

Lines from 'I think continually about those who were truly great' by Stephen Spender from *The Collected Poems*, and 'Little Gidding' from 'Four Quartets' by T.S. Eliot used by permission of Faber and Faber Limited.

Lines from Sonnet 4 from *Sonnets to Orpheus* by Rainer Maria Rilke, edited/translated by C.F. MacIntyre, copyright © 1960 by C.F. MacIntyre used by permission of the University of California Press.

Lines from *The Lord of the Rings* by J.R.R. Tolkien used by permission of HarperCollins Publishers.

Lines from *The Duino Elegies* by Rainer Maria Rilke, translated by Stephen Cohn, used by permission of Carcanet Press Limited.

Lines from *Gitanjali* by Rabindranath Tagore used by permission of Visva-Bharati, Publishing Department, Visva-Bharati University, Calcutta.

Lines from *Rilke on Love and Other Difficulties* by Rainer Maria Rilke, translated by J.J.L. Mood © 1975 used by permission of W.W.Norton & Co., New York.

To the memory of my father, Donald E. Logan,
Toledo, Ohio, 1919–81

AUTHORS' NOTE

Although this book is written in the first person by Danah Zohar, its contents are the joint work of the authors

CONTENTS

CONTENTS

Part IV: Using SQ

Part V: Can We Improve Our SQ?

It doesn't interest me what you do for a living.

I want to know what you ache for, and if you dare to dream of
    meeting
your heart's longing.

It doesn't interest me how old you are.

I want to know if you will risk looking like a fool for love, for dreams,
for the adventure of being alive.

It doesn't interest me what planets are squaring your moon.

I want to know if you have touched the center of your own sorrow, if
you have been opened by life's betrayals or have become shriveled
    and closed
from fear of further pain! I want to know if you can sit with pain,
    mine
        or your own, without moving to hide it or fade it or fix it. I want
        to know if you can be with joy, mine or your own;
if you can dance with wildness and
let ecstasy fill you to the tips of your fingers and toes without
    cautioning us to be careful, be realistic, or to remember the
limitations of being a human.

It doesn't interest me if the story you're telling me is true.

I want to know if you can disappoint another to be true to yourself;
    if you
can bear the accusation of betrayal and not betray your own soul.
I want to know if you can be faithful and therefore trustworthy. I
    want to know if you can see beauty even if it's not pretty every day,
        and if you can
source your life from God's presence. I want to know if you can live
    with failure, yours and mine, and still stand on the edge of a
    lake and shout to the silver moon, 'Yes!'

It doesn't interest me where you live or how much money you have.

I want to know if you can get up after the night of grief and despair,
    weary, bruised to the bone, and do what needs to be done for the
    children.

It doesn't interest me who you are, how you came to be here.

I want to know if you will stand in the center of the fire with me
and not shrink back.

It doesn't interest me where or what or with whom you have studied.

I want to know what sustains you from the inside, when all else falls
    away.
I want to know if you can be alone with yourself; and if you truly
like the company you keep in the empty moments.

The Invitation, inspired by Oriah Mountain Dreamer,
Native American Elder, May 1994[1]

Part I

WHAT IS SQ?

1. INTRODUCING SQ

In the early part of the twentieth century, IQ became the big issue. Our intellectual or rational intelligence is what we use to solve logical or strategic problems. Psychologists devised tests for measuring it, and these tests became the means for sorting people into degrees of intelligence, known as their intelligence quotient or IQ, that could allegedly signpost their abilities. The higher a person's IQ, the theory went, the higher their intelligence.

In the mid-1990s, Daniel Goleman[1] popularized research from many neuroscientists and psychologists showing that emotional intelligence – which, as a convenient shorthand, I term EQ – is of equal importance. EQ gives us our awareness of our own and other people's feelings. It gives us empathy, compassion, motivation and the ability to respond appropriately to pain or pleasure. As Goleman pointed out, EQ is a basic requirement for the effective use of IQ. If the brain areas with which we *feel* are damaged, we *think* less effectively.

Now, at the end of the century, an array of recent but so far undigested scientific data shows us that there is a third 'Q'. The full picture of human intelligence can be completed with a discussion of our spiritual intelligence – SQ for short. By SQ I mean the intelligence with which we address and solve problems of meaning and value, the intelligence with which

3

we can place our actions and our lives in a wider, richer, meaning-giving context, the intelligence with which we can assess that one course of action or one life-path is more meaningful than another. SQ is the necessary foundation for the effective functioning of both IQ and EQ. It is our ultimate intelligence.

In his book *Multiple Intelligences*, Harvard's Howard Gardner argues there are at least seven kinds of intelligence, including musical, spatial and sporting as well as rational and emotional. But I will argue in this book that all our possibly infinite intelligences can be linked to one of three basic neural systems in the brain, and that all of the intelligences Gardner describes are actually variations of the basic IQ, EQ and SQ and their associated neural arrangements.

Webster's dictionary defines spirit as 'the animating or vital principle; that which gives life to the physical organism in contrast to its material elements; the breath of life'. Human beings are essentially spiritual creatures because we are driven by a need to ask 'fundamental' or 'ultimate' questions. Why was I born? What is the meaning of my life? Why should I go on when I am tired, or depressed, or feel beaten? What makes it all worth while? We are driven, indeed we are defined, by a specifically human longing to find meaning and value in what we do and experience. We have a longing to see our lives in some larger, meaning-giving context, whether this is the family, the community, a football club, our life's work, our religious framework or the universe itself. We have a longing for something towards which we can aspire, for something that takes us beyond ourselves and the present moment, for something that gives us and our actions a sense of worth. Some anthropologists and neurobiologists argue that it is this longing for meaning, and the evolutionary value it confers, that first brought human beings out of the trees some two million years ago. The need for meaning, they say, gave rise to the symbolic imagination, to the evolution of language, and to the extraordinary growth of the human brain.[2]

Neither IQ nor EQ, separately or in combination, is enough to explain the full complexity of human intelligence nor the vast richness of the human soul and imagination. Computers have high IQ: they know what the rules are and can follow them without making mistakes. Animals often have high EQ: they have a sense of the situation they are in and know how to respond appropriately. But neither computers nor animals ask *why* we have these rules or this situation, or whether either could be different or better. They work *within* boundaries, playing a 'finite game'. SQ allows human beings to be creative, to change the rules and to alter situations. It allows us to play *with* the boundaries, to play an 'infinite game'.[3] SQ gives us our ability to discriminate. It gives us our moral sense, an ability to temper rigid rules with understanding and compassion and an equal ability to see when compassion and understanding have their limits. We use SQ to wrestle with questions of good and evil and to envision unrealized possibilities – to dream, to aspire, to raise ourselves out of the mud.

It is in its transformative power that SQ differs mainly from EQ. As Daniel Goleman defines it, my emotional intelligence allows me to judge what situation I am in and then to behave appropriately within it. This is working *within* the boundaries of the situation, allowing the situation to guide *me*. But my spiritual intelligence allows me to ask if I want to be in this particular situation in the first place. Would I rather change the situation, creating a better one? This is working *with* the boundaries of my situation, allowing me to guide the *situation*.

Finally, because as we shall see when we look at the neurological basis of SQ, it literally operates out of the brain's centre – from the brain's neurological unifying functions – it

integrates *all* our intelligences. SQ makes us the fully intellectual, emotional and spiritual creatures that we are.

Ideally, our three basic intelligences work together and
support one another. Our brains are designed so that they can
do this. But each of them – IQ, EQ and SQ – has its own area
of strength, and they can function separately. That is, we
aren't necessarily high or low in all three simultaneously. One
needn't be high in IQ or SQ to be high in EQ. One could be
high in IQ but low in both EQ and SQ, and so on.

THREE PSYCHOLOGICAL PROCESSES

The whole of Western psychology rests on two processes. SQ
introduces a third, and thus calls for an expansion of psychology as a science and for an expanded understanding of the
human self.

Freud initially defined the two psychological processes as
primary and secondary. The primary process is associated with
the id, with instincts, the body, emotions and the unconscious. The secondary process is associated with the ego, with
conscious, rational mind. For Freud, the secondary process
was higher and superior: 'Where Id was, there Ego shall be.'
Others, after Freud, sometimes emphasized the greater importance of the primary process. But all of subsequent psychology, including cognitive science, has kept this two-
process structure. The primary process could be called EQ
(based on 'associative neural wiring' in the brain), the secondary IQ (based on 'serial neural wiring' in the brain).

Based as it is on these two processes, Western psychology
effectively places a hole at the centre of the self. The primary
and secondary processes vie with each other for control and
expression. Neither reason nor the emotions can appeal to
anything beyond themselves. They have no further common
source through which they can be integrated and transformed.

6

They have no transpersonal dimension. The Jungian 'self', or the Jungian 'transcendental function', was an attempt to bridge this divide, but neurology was insufficiently developed in Jung's lifetime (he died in 1961) to offer him a scientific basis for his further psychology.

SQ (based on the brain's third neural system, the synchronous neural oscillations that unify data across the whole brain) offers us a viable tertiary process for the first time. This process unifies, integrates and has the potential to transform material arising from the other two processes. It facilitates a dialogue between reason and emotion, between mind and body. It provides a fulcrum for growth and transformation. It provides the self with an active, unifying, meaning-giving centre.

THE LOTUS OF THE SELF

The discovery that SQ gives psychology a tertiary process requires the development of a new psychological model of the human self and of human personality. Previous models have had two 'layers': the outer, conscious, rational personality and the inner, largely unconscious associations, motivations, neuroses and so on. The tertiary process introduces a third layer, a central core.

In this book, the self is presented as a lotus with six petals. The outer layer of each petal represents the ego, distributed among the six possible personality types or functions recognized by many psychologists. I shall rely principally on three extensively researched sources: J.F. Holland's work on career guidance and six personality types; Jung's six types as used in Myers–Briggs (introversion, extroversion, thinking, feeling, sensation, intuition); and Cattell's work on motivation.

Each of us would find the main aspects of our conscious personalities distributed among the petals of the lotus. Deeper

7

in, each petal has its primary process layer, its unconscious and partly bodily associations, motivations and so forth. At the deepest part of this unconscious layer lies the collective unconscious with its archetypes, as described by Jung. At the centre of the lotus is the tertiary layer, the core of the self from which we draw the energy and potential to transform. The six petals of the lotus and its centre also correspond to the seven chakras described by Hinduism's Kundalini yoga, and to many other mystical and mythological structures found within Buddhism, ancient Greece, Jewish cabalistic thought and the Christian sacraments.

Using the model of the lotus with its six petals/personality types, we can discuss six ways to be spiritually stunted and six ways to be spiritually intelligent. This gives readers a map on which to find their own personality, their own strengths and weakness, and their own best path to growth and transformation.

SQ IS NOT ABOUT BEING RELIGIOUS

The major issue on people's minds today is meaning. Many writers say the need for greater meaning is the central crisis of our times. I sense this when I travel abroad each month, addressing audiences from countries and cultures all over the world. Wherever I go, when people get together over a drink or a meal, the subject turns to God, meaning, vision, values, spiritual longing. Many people today have achieved an unprecedented level of material well-being, yet they feel they want more. Many speak of an emptiness 'here', pointing to their abdomens. This 'more' that would fill the emptiness seldom has any connection with formal religion. Indeed, most people seeking some spiritual fulfilment see no relation between their longing and formal religion.

SQ has no necessary connection to religion. For some

people, SQ may find a mode of expression through formal religion, but being religious doesn't guarantee high SQ. Many humanists and atheists have very high SQ; many actively and vociferously religious people have very low SQ. Some studies done by the psychologist Gordon Allport fifty years ago showed that more people have religious experiences *outside* the confines of mainstream religious institutions than within them.

Conventional religion is an externally imposed set of rules and beliefs. It is top-down, inherited from priests and prophets and holy books, or absorbed through the family and tradition. SQ, as described in this book, is an *internal*, innate ability of the human brain and psyche, drawing its deepest resources from the heart of the universe itself. It is a facility developed over millions of years that allows the brain to find and use meaning in the solution of problems. The rapid changes in the Western world over the past three centuries have left conventional religions struggling to be meaningful. We now have to use our innate SQ to forge new paths, to find some fresh expression of meaning, something that *touches* us and that can guide us from within.

Spiritual intelligence is the soul's intelligence. It is the intelligence with which we heal ourselves and with which we make ourselves whole. So many of us today live lives of wounded fragmentation. We long for what the poet T. S. Eliot called 'a further union, a deeper communion',[4] but we find little resource within our ego-bound selves or within the existing symbols or institutions of our culture. SQ is the intelligence that rests in that deep part of the self that is connected to wisdom from beyond the ego, or conscious mind, it is the intelligence with which we not only recognize existing values, but with which we creatively discover new values. SQ is not culture-dependent or value-dependent. It does not follow *from* existing values but rather *creates* the very possibility of having values in the first place. Throughout human history, every known culture has had *some* set of values, though the specific values differ from culture to culture. SQ is, thus, prior to all specific values and to any given culture. It is also, therefore, prior to any form of religious expression that it might take. SQ makes religion possible (perhaps even necessary), but SQ does not depend upon religion.

The thirteenth-century Sufi mystic poet Rumi might have been thinking about this relation between SQ, values and religion when he spoke the following words:

> I am not a Christian, I am not a Jew, I am not a Zoroastrian,
> I am not even a Muslim.
> I do not belong to the land, or to any known or
>   unknown sea.
> Nature cannot own or claim me, nor can heaven.
> Nor can India, China, Bulgaria,
> My birthplace is placelessness,
> My sign to have and give no sign.
> You say you see my mouth, ears, nose – they are not
>   mine.
> I am the life of life.
> I am that cat, this stone, no one.
> I have thrown duality away like an old dishrag.
> I see and know all times and worlds,
> As one, one, always one.
> So what do I have to do to get you to admit who is
>   speaking?
> Admit it and change everything!
> This is your own voice echoing off the walls of God.[5]

What I am calling SQ, or spiritual intelligence, here is the voice echoing off the walls of Rumi's God. As we go further together in this book, we will see there is little difference.

SCIENTIFIC EVIDENCE FOR SQ

SQ is an ability as old as humanity, but the concept is only developed fully for the first time in this book. So far, science and scientific psychology have been at a loss to discuss meaning and its role in our lives. Spiritual intelligence has been awkward for academics because existing science is not equipped to study things that can't objectively be measured.

A great deal of scientific evidence for SQ does exist, however, in recent neurological, psychological and anthropological studies of human intelligence and is studies of human thinking and linguistic processes. Scientists have already done most of the basic research revealing the neural foundations of SQ in the brain, but the dominating IQ paradigm has overshadowed further inquiry into their own data. This book will bring together four specific streams of research that have so far remained separate owing to the highly specialized nature of existing science.

First, in the early 1990s research was carried out by neuropsychologist Michael Persinger, and more recently, in 1997, by neurologist V.S. Ramachandran and his team at the University of California, on the existence of a 'God spot' in the human brain. This built-in spiritual centre is located among neural connections in the temporal lobes of the brain. On scans taken with positron emission topography these neural areas light up whenever research subjects are exposed to discussion of spiritual or religious topics. These vary with cultures, Westerners responding to mention of 'God', Buddhists and others responding to symbols meaningful to them. Such temporal lobe activity has been linked for years to the mystical visions of epileptics and people who take LSD. Ramachandran's work is the first to show it active in normal people. The 'God spot' does not prove the existence of God, but it does show that the brain has evolved to ask 'ultimate questions', to have and to use a sensitivity to wider meaning and value.

Second, the work of Austrian neurologist Wolf Singer in the 1990s on 'the binding problem' shows that there is a neural process in the brain devoted to unifying and giving meaning to our experience – a neural process that literally 'binds' our experience together. Before Singer's work on unifying, synchronous neural oscillations across the whole brain, neurologists and cognitive scientists only recognized two forms of brain neural organization.

One of these forms, serial neural connections, is the basis of our IQ. Serially connected neural tracts allow the brain to follow rules, to think logically and rationally, step-by-step. In the second form, neural network organization, bundles of up to a hundred thousand neurones are connected in haphazard fashion to other massive bundles. These neural networks are the basis of EQ, our emotion-driven, pattern-recognizing, habit-building intelligence. Both serial and parallel computers exist and have different abilities, but neither kind can operate with meaning. No existing computer can ask 'Why?' Singer's work on unifying neural oscillations offers the first hint of a third kind of thinking, unitive thinking, and an accompanying third mode of intelligence, SQ, that can deal with such questions.

Third, as a development of Singer's work, Rodolfo Llinas's mid-1990s work on sleeping and waking consciousness and the binding of cognitive events in the brain has been greatly enhanced by new MEG (magneto-encephalographic) technology allowing whole-skull studies of the brain's oscillating electrical fields and their associated magnetic fields.

Fourth, Harvard neurologist and biological anthropologist Terrance Deacon has recently published new work on the origins of human language (*The Symbolic Species*, 1997). Deacon shows that language is a uniquely human, essentially symbolic, meaning-centred activity that co-evolved with rapid development in the brain's frontal lobes. Neither existing computers nor even higher apes (with rare and limited exception) can use language, because they lack the frontal lobe facility for dealing with meaning. This book will show that Deacon's whole research programme for the evolution of symbolic imagination and its consequent role in brain and social evolution underpins the intelligence faculty we are calling SQ.

USING SQ

In evolutionary terms, Deacon's neurobiological work on language and symbolic representation shows that we have used SQ literally to grow our human brains. SQ has 'wired' us to become the people we are and gives us the potential for further 'rewiring' – for growth and transformation, for further evolution of our human potential.

We use SQ to be creative. We call upon it when we need to be flexible, visionary or creatively spontaneous.

We use SQ to deal with existential problems – problems where we feel personally stuck, trapped by our own past habits or neuroses or problems with illness and grief. SQ makes us aware that we have existential problems, and it enables us to solve them – or at least to find peace about them. It gives us a 'deep' sense of what life's struggles are about.

SQ is our compass 'at the edge'. Life's most challenging existential problems exist outside the expected and the familiar, outside the given rules, beyond past experience, beyond what we know how to handle. In chaos theory, 'the edge' is the border between order and chaos, between knowing comfortably what we are about and being totally lost. It is the place where we can be at our most creative. SQ, our deep, intuitive sense of meaning and value, is our guide at the edge. SQ is our conscience. (In Hebrew, the words for 'conscience', 'compass' and 'the hidden, inner truth of the soul' all have the same root.)

We can use SQ to become more spiritually intelligent about religion. SQ takes us to the heart of things, to the unity behind difference, to the potential beyond any actual expression. SQ can put us in touch with the meaning and essential spirit behind all great religions. A person high in SQ might practise any religion, but without narrowness, exclusiveness, bigotry or prejudice. Equally, a person high in SQ could have very spiritual qualities without being religious at all.

SQ allows us to integrate the intrapersonal and the interpersonal, to transcend the gap between self and other. Daniel Goleman wrote about intrapersonal, or within-the-self, emotions and interpersonal emotions – those we share with others or use to relate to others. But mere EQ cannot help us to bridge the gap. It takes SQ to have an understanding of who we are and what things mean to us, and how these give others and their meanings a place in our own world.

We use SQ to reach more fully towards the developed persons that we have the potential to be. Each of us forms a character through a combination of experience and vision, a tension between what we actually do and the bigger, better things that we might do. On the pure ego level we are I-centred, selfish, materially ambitious, and so on. But we do have transpersonal visions of goodness, beauty, perfection, generosity, sacrifice and so on. SQ helps us to outgrow our immediate ego selves and to reach beyond to those deeper layers of potentiality that lie hidden within us. It helps us to live life at a deeper level of meaning.

And finally, we can use our SQ to wrestle with problems of good and evil, problems of life and death, the deepest origins of human suffering and often despair. Too often we try to rationalize such problems away, or else we become emotionally swamped or devastated by them. To come into full possession of our spiritual intelligence we have at some time to have seen the face of hell, to have known the possibility of despair, pain, deep suffering and loss, and to have made our peace with these. 'When you are at one with loss,' says the ancient Chinese text known a the *Tao Te Ching*, 'the loss is experienced willingly.' We have to have longed deeply, in the bowels of our being, for a meaning that will touch us, for the intimation of something fresh, something pure, something enlivening. In such longing we may hope to find that for which we long, and we may share the fruits of that creative discovery with others. The twentieth-century Jewish mystic Rabbi Abraham Heschel said, 'We are closer to God when we are asking questions than when we think we have the answers.'[6] In the same vein, the seventeenth-century French philosopher mystic Blaise Pascal wrote in God's name, 'You would not be seeking me unless you had already found me.'

TESTING FOR SQ

The indications of a highly developed SQ include:

☐ the capacity to be flexible (actively and spontaneously adaptive)
☐ a high degree of self-awareness
☐ a capacity to face and use suffering
☐ a capacity to face and transcend pain
☐ the quality of being inspired by vision and values
☐ a reluctance to cause unnecessary harm
☐ a tendency to see the connections between diverse things (being 'holistic')
☐ a marked tendency to ask 'Why?' or 'What if?' questions and to seek 'fundamental' answers
☐ being what psychologists call 'field-independent' – possessing a facility for working against convention

A person high in SQ is also likely to be a servant leader – someone who is responsible for bringing higher vision and value to others and showing them how to use it, in other words a person who inspires others. This book will pose questions through which readers can assess their own SQ, and will discuss some famous people who are high and low in SQ.

IMPROVING SQ

Collective SQ is low in modern society. We live in a spiritually dumb culture characterized by materialism, expediency, narrow self-centredness, lack of meaning and dearth of commitment. But as individuals we can act to raise our personal SQ – indeed, the further evolution of society depends upon enough individuals doing so. In general, we can raise our SQ by raising our use of the tertiary process – our tendency to ask why, to look for the connections between things, to bring to the surface the assumptions we have been making about the meaning behind and within things, to become more reflective, to reach beyond ourselves a little, to take responsibility, to become more self-aware, to be more honest with ourselves and more courageous.

The book finishes with a chapter on how to be spiritually intelligent in a spiritually dumb culture. Western-type culture, wherever it is found on the globe, is awash with the immediate, the material, the selfish manipulation of things and experience and others. We misuse our relationships and our environment just as we misuse our own deepest human meanings. We suffer a dreadful poverty of the symbolic imagination. We ignore the human qualities and concentrate on ever more frenzied doing, on acts of 'getting and spending'. We dreadfully neglect the sublime and the sacred within ourselves and others and our world. As American playwright John Guare writes in *Six Degrees of Separation*:

One of the great tragedies of our times is the death of the imagination. Because what else is paralysis?

I believe that the imagination is the passport we create to take us into the real world. [It] is another phrase for what is most uniquely us.

To face ourselves. That's the hard thing. The imagination [is] God's gift to make the act of self examination bearable. [It] teaches us our limits and how to grow beyond our limits . . . the imagination is the place we are all trying to get to . . .[7]

Through a more cultivated use of our spiritual intelligence, and through the personal honesty and courage that such cultivation requires, we can reconnect with the deeper sources and deeper meanings within ourselves, and we can use that reconnection to serve causes and processes much larger than ourselves. In such service we may find our salvation. Our deepest salvation may lie in serving our own deep imagination.

2. THE CRISIS OF MEANING

Man's search for meaning is the primary motivation in his
life and not a 'secondary rationalization' of instinctual
drives. This meaning is unique and specific in that it must
and can be fulfilled by him alone; only then does it
achieve a significance which will satisfy his own *will* to
meaning.
Viktor Frankl, *Man's Search for Meaning*

One of the most profound new insights of twentieth-century
science is that wholes can be greater than the sum of their
parts. The whole contains a richness, a perspective, a dimen-
sionality not possessed by the parts. So the whole is not just a
larger quantity, but has added quality too.

Here science helps us to understand the spiritual. As the
concept is used in this book, to experience 'the spiritual'
means to be in touch with some larger, deeper, richer whole
that puts our present limited situation into a new perspective.
It is to have a sense of 'something beyond', of 'something
more' that confers added meaning and value on where we are
now. That spiritual 'something more' may be a deeper social
reality or social web of meaning. It may be an awareness of
or attunement to the mythological, archetypal or religious
dimensions of our situation. It may be a sense of some more

profound level of truth or beauty. And/or it may be an attunement to some deeper, cosmic sense of wholeness, a sense that our actions are part of some greater universal process.

Whatever our specific sense of the spiritual, without it our vision is clouded, our lives feel flat and our purposes dreadfully finite. As the poet William Blake wrote, 'If the doors of perception were cleansed, everything would appear to us as it is, infinite.'

As Viktor Frankl says, our search for meaning is the primary motivation in our lives. It is this search that makes us the spiritual creatures that we are. And it is when this deep need for meaning goes unmet that our lives come to feel shallow or empty. For a great many of us today this need is not met, and the fundamental crisis of our times is a spiritual one.

Very recently I received an urgent e-mail from a senior business executive in Sweden asking to meet me on my next visit to Stockholm. He said that he had to make a major decision about the future direction of his life, and hoped we could discuss it together. When we did meet, he was nervous and intense, wanting to get straight to the point.

'Anders', as I shall call him, told me that he was in his mid-thirties. 'I am,' he said, 'managing a large and successful company here in Sweden. I have good health, I have a wonderful family, position in the community. I suppose I have "power". But still I'm not certain what I'm doing with my life. I'm not certain I am on the right path doing the job that I do.' He continued that he was very worried about the state of the world, especially the state of the global environment and the breakdown of community, and said he felt people were avoiding the real scale of the problems facing them. Big businesses like his, he felt, were especially guilty of not facing such problems. 'I want to do something about it,' he continued, 'want, if you like, to use my life to

19

serve, but I don't know how. I just know that I want to be part of the solution. Not the problem.'

Anders described his own unrest as a 'spiritual problem', and himself as going through a 'spiritual crisis'. It is a typical one today amongst sensitive young people. When I told Anders' story the next day to a group of business executives to whom I'd been asked to give a lecture, four of them came up to me separately afterwards and asked, 'How did you know my story?' Later in the day, a group of Swedish high school students who were interviewing me raised the same question about their own futures. 'We want to serve. We want to change the world. We don't want to repeat the crap that your generation has dumped on us. What can we do? Do we join the system, or stay outside?' Nothing to do with belief or religion, these young people describe themselves as having a spiritual problem because they wonder how to lead mean-ingful lives. They long to live their lives within some larger context of meaning and value. They have what Viktor Frankl calls a *will* to meaning, yet they feel that will frustrated in today's world.

The search for meaning is evident in so many aspects of our lives. What is my life all about? What does my job mean? This company I have founded or work for? This relationship? Why am I studying for this degree? What does it mean to be me? What does it mean that I am going to die some day? Why commit myself to one thing or another, to one person or another – or to anything? Two of the top ten causes of death in the Western world, suicide and alcoholism, are frequently related to this kind of crisis of meaning.

People living in earlier societies would not even have asked such questions. Their lives were culturally embedded in a set framework. They had living traditions, living gods, living communities, functioning moral codes, problems that had known boundaries and fixed goals. But in modern times we have lost what some philosophers call the 'taken-for-grant-edness' of life. We are left with existential or spiritual problems, and with the need to cultivate a kind of intelligence that can deal with them. Mere IQ or rational intelligence isn't enough. The reasons people seek for living their lives are not rational ones; nor are they purely emotional ones. It isn't enough for people to find happiness within their existing framework. They want to question the framework itself, to question the value of how they are living their lives, and to find new value, that elusive 'more'. Just by asking such questions they are showing a need to use their spiritual intelligence.

What is this 'more' that people seek, and why do we need spiritual intelligence to find it? Why do we say that meaning is the fundamental issue of our times? Have the times changed, or have people's needs grown, or has intelligence itself entered a new stage of evolution? These are some of the questions we need urgently to consider.

In my own life meaning has always been a burning issue because there was never any obvious, *given* meaning. My parents were separated before I was three and divorced by the time I was five. I never knew my father or his working-class, Polish immigrant family. I spent my early years with grandparents whose lives were embedded in a timeless rural culture and a traditional religion, but to my mother and her contemporaries these were meaningless forms to be clung to to 'impress the neighbours'. My mother taught me rules that she didn't follow and gave me reasons in which she didn't believe. I grew up in an America going through McCarthyism and headed towards Vietnam. The national leaders who spoke of ideals and values and who were my heroes were assassinated: JFK, Martin Luther King and Bobby Kennedy.

We were a comfortable middle-class family, but my stepfather drifted from job to job and into and out of extra-marital affairs, while my highly intelligent mother took pills 'so I don't have to think too much'. Later, she committed suicide so as not to have to think at all. There were few close relatives in my later childhood, most having moved to other cities or other states, and the neighbours were equally mobile. I attended six different schools. I sought roots first in my grandparents' religion, then in others, but a lifetime's exploration has never found me satisfied with any formal religion. Like Anders, all my adult life I have sought some meaning, some way to live or some vision to live by that could put my actions, my parenting and my work in some larger framework.

My story is not atypical. Our modern age is defined by such things as the breakdown of family and community and traditional religion, and the loss or absence of heroes, and peopled by young humans trying to make sense of them. We live at a time when there are no clear goalposts, no clear rules, no clear values, no clear way to grow up, no clear vision of responsibility.

We lack an overall context for our lives, a natural flow of meaning of which we can simply be a part. In many ways this spiritual desert has come about as a product of our high human IQ. We have reasoned ourselves away from nature and our fellow creatures, and we have reasoned ourselves beyond religion. In our great technological leap forward, we have left traditional culture with its embedded values behind. Our IQ has diminished labour, increased wealth and longevity and invented countless trinkets, some of which threaten to destroy both us and our environment. But we haven't found a way to make it all worthwhile.

Modern culture is spiritually dumb, not only in the West but also, increasingly, in those Asian countries influenced by the West. By 'spiritually dumb' I mean we have lost our sense of fundamental values – those attached to the earth and its seasons, to the day and its passing hours, to the implements and daily rituals of our lives, to the body and its changes, to sex, to labour and its fruits, to the stages of life, and to death as a natural ending. We see and use and experience only the immediate, the visible and the pragmatic. We are blind to the deeper levels of symbol and meaning that place our objects, our activities and ourselves in a larger existential framework. We are not colour-blind, but meaning-blind. How did we get this way?

THE MISSING MIDDLE

While I have been writing this book, our family has spent a month at Christmas each year in Nepal. This magical time in a pre-modern Hindu and Buddhist culture so rich in colour, sound, scent and meaning has deeply affected us all. It has certainly influenced many of the thoughts I express through-out the book. Being young and romantic, our teenage children have been ready to trade all their Western wealth and comfort for Nepalese poverty. 'Let us never go home!' they plead at the end of each visit. My own and my husband's reactions have been more complex.

Nepalese society embraces things that are missing at home – strong local communities and extended families, living spiri-tual traditions shared by the whole culture, the spontaneity and urgency of daily life and the symbolic richness of daily dressing, eating, living and dying, the care and awe devoted to the design of everyday implements like eating bowls and rickshaws, the simple, repetitive pattern of everyday life, seasonal crops and festivals. But we know that these are not features of our culture. Nepal is deeply spiritual (filled with over-arching meaning) because its daily life is embedded in a cultural spiritual richness. But it is not our culture, nor is it the culture of any likely future.

The few surviving traditional cultures like Nepal belong to an earlier stage of human consciousness. I call them 'associative cultures' because their habits and values are underpinned by the style of thinking called 'associative thinking' – habit-bound and tradition-bound, it thrives on recognition and repetition of familiar patterns (there will be more on that in Chapter 3). I also call them cultures of the 'healthy middle', because their strengths and weaknesses are those of the self's middle layer, the layer that Freud called the 'primary process' or that Ken Wilber calls 'prepersonal', and that I place in the middle layer of the Lotus of the Self, along with mythological images and Jung's archetypes of the unconscious.

In the lotus image used throughout this book, the self has an ego (rational) periphery, an associative (emotional) middle and a unitive (spiritual) centre. A well-balanced, spiritually intelligent self needs something of each layer. But in traditional societies – both those in the West that preceded Descartes and the beginning of the Age of Reason in the seventeenth century and those today in the so-called undeveloped world like Nepal – the centre, the inspiring, energy-giving, meaning-giving, unifying spiritual level of existence, is held in the middle layer. The traditions of the community encapsulate deeper spiritual insights and values, so that the individual relates to the spiritual centre *through* his culture and its traditions. He does not have to relate directly to the centre on his own, as an individual.

Few of the craftsmen who built the great European cathedrals of the Middle Ages, for instance, consciously knew the principles of sacred architecture, but absorbed them as they learned their craft. Few medieval peasants had to consider the meaning of life or the meaning of their work because these were embedded in the necessities and traditions of daily life. Defining his personal values to me, a young member of a traditional tribe in Nigeria said, 'They are the things handed down to me by my parents. I build on them, but the core doesn't change.' The whole of life in those traditional societies was or is less conscious, or at least less self-conscious, than our own today. Just as when we drive a car or ride a bicycle we don't think consciously of our every move, so in societies with a healthy middle layer people rely on spiritual values, webs of meaning and habits of relationship that are skills of the community.

That shared community simply does not exist for most urban people in today's world. We are deeply undernourished in that whole associative, middle layer of the self. We have few collective traditions that point beyond the prosaic, every-day level of life, that ground us in the deeper origin and meaning of our communities and of our life within them. We have few 'gods' and 'goddesses', collective heroes whose lives exemplify some deeper layer of human possibility or aspiration and touch our own with a sense of grace. The global mourning that followed the death of Diana, Princess of Wales, exposed the extent and depth of our need for such figures. Hers was a life that exemplified a spontaneity, a warmth, a quality of love, a vulnerability that we long to contact through some collective symbol or icon.

In the absence or poverty of this healthy associative middle, we are left to find or create our own meanings, or just to feel their loss. Too often we have sought to compensate with an overblown importance of our own individual selves, lives, ambitions and perceived needs. We have looked to the ego layer of the self for resources it does not possess. Deprived of the deep, meaningful centre that was held and mediated by the middle, we are caught on the fragmented periphery of life, isolated on the outer petals of the Lotus. As a result, too often we seek meaning in distorted or peripheral activities like materialism, promiscuous sex, pointless rebellion, violence, drug abuse or New Age occultism.

THE ROLE OF SCIENCE

In the West, traditional culture and all the meanings and values that it preserved began to unravel as a result of the seventeenth-century scientific revolution and the accompanying rise of individualism and rationalism. The thinking of Isaac Newton and his colleagues gave rise not only to the technology which led to the Industrial Revolution but also to a deeper erosion of the religious beliefs and philosophical outlook that had hitherto underpinned society. The new technology provided many blessings but also moved people from the land into big cities, disrupted communities and families, displaced traditions and crafts, and made reliance on habit and repetition virtually impossible. Associative meanings and values were uprooted from the soil in which they had grown. The accompanying philosophical revolution has uprooted the human soul.

The most central tenets of Newtonian philosophy can be captured in the words 'atomism', 'determinism' and 'objectivity'. Although they sound abstract and remote, the concepts that these words represent have touched us at the centre of our being.

Atomism is the view that the world ultimately consists of fragments – particles, each isolated in space and time. Atoms are hard, impenetrable things with hard-and-fast boundaries: they cannot get inside each other, but relate instead through action and reaction. They push each other about or seek ways to avoid each other. John Locke, the eighteenth-century founder of liberal democracy, used atoms as his model for individuals, the basic units of society. The social whole, he asserted, was an illusion; the rights and needs of the individual were primary. Atomism is also the cornerstone of Sigmund Freud's view of psychology and his 'Theory of Object Relations'.

26

According to that theory, each of us is isolated within the impenetrable boundaries of the ego. You are an object to me and I am just an object to you. We can never know each other in any fundamental way. Love and intimacy are impossible. 'The commandment to love thy neighbour as thyself,' Freud said, 'is the most impossible commandment ever written.' The whole world of values, he believed, was a mere projection of the superego, the expectations of parents and society. Such values placed an impossible burden on the ego and made us ill, which he termed 'neurotic'. A thoroughly modern person, according to Freud, would be liberated from such unreasonable expectation and follow such principles as every man for himself, survival of the fittest and the fastest, and so on.

Newtonian determinism taught that the physical world is governed by iron laws: the three laws of motion and the law of gravitation. Everything in the physical world is predictable and thus ultimately controllable. B will always follow A in the same circumstances. There can be no surprises. Freud took this determinism, too, into his new 'scientific psychology', stating that the helpless ego is pushed about from below by the dark forces of instinct and aggression in the id, and pressured from above by the impossible expectations of the superego. Our experiences and behaviour throughout life are fully determined by these conflicting forces and by the experience of our first five years. We are the victims of our experience, hapless bystanders in a script written by others. Sociology and the modern legal system have reinforced this feeling.

Although the majority of the population may know little of Newtonian determinism or of Freud's id and superego, the notion that we are isolated, passive victims of forces larger than ourselves, that we are helpless to change our own lives, never mind the world, is endemic. We feel concerned, but we don't know how to take responsibility. A man in his early twenties told me, 'I have become overwhelmed by the confusing fragmentation of the world, and being unable to make sense of it or to do anything about it, I have lapsed into apathy and depression.'

Newtonian objectivity, or 'objectivism' as I prefer to call it, has reinforced this sense of isolation and helplessness. In founding his new scientific method Newton drew a sharp split between the observer (the scientist) and what he observes. The world is divided into subjects and objects: the subject is 'in here', the world 'out there'. The Newtonian scientist is a detached observer who simply looks at his world, weighs and measures it and performs experiments on it. He manipulates and controls nature.

The average modern person experiences himself or herself as just *in* the world – not *of* the world. In this context 'the world' includes other people, even would-be intimates, as well as institutions, society, objects, nature and the environment. Newton's observer/observed split has left us with a sense that we are just here, to do the best for ourselves that we can. Again, it leaves us not knowing how to take responsibility, with little sense of whom or what we might be responsible for. We don't own our relationships, don't know how to own our possible effectiveness.

And finally, the cosmos as portrayed by Newtonian science is cold, dead and mechanical. There is no place in Newton's physics for mind or consciousness, no place for any aspect of the human struggle. Paradoxically, the biological and social sciences developed in the nineteenth and twentieth centuries bought into this mechanism, portraying human beings, human minds and human bodies in this same mechanical paradigm. We are mind–machines or gene–machines, our bodies are a collection of parts, our behaviour is conditioned and predictable, our souls an illusion of archaic religious language, our thinking the mere activity of cells in our brains. Where can we find the meaning of our human experience in this picture?

'DISEASES OF MEANING'

One of the commonest ways by which we meaning-deprived people seek wholeness is an obsession with health. The two words have the same Germanic root: to be healthy is to be whole. And so we grab at every health fad, vitamin diet and fitness regime that we can crowd into our busy lives. Yet mainstream modern medicine is very Newtonian. It sees the body as a mechanism, a well-oiled gene machine; disease as something to be eradicated or 'cured'; ageing and death as 'faults' or 'enemies' of the system.

Some doctors and healthcare professionals, however, are starting to see disease differently. They regard it as a crying out of the body and its person for attention to something in our lives which, if left unattended, will lead to irrevocable damage or lasting physical, emotional, and/or spiritual distress and even death. It may be our attitudes or lifestyles that are causing the problem, rather than any chemical imbalances. In the words of doctors, patients, scientists and policymakers who in June 1999 attended an international meeting in Britain to explore these ideas, much of our suffering, even chronic physical conditions, consists of 'diseases of meaning'.[1] Cancer, heart disease, Alzheimer's and other dementias that may be preceded by depression, fatigue, alcoholism or drug abuse are evidence of the crisis of meaninglessness brought home to the very cells of our bodies. Ultimately death, too, is experienced with pain and terror because we have no meaningful context in which to place the natural ending of this life, no way to die with blessedness, peace or grace.

The conference delegates argued that the medical and scientific establishment increases the prevalence of diseases of meaning by ignoring the more complex origins of much illness. Instead, it chains itself to 'the medicalisation of disease – finding the "right" gene, designing the "right" drug to

block or eradicate the disturbance, while ignoring that many
of our pathologies are not primarily physical, but rather
spiritual and psycho-physical'. In his poem 'Healing' D. H.
Lawrence wrote:[2]

> I am not a mechanism, an assembly of various sections.
> And it is not because the mechanism is working
>   wrongly that I am ill.
> I am ill because of wounds to the soul, to the deep
>   emotional self
> and the wounds to the soul take a long, long time, only
>   time can help
> and patience, and a certain difficult repentance
> long, difficult repentance, realisation of life's mistake,
>   and freeing oneself
> from the endless repetition of this mistake
> which mankind at large has chosen to sanctify.

THREATS OF EXTINCTION

The technology of the twentieth century has introduced
another crisis of meaning. Previously, human beings knew
catastrophe and natural cataclysm, but as a species we could
always assume that human life, or life in general, would go on
for millions of years. The personal drama of each generation
was part of a larger process and flow of time. But since the
1940s we have lived first with the prospect of mass extinction
through nuclear warfare, and in more recent decades with the
added threat of ecological disaster.

It will be made increasingly clear throughout this book that,
in order for meaning to *have* meaning, it must have a framework or boundaries. When our boundaries are violated, we
feel outrage and take action. But when boundaries cease to
exist, we feel sheer horror: our experience loses all meaning

30

and we simply can't deal with it. The Nazi killing machines of the Second World War removed all boundaries on the scale of evil that human beings were willing to commit against each other, and as a result we have never really been able to grasp the scale of the Holocaust or come to terms with it. It is outside the context of human expectation and values. How much more so is the very real possibility that *all* life will cease in the foreseeable future.

Most of us don't think about these matters very much because we can't bear to. But threats of global extinction do affect the way we think and behave, throwing us back more on to more immediate concerns: 'Live today, there may never be another tomorrow.' We seek pleasure and satisfaction as though we were drinking in the Last Chance Saloon, we exploit our fellow humans and rape the earth even faster to ensure today's comfort, today's profit. Our whole time-frame shrinks, and with it the context of meaning and value within which we live our lives.

THE POVERTY
OF WESTERN HUMANISM

A further reason why we throw ourselves into immediate pleasure and satisfaction is that we have lost our capacity to imagine much else. For the past two or three hundred years we have limited our horizons to the merely human, falling increasingly into a self-centredness that cuts us off from wider meaning and broader perspective. The great eighteenth-century Enlightenment thinkers asserted that man was the measure of all things. In itself, this view is not alien to the biblical notion that God created all things for our benefit. Human self-centredness is a fundamental tenet of the Western tradition. But Enlightenment thinking took us deeper into a narrowing humanism because its own concept of the human was more limited.

Taking their lead from Aristotle's philosophy, Enlightenment thinkers defined man as a rational animal. The roots of
the truly human lay in reason (in modern terms, in our IQ)
and in the products of reason – science, technology, the
logical, the pragmatic. Social and political philosophers followed suit by stressing the *rights* of man over service or duty.
Alienated from nature by the general spread of Newtonian
thinking and the move to big cities, alienated from God by the
slow death of Western religious traditions, alienated from
magic and mystery by reductionist scientific thinking, encouraged by Freud and his followers to see the ego and its
petty conceits as the true self, Western humanism has become
a mixture of conceit and despair. We're the best, we're top of
the evolutionary tree – but so what?

In the East, humanism is the basis of true spirituality.
Buddhists and Hindus criticize Western religions for being
insufficiently humanist, for putting gods above man. When
I've tried to argue that humanism is the whole root of our
problem, Asians shake their heads in disbelief. The basis of the
misunderstanding is that theirs is a higher humanism, a higher
'selfishness', based on far more than power and rationality. In
the traditional Eastern sense, a humanist has a deep sense of the
interconnectedness of life and all its enterprises. He has a deep
sense of engagement with, and responsibility for, the whole
world and all that it contains. He is aware that all human
endeavour, whether in business, the arts or religion, is a part of
the larger, richer fabric of the whole universe. And Asian
humanists are not arrogant. Their view of the true self and its
origin in the deepest ground of being fill them with a sense of
humility and gratitude. They are constantly aware of the
source from which self, meaning and values emerge. In the
language of this book, I would say that post-eighteenth-
century Western humanism is spiritually dumb, and that
Asian humanism is spiritually intelligent.

THE CONCEPT
OF THE SERVANT LEADER

Despite our material richness and technological expertise, our lives lack something fundamental. For some people, that might be the ability to turn a mere job into a vocation. But this sense of vocation won't be found within the existing value structure of the business community. Most of us won't find it within the existing value structure of *any* profession, nor within the wider culture. So we have to invent or discover for ourselves something that is at present *beyond* anything provided by or missing from our culture. We have to take personal responsibility for meaning, to create new access to it and use it intelligently. Usually, we have to do so by transforming or making best use of whatever situation we are in.

In business and in most other fields of life, the concept of the servant leader brings together service and meaning. The original notion was first published by the American Robert Greenleaf in the 1980s. American thinkers have taken it to mean a leader who has a sense of deep values and who consciously serves these values in his or her leadership style. But in American business, particularly, deep values refer to matters such as excellence, fulfilling one's potential and allowing others to do so, achievement, quality of products and services, and a commitment to never-ending growth. By contrast, in keeping with the spirit of Eastern humanism, traditional Eastern values centre on areas like compassion, humility, gratitude, service to one's family and service to the ground of being itself.

In the Eastern sense, and in the sense that I use the word, a servant leader serves the ultimate source of meaning and value. He or she is attuned to the basic life forces of the universe and, in serving them, naturally serves his or her colleagues,

company, society or whatever. Great twentieth-century figures who are or were obvious servant leaders in this sense
include Mahatma Gandhi, Mother Teresa and Nelson Mandela. All have been great spiritual leaders as well as serving
their societies. Each 'raised the game' of meaning, morality
and service. The Dalai Lama is another obvious example of
such leadership, and that is why his leadership inspires not just
Tibetans and Buddhists but large sections of humanity as a
whole.

SINGING OUR SONG

A few years ago I was participating in a UNESCO conference
in Tbilisi, capital of the civil war-torn Republic of Georgia,
formerly part of the Soviet Union. The conference took place
in a modern, Western-style hotel that contrasted sharply with
the destruction, despair and hunger outside.

One night we were taken to the city's theatre: the Georgian
people wanted to show off their rich culture, the remains of
their proud and flourishing past.

Inside, there were cracks and burn marks on the ceiling.
The walls were pocked with holes where the plaster had been
blown away by bombs and mortar shells. The only evidence
left of the works of art that had once decorated these walls
were musty discolourations in the chipped paint. The light
was very dim because the damaged generators could produce
only scant power. There was no air-conditioning and the
temperature was sweltering.

When the orchestra appeared in their limp white shirts and ill-
fitting black trousers, their playing was limp and dispirited. They
could not lift their performance above their own and their city's
depression. The audience grew bored and many, including me,
fell asleep. It seemed that the torture of sitting there would go on
forever. Then, in an instant, the atmosphere changed.

Into the centre of the stage walked an elegantly dressed singer in a black dinner jacket, Zurab Sotkilava. A much-loved Georgian, Sotkilava was now the leading tenor of Moscow's famous Bolshoi Opera. He was making a guest appearance in the city of his birth to honour its UNESCO guests. Puffing up his chest, he let out a great torrent of sound, beginning with arias from Verdi and then moving on to traditional Georgian songs.

As he sang, the theatre came alive. This voice seemed to come not from his throat but from somewhere far back in the Georgian past – indeed from somewhere in the collective pool of the human unconscious, linking it to the suffering and tragedy of the Georgian present. It was a channel that brought energy and hope from those other dimensions to the stifled and dispirited orchestra and audience. His voice was, in short, soulful. It was the soul in action, playing its role as transmitter from the depths to place the present in a broader and richer context – a powerful instance of spiritual intelligence.

That Georgian tenor's performance symbolized for me what each of us must do to raise the game of meaning and value. Each of us must 'sing our song'. We must all, through our own deepest resources and through the use of our spiritual intelligence, access the deepest layer of our true selves and bring up from that source the unique 'music' that each human being has the potential to contribute.

The task of using our SQ will not come easily. We have forgotten many of our meaning skills. Our culture is even spiritually dumb in the literal sense – we have no adequate language to express the richness of the human soul. Words like 'joy', 'love', 'compassion' and 'grace' allude to so much more than we can articulate. Using our SQ means stretching the human imagination. It means transforming our consciousness. It means discovering deeper layers of ourselves than we are used to living. It requires us to find some grounding in the self for meaning that transcends the self. This will not be a simple task for a people who have grown used to five-easy-steps-to-self-improvement.

A TIME FOR QUESTIONS

I hope that I have laid the foundations for what spiritual intelligence is and why we need it so particularly today. But we live in a scientific age, and if we are to make a really solid case for SQ we must ask how we have it and how it functions in the human brain. What is it about our brains that gives us a meaning-centred intelligence? What role has that played in human evolution? Why and how do our brains have the capacity to work outside the box, to stretch the boundaries? How do we recontextualize or reframe our experiences? What is it in the nature of the brain that might give our minds access to intelligence or consciousness from beyond the individual brain and its neural structures? What might it mean, in terms of neurology and physics, that our ego-level selves can access some deeper layer of knowing? Why, in short, are we biologically equipped by our brains to be spiritual crea-tures? In Chapters 3–5 I shall deal with these questions, offering whatever relevant scientific research is available.

Part II

THE SCIENTIFIC
EVIDENCE FOR SQ

3. THREE KINDS OF THINKING, THREE KINDS OF INTELLIGENCE[1]

Human intelligence has its roots in our genetic code, and in the whole evolutionary history of life on this planet. It is influenced by our daily experience, our physical and mental health, our diet, the amount of exercise we get, in the kinds of relationships we form, and by many other factors. But neurologically speaking, everything that bears on intelligence is routed through or controlled by the brain and its neural extensions into the body. One kind of neural organization enables us to do rational, logical, rule-bound thinking. It gives us our IQ. Another kind allows us to do our associative, habit-bound, pattern-recognizing emotive thinking. It gives us our EQ. A third kind makes it possible for us to do creative, insightful, rule-making, rule-breaking thinking. It is the thinking with which we reframe and transform our previous thinking. This gives us our SQ. If we want fully to understand IQ, EQ and SQ, a very important part of the story lies in understanding the brain's different thinking systems and their neural organization.

The brain is the most complex organ in the body. It produces the mystery of conscious mind, our awareness of ourselves and our world and our ability to make free choices about engaging with the world. It generates and structures our thoughts, enables us to have emotions and mediates our spiritual lives – our sense of meaning and value and the proper context within which to make sense of our experience. The brain gives us touch, sight, smell and language. It is the storehouse for our memories. It controls the beating of our hearts, the rate at which we sweat, the pace of our breathing and countless other bodily functions. Its outward-reaching neural fibres extend to every region of the body. It is the bridge between our inner lives and the outer world. The brain can do all these things because it is complex, flexible, adaptive and self-organizing.

THE BRAIN'S INFINITE CAPACITY TO GROW

Scientists used to think the brain was 'hard-wired'. We are born, so the theory went, with a certain number of neurones connected in particular ways, and as we age the whole network slowly breaks down. People were thought to be in their mental prime at about the age of eighteen, after which gradual but constant deterioration took place. Today neuro-scientists know better. True, we are born with a certain number of neurones and we lose many of them as we go through life. A pensioner has fewer neurones than a baby. But we grow new neural *connections* throughout our lives – or at least we have the capacity to do so.[2] Conversely, neural systems that are little used shrink, disappear or are taken over for other purposes.

And it is the neural connections that give us our intelli-gence. The human infant is born with the basic necessities for maintaining life – neural connections to regulate breathing, heartbeat, body temperature and so on. But infants can't see faces and objects, form concepts or utter coherent sounds. These capacities evolve over time: through experience of the world, the brain lays down new neural connections. The richer and more varied that experience, the greater and more complex the maze of neural connections that forms. This is why we can boost young children's intelligence and even physical coordination through offering them frequent and varied stimulation – brightly coloured objects to look at, different sounds and voices to hear, a range of things to smell and taste, back rubs and emotional warmth. With increasing maturity, new neural connections give children language and concept formation; these connections store the facts and experiences of memory, enabling reading, writing and general learning to take place. There is no definable limit to the number and complexity of neural connections that a child's brain can grow.

In a highly complex culture like our own, if it were stable, most of us would have grown enough neural connections by about the age of eighteen to cope for the rest of our lives. We would have created an overall picture of our world and its ways. We would have formed mental habits and emotional patterns, patterns of response to people and situations. In short, we would have 'wired in' our basic, underlying and largely unconscious set of assumptions and values – things we could take for granted.

But our culture is not stable. There is too much rapid change, ambiguity and uncertainty for us to be able to rely on wiring diagrams established in our first eighteen years to get us through the rest of life. We have to use that third kind of thinking which involves creative rule-making and rule-breaking, so that we constantly rewire our brains as we go along (the mechanism for doing so will be explained later in this chapter). And relying more heavily on those brain structures that give us our SQ takes a great deal of energy.

A SHORT HISTORY OF THE BRAIN

By nature, the brain is quite conservative. It carries the whole long history of the evolution of life on this planet within its complex structures. Its architecture is like the twisting alleyways and jumbled buildings of a centuries-old city – layer upon layer of archaeological history built one on top of the other and all somehow being lived in.

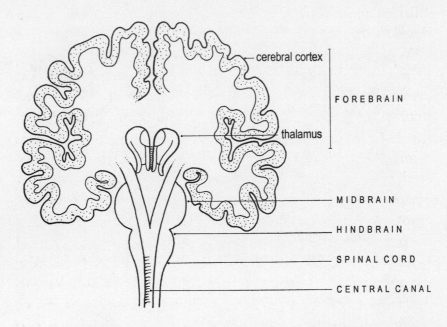

External anatomy of the brain.

In the simplest layer of our bodily organization – the part corresponding to the lowest archaeological level of the ancient city – we find structures like those of single-celled animals such as the amoeba. They have no nervous system; all the sensory coordination and motor reflexes of these animals exist within one cell. Our own white blood cells, as they scavenge for rubbish and eat up bacteria, behave in the bloodstream much like amoeba in ponds. Simple many-celled animals like jellyfish still have no central nervous system, but they do have a network of nerve fibers that allow communication between cells so that the animal can react in a coordinated way. In our bodies, the nerve cells in the gut form a similar network that coordinates peristalsis, the muscular contractions that push food along. More evolved animals develop increasingly complex central nervous systems.

With the evolution of mammals a forebrain developed – first the primitive forebrain of the lower mammals, ruled primarily by instinct and emotion, and then the cerebral hemispheres with all their sophisticated computing ability, the 'little grey cells' that most of us identify with the human mind. The prefrontal lobes of the cortex are the most recently evolved of all, and are essential to rational ego abilities. Yet drunkenness, the use of tranquillizers, great stress, violent emotion or damage to the higher forebrain result in regression to primitive, more spontaneous, less calculating types of behaviour, of the kind found in lower animals. So despite the increasing centralization and complexity of the nervous system as it evolves, even in human beings the more primitive nerve nets remain, both within our expanded brain and throughout the body.

Our Western model of 'thinking', then, is inadequate. Thinking is not an entirely cerebral process, not just a matter of IQ. We think not only with our heads but also with our emotions and our bodies (EQ) and with our spirits, our visions, our hopes, our sense of meaning and value (SQ). We think with all the complex nerve nets woven throughout our organisms. These are all part of our intelligence. Everyday

43

language recognizes this when we say things like, 'He thinks with his guts,' or 'She thinks with her heart.' Many people speak of having a 'feel for the situation' sometimes described as almost tactile.

Let's look more closely now at the neural wiring that underpins each of our three basic kinds of intelligence. We will begin with the neurone itself, the basic building block of all neural processes.

THE NEURONE

The human brain contains between 10,000,000,000 and 100,000,000,000 neural cells or neurones. There are about one hundred different sorts, and half of them are located in the brain's most evolved part, the cerebral cortex. A typical neurone is shaped like a tree, with 'roots' (dendrites), a 'cell body' (soma), a 'trunk' (axon) and 'branches' (axon terminals). Each neurone receives sensory inputs to its dendrites which can stimulate or inhibit it. These inputs travel towards the cell body, fading as they go. If enough stimulus reaches the cell body at any given moment, it fires an action potential along its axon. The action potential travels like a lit fuse until it reaches the axon terminals. These axon terminals in turn form synapses (junctions) on to the dendrites of other neighbouring neurones.

A cortical pyramidal neurone has between one thousand and ten thousand synapses which communicate directly with many other neurones, mostly nearby in the cortex. Most synapses work by chemical signalling. The axon terminal of one neurone secretes a tiny drop of a chemical known as a neurotransmitter, which in turn excites or inhibits the dendrite it contacts. Over a dozen such neurotransmitters are known to be used in different brain systems affecting our mental and emotional abilities or states.

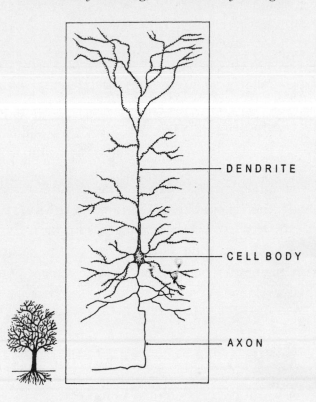

A single neurone.

Noradrenaline, for instance, stimulates the whole brain. Too little can contribute to depression, too much can give rise to mania. Acetylcholine wakens the outer layer of the cortex and enables the kind of coherent neural oscillations responsible for consciousness. A shortage of acetylcholine disturbs these oscillations and is implicated in the cause of Alzheimer's disease. Serotonin stimulates specific systems in the brain, and lack of it is implicated in depression. The famous antidepressant Prozac acts to boost serotonin levels. If both serotonin and acetylcholine levels are too low, Alzheimer's symptoms are very much worse. A fourth widely acting neurotransmitter, dopamine, also stimulates specific systems in the brain. In depression there is often too little dopamine present in some areas; in schizophrenia there is far too much in other areas. Nearly all drugs that affect mental function – tranquillizers, stimulants, opiates, antidepressants and so on – do so through acting on one or more neurotransmitters.

Neurones function as signalling devices, rather like the electronic elements in a telephone network or a computer. Action potentials mediate this function. But the dendrites themselves function in a more subtle way. Most dendrites, when stimulated, do not produce action potentials. Instead, they affect neighbouring parts of the same neurone, or adjacent neurones, by way of electrical fields, and then return to normal. Systems of interacting neurones can produce oscillating electrical fields in the dendrites.

SERIAL THINKING – THE BRAIN'S IQ

The simplistic model of 'thinking' as something linear, logical and dispassionate is not wrong – it is just not the full story. It is derived from formal, Aristotelian logic and from arithmetic: 'If x, then y', or '$2 + 2 = 4$'. Human beings are very good at this kind of thinking, surpassing all lower animals. Computers are even better at it. The brain can do it because of a very distinctive sort of neural wiring known as neural tracts.

Neural tracts resemble a series of telephone cables. The axon of one neurone or group of neurones stimulates the dendrites of the next one or group, and an electrochemical signal passes along the chain of linked neurones being employed for any thought or series of thoughts. Each neurone in the series is switched either on or off, and if any part of the chain gets damaged or switched off the whole chain ceases to function, like a chain of Christmas tree lights wired serially.

Neural tracts learn (are wired) according to a fixed program, the rules of which are laid down in accordance with formal logic. The learning involved is thus step-by-step and rule-bound. When we teach children their times tables by rote, we are encouraging them to wire their brains for serial processing. It produces the kind of thinking that is useful for solving rational problems or achieving definite tasks. It is goal-oriented, how-to thinking, the sort with which we manage the rules of grammar or of a game. It is rational and logical: 'If I do this, a certain consequence will follow.' Serial thinking ability is the kind of mental ability tested for in standard IQ tests.[3]

The neural tracts and circuits needed for serial thinking are found elsewhere in the body and in the lower animals. Simple, fixed-program serial computation in the brain stem and spinal cord is responsible for the knee-jerk reflex, the regulation of body temperature and blood pressure, and similar simple functions. At this level, serial neural wiring functions like the control thermostat of a central heating system. Conditioned reflexes are almost as simple.

Serial thinking or processing requires precise point-to-point wiring. There are neural tracts mapping, for example, each point on the retina of the eye on to an associated point on the thalamus and then point-to-point on to the primary optic cortex, and so on down the chain of visual processing. Other senses like smell, hearing and touch use other neural tracts.

Much of the instinctual behaviour in the lower animals is also accounted for by serial processing. An instinct can be thought of as a fixed program, as in the imprinting instinct in ducks and other birds — where the newly hatched bird identifies as its mother the first caring object or person it meets, and remains stuck on that identification. Some over-rational human beings (and many bureaucrats!) can get stuck in a programmed mode of thinking in the same way, finding it difficult to bend the rules or to learn new ones.

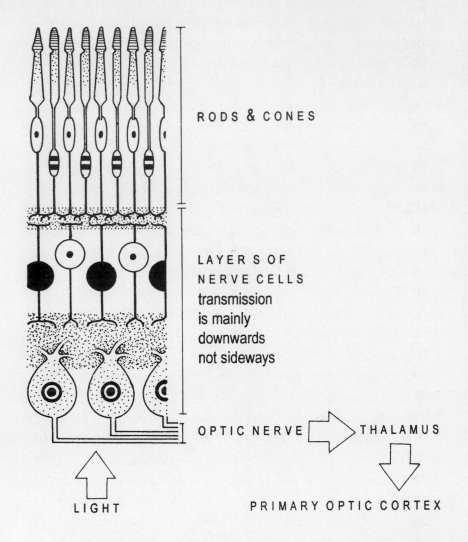

RODS & CONES

LAYERS OF
NERVE CELLS
transmission
is mainly
downwards
not sideways

OPTIC NERVE ⇒ THALAMUS

LIGHT

PRIMARY OPTIC CORTEX

Neutral tracts in the retina and optic nerve. The retina is connected in serial fashion, like telephone cables. The same kind of wiring continues on to the thalamus and the primary optic cortex.

Serial thinking is very similar to the serial processing done by many computers. Indeed, because of this similarity cognitive science has tended to put the cart before the horse, explaining human thinking in terms of computer processing.[4] In a serial computer, data is represented as an array of 'bits' – for example, spots on a magnetic tape or electrical impulses – representing information. This information is manipulated according to certain rules (the 'program'). But computers can't think for themselves. They can't ask whether they are following a good program, or whether there is a better one. And they can't respond to or manipulate any data not covered by their program – they can't learn creatively. For human thinking we need a wider model, including the possibility of consciousness. That will be discussed a little later, when we see how different neural systems cooperate in the human brain.

A great deal of thinking used in practical day-to-day life in our culture is of the serial or IQ kind. Mental arithmetic is a simple example. The analysis phase of any project involves breaking a problem or situation down into its simplest logical parts and then predicting the causal relationships that will emerge. All strategic planning assumes a game plan and a step-by-step rationale for enacting it. In business, 'management by objectives' assumes that it is best to set clear goals and then work out a logical series of actions for achieving them. Serial computers that play chess do so by analyzing all possible outcomes of each position and then calculating, step-by-step, the strongest move.

The advantages of serial thinking and of IQ intelligence are that it is accurate, precise and reliable. But like the kind of thinking that underpins Newtonian science, it is linear and deterministic: B always follows A in the same way. This kind of thinking does not tolerate nuance or ambiguity: it is strictly on/off, either/or. Fantastically effective within its given set of rules, the serial thinking process breaks down if someone moves the goalposts. It is like a computer asked to do a task not covered by its program.

In the metaphor of American philosopher James Carse, serial thinking is a 'finite game'. It functions within boundaries.[5] It is of no use when we have to scan the horizon for new possibilities or deal with the unexpected. So now let's look at the first of the other two neural systems that work in tandem with serial processing and enrich its abilities considerably.

ASSOCIATIVE THINKING – THE BRAIN'S EQ

This kind of thinking helps us to form associations between things like hunger and the food that will satisfy it, between home and comfort, mother and love, barking dogs and danger, the colour red and emotions of excitement or danger. Associative thinking underlies most of our purely emotional intelligence – the link between one emotion and another, between emotions and bodily feelings, emotions and the environment. It also enables us to recognize patterns like faces or smells, and to learn bodily skills like riding a bicycle or driving a car. It is 'thinking' with the heart and the body. EQ, while normally thought of as our 'emotional intelligence', is also the body's intelligence. It is the intelligence used to great effect by a gifted athlete or by a pianist who has practised painstakingly.

The structures within the brain with which we do our associative thinking are known as neural networks. Each of these networks contains bundles of up to a hundred thousand neurones, and each neurone in a bundle may be connected to as many as a thousand others. Unlike the precise wiring of neural tracts, in neural networks each neurone acts upon, or is acted upon by, many others simultaneously.

At its simplest, associative thinking is done via conditioned

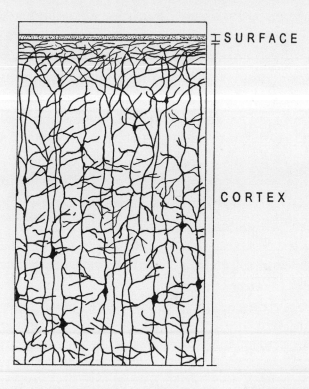

Neural network, showing in simplified form pyramidal cells in the cortex.

response, as in the experiments of the Russian scientist Pavlov with dogs. The animals learned to salivate at the sound of a bell after repeated presentations of food and the bell together. Neural networks allow much more complex associative patterns to be learned. Learning input takes place via some of the elements in a neural network, behavioural output via others; still other elements mediate between the two. A single element in a network is activated if a large enough number of its inputs 'fire' at once. The strength of interconnections between elements is modified by experience, thus allowing the system to 'learn', as we shall see.

51

Neural networks in the brain are connected to further neural networks throughout the brain and body. Those in the brain stem, the oldest part of the brain, are known as the reticular formation and they process incoming sensory information and the associated outgoing motor commands, for instance walking or swallowing – commanded from higher brain levels, but coordinated in the lower brain or spinal cord. They are also responsible for the sleep/wakefulness cycle. For example, a mother may sleep through the noise of heavy traffic but waken at the much fainter sound of her baby. The reticular formation processes this arousal reaction. Its most sophisticated part, the thalamic reticular formation, can arouse just one part of the brain at a time, which is how we can be selectively attentive.

Unlike serial neural tracts, which are rule-bound or program-bound and thus unable to learn, neural networks have the ability to rewire themselves in dialogue with experience. Each time I see a pattern, the neural network connections which recognize that pattern grow stronger, until recognition becomes something automatic. If the pattern alters, my ability to perceive it will alter slowly, too, until my brain has rewired itself to see the new pattern. The connections between neurones in the network may have different strengths, and any one element may tend to excite or inhibit the other elements to which it is connected. Learning changes these strengths between the connections: neural elements that fire together gradually tend to become more strongly interconnected.[6]

While learning to drive a car, for instance, every movement of my hands and feet is thoughtful and deliberate, and my control of the car is only slight. With each practice run, coordination between hands, feet and brain is more strongly wired into the brain's neural networks until eventually I don't think (with my head) about driving unless there is some emergency.

All associative learning is done by trial and error. When a rat learns to run a maze it doesn't follow rules, it practises. If a trial run fails, no neural connection is wired in; if it succeeds, the brain strengthens that connection. This kind of learning is heavily experience-based: the more times I perform a skill successfully, the more inclined I will be to do it that way the next time. Associative learning is also tacit learning – I learn the skill, but I can't articulate any rules by which I learned it and usually can't even describe how I did so. We don't learn to ride a bicycle by reading a manual. Neural networks are not connected with our language faculty, nor with our ability to articulate concepts. They are simply embedded in experience. We *feel* our skills, we *do* our skills, but we don't think or talk about them. We develop our skills because they give us a sense of satisfaction or a feeling of reward, or because they help us avoid pain.

The brain's associative neural networks cover more than those things we readily identify as emotions, but we can easily see how our emotional life fits into the associative pattern, and how it would be based largely in these neural networks. The limbic system, which is the central seat of emotional control in the brain, has both serial neural tracts and associative neural networks. Some emotions, like a fear of snakes, are innate, and are probably grounded in serial wiring within the limbic system. But most emotions are trial-and-error, a slow associative build-up of response to certain stimuli. And they are quite habit-bound. Once I have learned to feel anger at a given stimulus, it is difficult for me to react differently next time. Much of psychotherapy exists to help people break the habit of long-standing but inappropriate emotional association.

Like other aspects of associative intelligence, emotions are not immediately verbal. We often have trouble talking about them, at least with any accuracy, and they are certainly not always 'rational' in the sense of obeying rules or predictions.

They often respond to incomplete data in an unpredictable way.

Similarly, in pattern recognition all the pieces of data from a
given pattern are allowed to interact. Some pieces may be
missing, or different, from an original learned pattern, but
what emerges is a 'best fit'. Thus associative intelligence is able
to deal with ambiguous situations, but it also 'approximates'. It
is more flexible but less accurate than serial thinking.[7] Emotions cover a wider range of experience than reason, but they
are often less accurate.

One-off memory is enabled by precise neural wiring in a
part of the brain known as the hippocampus (see pp. 94–5).
This can deteriorate with age. But we also have a slower,
long-term memory system based on associative neural networks located throughout the brain. This memory system can
gradually learn new things like bodily skills and a memory for
faces, even when our memory for new events weakens. It is
difficult to teach an elderly person new serially wired skills,
but we can learn new motor skills at any age, even if very
slowly. Swimming, or the rote learning of a song, are two
examples here. Again, many of our emotional reactions are
held in the long-term memory system, because their associative base has been built up over time.

The two memory systems have not only different neural
wiring but also different biochemistries. The biochemical
learning mechanism found at the synapses (nerve junctions)
in associative memory changes slowly and gradually, becoming stronger by repetition whenever two neurones fire together, The biochemical learning mechanism in short-term
memory, by contrast, relies on a one-off signal.[8]

As with serial computation in the brain, there are computer
analogues of the brain's associative or parallel computation.
These are known as neural networks or parallel processors.
Like the associative wiring in the brain, they consist of large

numbers of complex, interconnected computer elements. As in the brain, each time a connection between these elements fires, the connection is strengthened, so the computer slowly 'learns' new behaviour. This is unlike serial processors, which can never learn. They can only be reprogrammed. Parallel computers slowly learn from their environment and alter their own internal wiring.

Whereas a serial computer fails if even one link in its chain of communication is blocked, a parallel computer is more robust. Even if slightly damaged, it can still give a good performance because various parallel connections take over the job of damaged neighbours. Since in human beings brain cells are dying every day, it is a clear advantage that we have our parallel abilities!

Where serial processors have a 'language', a set of symbols that manipulate their calculations, parallel processors are 'dumb'. They proceed, instead, by trial-and-error learning. Such computers are used today to recognize handwriting, to read postal codes, to discriminate tastes and smells, and to 'see' faces. They can be used to build up a photo-fit image from a partial description of someone's face or appearance.

The advantages of associative thinking are that it is in dialogue with experience and can learn through experimentation as it goes along. It can feel its way with untried experience. It is also a kind of thinking that can handle nuance and ambiguity – we can remove up to 80 per cent of a given pattern and the brain can still recognize what is left. A neural network computer can recognize a postal code written in millions of different samples of handwriting. The disadvantages of this kind of thinking are that it is slowly learned, inaccurate and tends to be habit-bound or tradition-bound. We *can* relearn a skill or an emotional response, but it takes time and much effort. And because associative thinking is tacit, we have difficulty sharing it with others. We can't just write out a formula and tell someone else to get on with the job. All of us must learn a skill in our own way, for ourselves. No two brains have the same set of neural connections.

Similarly, no two people have the same emotional life. I can recognize your emotion, I can empathize with it, but I don't *have* it.

COOPERATION BETWEEN IQ AND EQ

The human brain is much more complex than any computer. There are the obvious differences, like brains being made of flesh and blood while computers are made of silicon chips, or the fact that brains have *evolved* in complex fashion over millions of years whereas computers are *designed* by human beings with specific goals in mind. But it is also the case that brains cooperate across thinking systems. The brain does not consist of isolated 'intelligence' modules, or an isolated serial processing system alongside an isolated associative system. The two systems interact and enhance each other, giving us a kind of intelligence that neither could on its own. IQ and EQ support each other.

In 1993, Seymour and Norwood described experiments done with chess players to see what kind of thinking lay behind their strategies.[9] Experts and poor chess players were briefly shown a range of positions, some common and others almost nonsensical. Both groups were then asked to reproduce the positions shown. The experts were much better than the poor players at reproducing the common positions, but both groups performed the same at reproducing the absurd positions. The difference was found to be the use of associative thinking combined with serial thinking in the case of the experts reproducing common positions, whereas poor chess players use only serial thinking for everything.

A chess grandmaster, it was found, has over the years built up associative patterns for perhaps fifty thousand common types of chess position. So when confronted with a problem in actual play, he does not calculate serially the consequences of each possible move. He instantly recognizes the promising moves and then devotes his serial (rational) analyses to these moves only. A poor player, by comparison, tries to analyze every possible move, and so wastes time and energy.

At the most general level, psychologists agree that the human brain has a large-capacity set of associative processors, together with a small-capacity serial processor that attends selectively to one or another of them. One metaphor is a searchlight picking out something from a dim background.[10] What is not attended to is forgotten within a few seconds, though meanwhile it may have produced a subliminal effect (like subliminal advertising). For example, most people can remember a seven-figure telephone number for a few seconds. The memory lasts longer if we keep repeating the number to ourselves, but gets lost if we are distracted. This short-term 'working memory' is backed by a great deal of experimental evidence.

Working memory is an essential feature of human serial thinking. It provides a mental note of where we are in any given serial task such as cooking, reading or reasoning. If the mind is presented with many alternatives at some branch point in this process of serial thinking, the working memory allows us to remain aware of the alternatives long enough to decide between them.

This type of memory, in which all the relevant alternatives are held in full consciousness while a response is selected, is a function of the prefrontal cerebral cortex. People who suffer prefrontal damage, as in Alzheimer's disease or in some strokes or traumas, show signs of damage to their working memory and have difficulty sustaining attention and forming concepts or using them flexibly.

If there is only one possibility present in our consciousness, our mental response becomes automatic. The attention sys-

57

tem becomes less active and consciousness diminishes. Similarly a simple manual activity like driving a car can become programmed, replacing most of the need for conscious attention. Hence our intermittent human hunger for new experiences and challenges – something that will require fresh decisions and thus more consciousness.

The attention system as described here is close to Freud's concept of the ego. It has a heightened degree of consciousness compared to the associative background (the id). It can deal with possibilities, abstractions and rational arguments – all an important part of civilization.

Another, dramatic, instance of cooperation between the serial and the associative to boost intelligence is provided by Dr Antonio Damasio's studies of brain-damaged patients. In one famous case discussed by Damasio in his book *Descartes' Error* and highlighted again in Daniel Goleman's *Emotional Intelligence*, a patient named Elliot suffers impairment to his *rational* thinking abilities because of limited brain damage to his prefrontal cortices that resulted in *emotional* impairment.[11] None of the brain areas responsible for rational decision-making or IQ was affected by his tumour, and he continued to score highly on IQ tests. His memory was good and all his rational skills and knowledge remained intact. But his injury had resulted in 'flat' emotional responses that affected his rational decision-making abilities. The coordination between IQ and EQ had broken down, and as a result he had lost his 'common sense'.

Both the chess experiments and Damasio's observations illustrate a coordination between serial and associative processing, between IQ and EQ, that can be accounted for at least partially in present, formal models of thinking. But there are other obvious human mental abilities that remain mysterious. The brain has some further kind of intelligence for which cognitive science has as yet no explanation. Let's look at that now, and at the neurological experiments that shed some light on how that further intelligence operates.

UNITIVE THINKING – THE BRAIN'S SQ

We have seen that computers can simulate both serial and associative thinking. PCs can do something very like serial thinking faster and more accurately than human beings. Neural network computers can replicate some of our associative thinking abilities, and these machines will certainly get better as the technology develops. But there are a great many aspects of human mental life and intelligence that no computer so far built, or even envisaged, can replicate. These are capacities that in this book are called 'spiritual intelligence' – our meaning-giving, contextualizing and transformative intelligence.

Unlike machines, human beings are conscious. We are aware of our experience, and aware that we are aware. We respond to this experience with pain or laughter, with a sense of sorrow or a sense of humour. We laugh at jokes and feel toothache. Though we have been 'programmed' through the rules that we learn, and have formed deep habits through our lifelong associations, we retain free will. If we are willing to invest the commitment and the energy, we can change those rules and break those habits. Computers always work within programs, within boundaries. They play what we have called a finite game. But human beings can be infinite players. We can move the goalposts – we can play *with* boundaries.

We can do all this because we have a kind of thinking that is creative, insightful and intuitive. We *learn* language with our serial and associative thinking systems, but we *invent* language with some third thinking system. We *understand* common or given situations and behaviour patterns and rules with our first two kinds of thinking, but we *create* new ones with this third kind.

And we human beings are creatures of meaning. When given a programmed command, a computer does not ask, 'Why should I do this?' or 'What does this mean?' It just follows the command. Human beings very often ask such questions, and function more effectively when there are good answers. Computers can manipulate the syntax of language – they can figure out and order the correct grammatical (that is, rule-bound) arrangement of words. But only human beings understand semantics, the meaning of an arrangement of words, and thus have the ability to decode something like a metaphor.

One thing that all these further human abilities have in common is a sense of unity in our grasp of a situation or our reaction to it. Understanding is in essence holistic – an ability to grasp the overall context that links component parts. It is this contextual understanding that is lacking in schizophrenics, who cannot unify their experience and so cannot respond appropriately to it. In this book we call it 'unitive thinking'. This unitive ability is an essential feature of consciousness, and is the key to understanding the neurological basis of SQ.

Many of the vast number of neurones in the human brain are connected to one other in serial chains and circuits, whilst many others are closely connected to as many as ten thousand others in neural networks. But no sort of physical neural connection links all the neurones in the brain to each other, or even all the different chains or modules of neurones to each other. Physically speaking, the brain consists of lots of independent 'expert systems', some of which process colour, some sound, some tactile sensation and so on. When I look at the room in which I am working, all these expert systems are bombarded by millions of pieces of perceptual data – visual, auditory, tactile, thermal and so forth. Yet my consciousness sees the room as a whole: I have a unified perceptual field. The mystery of how this can possibly be so is known in neurology, psychology and philosophy as 'the binding problem'. How does my brain bind its disparate perceptual experiences together?

Further, as I look round my room I can distinguish many different objects in it – my desk, the computer, the CD player, pictures on the walls, the coffee cup beside me. This is a further part of the binding problem. There is no central CD player neurone or coffee cup neural model in my brain that can account for this discriminating ability. But it has been the subject of much research, and is now at least partially understood.

A research team led by Wolf Singer and Charles Gray in Frankfurt connected electrodes to neurones in different parts of the mammal brain. All parts of the brain, at all times, emit electrical signals which can be read by electroencephalographs and oscillate at various frequencies. The Singer team found that, when I perceive an object like a coffee cup, the neurones in every localized part of my brain involved in that perception oscillate in unison, at a frequency between 35 Hz and 45 Hz (35–45 cycles per second). The synchronous oscillations unite my many different localized perceptual responses to the cup – its roundness, its colour, its height and so on – and give me the experience of a single, solid object.[12]

Similarly, if electrodes are connected to neurones in the various localized areas of my brain that perceive the CD player, these too will be found to be oscillating in unison – but at a slightly different frequency (though still in the 35–45 Hz range) than those neurones perceiving the coffee cup. And so on for each of the objects in my room.

The study of neural oscillations for the unified perception of single objects is as far as the Singer research has yet gone. But neurological studies of people who meditate reinforce and extend these perceptual insights. Physiologically, practices like Buddhist vipassana meditation or raja yoga (for instance transcendental meditation) have been found to lower the blood pressure and slow the metabolism, suggesting that they are effective for stress relief. But EEG studies of the meditators' brain waves have also been carried out[13] and, usefully, unlike coffee cups and CD players, human meditators can describe their experience.

In Eastern practices the meditator first sits upright in a quiet room for at least twenty minutes. He or she focuses the attention on breathing, on some sound (known as a mantra), or on an object like a candle flame. Because there are no distractions the mind stills and the meditator becomes very relaxed. It is at this stage that blood pressure and metabolism effects are noted. Coherent alpha brain waves, characteristic of alert relaxation, are noted on EEG patterns.

In the second, deeper stage, the meditator moves into a state of consciousness that is aware but empty of specific thoughts or content. He may also be aware of particular deep insights. EEG studies of the meditator's mind during this stage of practice show increasingly coherent brain waves at several frequencies (including 40 Hz) across large areas of the brain. The experience, as described by meditators, of the contents of consciousness entering into a unity is accompanied by a unity of neural oscillations.

Until very recently there was no further research on the extent and role of 40 Hz neural oscillations in unitive thinking beyond Singer's and Gray's (or similar work), and the meditation studies. But in the 1990s new data began to appear in scientific research journals. A new technology, called magneto-encephalography, has been developed that permits more sensitive and larger-scale (across the whole brain) study of these oscillations and the role they play in human intelligence. As we shall see in Chapter 4, which is devoted entirely to this new research, there is now good evidence that synchronous neural oscillations in the 40 Hz range:

*　　　*　　　*

□ mediate conscious information processing between the serial and parallel neural systems in the brain, allowing the kind of coordination displayed in the chess experiments, or in the IQ–EQ link illustrated by Damasio's work

□ are the most likely neural basis for consciousness itself and of all unified conscious experience, including the perception of objects, the perception of meaning, and the ability to frame and reframe our experience

□ are the neural basis for that higher-order unitive intelligence that in this book we call 'SQ' or 'spiritual intelligence'.

THREE PSYCHOLOGICAL PROCESSES

In Freudian psychology, two basic processes for sifting and integrating psychological information are described. These are:

□ The primary process or the id, which is basically the unconscious – the world of sleep, of dreams, of unconscious motivations and slips of the tongue, of repressed memories and so on.

□ The secondary process, the world of consciousness or the ego, which is on the whole logical, rational and linear. Neurologically, we can see these two processes being underpinned by parallel or associative thinking (the primary process), and serial thinking (the secondary process).

□ But we have seen from the structure of the brain that there is a third kind of thinking, unitive thinking, which seems to be the neurological basis for what I shall call 'the tertiary process'.

Many students of religion, as well as many humanistic and transpersonal psychologists, have described three psychological processes. Ken Wilber, for instance, calls them the prepersonal (the instinctive), the personal (ego-level phenomena) and the transpersonal (going beyond the limited ego self to the core of its being).[14] There seems good reason to link these three processes to the brain's three kinds of neural thinking structures, and thus to its three kinds of intelligence. This is illustrated by a simple diagram of our mental life issuing from three layers of the self, where each of the concentric circles is a different psychological process. In Part III of this book, A New Model of the Self, I shall develop this idea in greater depth.

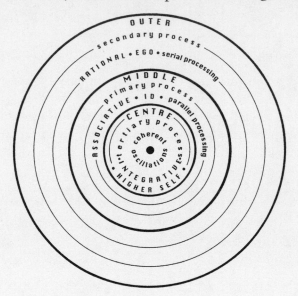

Each of the three concentric circles represents a different psychological process.

The rational, IQ, layer is used very often — perhaps too often — in our technology-driven Western culture, to interact efficiently with the public world of written texts, timetables and linear or goal-oriented planning. At home, in our private lives, we can relax into a mixed rational–associative (IQ–EQ) mode, where different sides of ourselves are given expression.

Both our emotions and our dreams are more associative, connected to the middle layer of the self. Beyond this are deep sleep, states reached in deep meditation, or a process drawn on when we need to be creative. It is from this third layer, the deep (SQ) centre of the self, that surface phenomena get put into wider context and integrated with one another. This tertiary process is associated with spirituality and spiritual intelligence in their widest sense.

HYPERTHINKING, THE TERTIARY PROCESS AND SQ

At its most simple neurological level, I have described SQ as an ability to reframe or recontextualize our experience, and thus an ability to transform our understanding of it. There is a mathematical theory known as 'hyperspace' that sheds some light on this at the most basic level. The gist is that there are not just three dimensions of space, or even four, but 'n' dimensions, each offering a further perspective on the last. In his book *Hyperspace*, physicist Michio Kaku uses the example of a family of goldfish swimming around in a bowl. From their present perspective, the fish have no sense that they are inside a bowl, or that it is filled with a fluid we would call water. This is just their world and they take it for granted.

But in Kaku's example, one of the fish suddenly takes a big leap that raises him above the surface of the water in his bowl. 'Ah!' he exclaims, 'Look where I've come from.' He sees the bowl and his fellow goldfish and the water from this further perspective, and he sees that he has come from a world of fishbowls and water. And now this goldfish knows there is a larger world outside the bowl, a medium in which to move other than water. He has recontextualized his original situation and transformed his view of reality.

Through small perceptual experiences like these, SQ allows

65

this recontextualizing, transformative power to exert itself on an almost daily basis. Whenever we look at the world afresh we see objects in new relationships to each other and to their surroundings. But this is only the most basic dimension of an intelligence and its accompanying neural processes that in more complex form touches and transforms our lives at every level. The expanding horizons of goldfish may be limited to seeing their bowls and fellow fish in a larger context. But in human beings, more complex variations of these same neural processes alter the *meaning* and existential substance of our lives.

In his book *The Tibetan Book of Living and Dying*, for instance, Sogyal Rinpoche describes the deep effect on his consciousness and 'the vast implications' for his life that resulted from his grasping, in a moment of insight, the true nature of impermanence. But what he says here about impermanence could apply to any insight gained through our SQ, or tertiary psychological process.

> It is as if all our lives we have been flying in an airplane through dark clouds and turbulence, when suddenly the plane soars above these into the clear boundless sky. We are inspired and exhilarated by this emergence into a new dimension of freedom . . . And as this new awareness begins to become vivid and almost unbroken, there occurs what the Upanishads [ancient Hindu writings] call 'a turning about in the seat of consciousness', a personal, utterly non-conceptual revelation of what we are, why we are here, and how we should act, 'which amounts in the end to nothing less than a new life, a new birth, you could say a resurrection'.[15]

This sense of resurrection is the experiential dimension of our spiritual intelligence. It is not just a state of mind but a way of knowing, a way of being, that utterly transforms our understanding and our lives.

4. MORE ABOUT 40 Hz NEURAL OSCILLATIONS, CONSCIOUSNESS AND SQ

Current theories of consciousness should de-emphasize the role of sensory inputs in determining ongoing cognitive events. Instead, we favor the view that the nervous system is essentially a closed system that generates oscillatory states based on the intrinsic membrane properties of its constitutive neurons and their connectivity. These oscillatory states shape the computational events elicited by sensory stimuli.

Denis Pare and Rodolfo Llinas, *Neuropsychologia*[1]

These few highly technical and tightly packed sentences challenge two thousand years of Western philosophizing about the nature of mind, and the past hundred years of theorizing by cognitive scientists and neurobiologists on the same subject. Ever since Plato we have believed that consciousness is 'consciousness *of* something'. We have been told that the mind is a blank slate (or set of neurones) set in motion through stimulation by the outside world. In the words of the seventeenth-century philosopher John Locke, 'All ideas come from sensation or reflection. Let us suppose the mind to be, as we say, white paper, void of all characters, without any ideas.'[2]

A related view led to Nobel laureate Francis Crick's 'astonishing hypothesis' in 1994 that, 'You, your joys and

67

your sorrows, your memories and your ambitions, your sense of personal identity and free will, are in fact no more than the behaviour of a vast assembly of nerve cells and their associated molecules.'[3] For neuroscientists like Crick, all that matters is behaviour – whether it be the behaviour of isolated nerve cells or of the whole individual. Consciousness, a mere side-effect of such behaviour, is something the scientist can ignore.

The very recent Pare-Llinas research on 40 Hz neural oscillations in the brain shows, by contrast, that consciousness is an intrinsic property of the brain. Consciousness just *is*, in and for itself, though this background, intrinsic consciousness can be modulated (given specific shape or form) by stimulation from the outside world, or from within the body itself. More like the view of Buddhist thinkers on consciousness these last two thousand years, or that of Western idealist thinkers like Kant, Hegel and Schopenhauer, the Pare-Llinas research shows, as we shall see, that all mammals at least share the property of having this intrinsic consciousness, and that consciousness itself is a transcendent process – that is, our consciousness puts us in touch with a reality far deeper and richer than the mere connection and vibration of a few nerve cells.

THE NEURAL BASIS
OF TRANSCENDENCE

Transcendence is perhaps the most essential quality of the spiritual. By 'transcendent', theologians and many religious people usually mean something that is beyond the physical world. In this book I mean something more humble and at the same time more fundamental. The transcendent, I suggest, is that which takes us beyond – beyond the present moment, our present joy or suffering, our present selves. It takes us beyond the limits of our knowledge and experience and puts these things in a wider context. The transcendent gives us a taste of the extraordinary, the infinite, within ourselves or within the world around us. Many who experience the transcendent call it 'God'; some say they have had a mystical experience; others sense it through the beauty of a flower, a child's smile or a piece of music.

It is usually such experiences of transcendence – had, psychologists say, by as many as 70 per cent of people[4] – that make us unwilling to accept something like Crick's 'astonishing hypothesis'. The behaviour of molecules and nerve cells is so finite; human beings can and do experience the infinite. This ability to access and use our experience of higher meaning and value is the basis of what we mean by SQ. Many of us would like a scientific understanding of it, but it must be one that does not diminish or explain away those very qualities of ourselves and our experience that make us feel most human.

A very simple example of a transcendent phenomenon in nature that is analogous to the neural oscillatory states referred to by Pare and Llinas is an absolutely still and transparent ocean on which waves have been created. The water in the ocean is in every wave, is the essence of every wave, yet when we look at the scene we see only the waves. If we *were* the waves, we would see only each other and not the ocean, though we might have some deeper sense of the ocean within us. The universe itself can be seen as just such a still and transparent ocean of energy, and all existing things and beings as waves upon it. This is described in the most sophisticated physics of the universe that we have so far – quantum field theory.

According to this theory, the universe and all its constitu-ents consist of energy in different states of excitation. People, tables, chairs, trees, stardust and so on are patterns of dynamic energy set against a background (the quantum vacuum) of still, unexcited energy, which therefore has no qualities that we can directly see or touch or measure. Any such quality would be an excitation (wave) of the vacuum, not the vacuum (the ocean) itself. The quantum vacuum, then, is almost transcendent to its qualities, transcendent to existence. Yet existence, too, is slightly sensitive to this transcendent dimension, as shown in what physicists call the 'Casimir Effect': when two metal plates are placed very close together, they are attracted to each other because of the subtle pressure that the quantum vacuum exerts on each.

The kind of transcendence illustrated by the quantum vacuum is similar to that described as the *Tao* or the Void (*Sunyata*) in many Taoist, Hindu and Buddhist texts. In the words of the *Tao Te Ching*:

> Look, it cannot be seen – it is beyond form.
> Listen, it cannot be heard – it is beyond sound.
> Grasp, it cannot be held – it is intangible.
> These three are indefinable;
> Therefore they are joined in one.
>
> From above it is not bright;
> From below it is not dark:
> An unbroken thread beyond description.
> It returns to nothingness.
> The form of the formless,
> The image of the imageless,
> It is called indefinable and beyond imagination.

But though Eastern sages felt they could *say* nothing about the Void, could not *grasp* the *Tao*, they did feel that practitioners of meditation could *experience* it in a state of Enlightenment, or in lesser experiences leading towards Enlightenment. Such experience is, if we like, a spiritual version of the physicists' Casimir Effect.

Excitations of the quantum vacuum are like guitar strings that have been plucked. Such strings vibrate or oscillate. This analogy brings us closer to the brain, whose neurones oscillate when stimulated. The work of Wolf Singer and Charles Gray on the 'binding problem' (see pp. 61–2) showed that bundles of neurones all over the brain oscillate simultaneously at similar frequencies (about 40 Hz) if they perceive the same object. Such coherent oscillations, they were able to show, give unity to our perceptions. At the neural level, this unity can be described as a transcendent dimension to the activity of individual neurones. Without it, our world would consist of meaningless fragments.

Going back to the ocean analogy, such coherent oscillations are the ocean of background consciousness, while specific perceptions, thoughts, emotions and so on are the waves on the ocean – modulations of the basic oscillatory activity. So at the very least, every single thought or emotion has its transcendent dimension against the wider oscillating background.

THE GENERAL PICTURE OF NEURAL OSCILLATIONS

In fact there are oscillations and waves of all sorts and frequencies in the brain, as demonstrated by EEG printouts of brain wave patterns. Neuroscientists have been able to associate some of these different wave patterns with specific levels of mental activity or alertness (see table).

All these various neural oscillations are known to be associated with electrical fields in the brain, which are generated by many dendrites oscillating in concert but not actually firing. Such oscillations are distinct from the action potentials that shoot along the neural axon; they are another way in which the brain can communicate with itself.

What Different Brain Wave Patterns Mean

Type	Speed	When/where mainly observed	What they mean
Delta	0.5–3.5 Hz	Deep sleep or coma. Also very prevalent in infants' brains	Brain doing nothing
Theta	3.5–7 Hz	Dreaming sleep, and in children 3–6 years	Episodic information passing from one area of brain to another – from hippocampus to more permanent storage in cortex
Alpha	7–13 Hz	Adults, or children 7–14 years	State of relaxed alertness
Beta	13–30 Hz	Adults	Concentrated mental work
Gamma	c.40 Hz	Conscious brain, either awake or during dreaming sleep	Credited by Singer and Gray with perceptual feature binding
	c.200 Hz	Recently discovered in hippocampus	Function as yet unknown

Until very recently, little more could be discovered about the nature, function or extent of neural oscillations because the EEG machine was the only technology available for observing them. The electrical fields in the brain are very weak, and the electrically conducting brain itself and the skull act as a barrier between them and the electrodes of the EEG when placed on the scalp (electrodes can be placed on or in the human brain only during necessary surgical operations). Readings were therefore crude and limited. Even the Singer–Gray work had been done by measuring oscillations in specific neurones with individual electrodes, and was therefore also limited. These measurements were enough to illustrate the existence of simultaneous oscillations at different points of the brain in connection with an individual perceptive (visual) act, but they could not give a broad picture of the extent of these oscillations at hundreds of points at once. Although interesting, the results were not enough to explain a whole-brain activity like consciousness, nor to illustrate a broad, transcendent dimension to our cognitive life. As late as 1994 Francis Crick dismissed the greater importance of the 40 Hz oscillations with the words, 'On balance, it is hard to believe that our vivid picture of the world really depends entirely on the activities of neurons that are so "noisy" and so difficult to observe.'[5]

MAGNETO-ENCEPHALOGRAPHY – THE MEG

The magneto-encephalograph (MEG) is an improvement on the older EEG. Whereas the EEG measures electrical activity generated by the brain, the MEG measures the associated magnetic activity. There is no problem with physical barriers because the brain, skull and scalp do not interfere with magnetic fields. MEG technology began in the late 1980s, but early machines could measure only small areas of the brain at any one time. With the development of whole-scalp MEGs in the late 1990s neuroscientists have at last been able to obtain a picture of neural oscillatory activity across the entire brain and deep within it.[6]

So far, MEG studies have produced masses of information about the brain's many complex oscillatory rhythms, their extent, their function and their relation to things like body movements, visual imagery, auditory commands and concentration. For our purposes, looking for the neural activity associated with consciousness and SQ, information generated by the 40 Hz oscillations is the most relevant.

40 HZ NEURAL OSCILLATIONS

A great deal of the research into the nature and function of 40 Hz oscillations across the brain has been done by Rodolfo Llinas and colleagues at the New York University School of

Medicine. Llinas' work has always been inspired by a passion to understand the 'mind–body problem'. 'As a neuroscientist,' he says, 'the single most important issue one can address concerns the manner in which brains and minds relate to one another.'[7] His work sheds further light on the Singer-Gray research into coherent neural oscillations and their role in solving the 'binding problem'.[8]

MEG studies have shown that the relatively fast 40 Hz oscillations are found all over the brain, in different systems and at different levels. At peripheral brain sites, they are found in the retina[9] and the olfactory bulb.[10] They are also found in the thalamus, in the thalamic reticular nucleus and in the neocortex. In fact the 40 Hz oscillations cover the whole cortex, moving in waves from front to back. Here in the cortex, they have two components. In the outermost layer of the cortex coherent 40 Hz waves behave like a smoothly flowing stream. These are thought to make possible the spatio/temporal binding of a specific perceptual or cognitive experience. Deeper into the cortex, where sensory inputs occur, more localized 40 Hz waves act like 'ripples' on the 'pond' of the smoothly flowing oscillations. These localized oscillations are thought to make possible the *content* of a given perceptual or cognitive experience.[11]

Both the local and more generalized oscillations transcend the abilities of any single neurone or localized group of neurones, in that they communicate and collate perceptual and intellectual processing across the whole brain. In other words they place the activity of a single stimulated neurone in a larger, more meaningful context (the beginnings of SQ). These oscillations are found in all mammal brains, and have also been discovered in some birds and in locusts, though we don't yet understand these animals' brains well enough to know whether their oscillations mean the same as in mammals.

Llinas' most recent research showed that 40 Hz oscillations are present in the brain during both full, waking alertness and dreaming or REM (rapid eye movements which probably follow the 'action' of the dream) sleep. The implications are vast, both for the nature of consciousness in general and for understanding the neural basis of our spiritual intelligence.

His work has shown, first, that the presence of conscious-ness (mind) in the brain is associated with the presence of 40 Hz neural oscillatory activity; such activity disappears if the brain is in coma or anaesthetized, and is only very slight in deep, dreamless sleep. Secondly, he has proved that 40 Hz oscillatory activity is fully present in a state of dreaming, REM sleep even though in the REM state the brain is not sensitive to external perceptual stimuli. The difference between the alert, waking brain and the dreaming brain, Llinas showed, was simply that – a difference in whether the brain was or was not sensitive to external sensory stimuli.[12] The dreaming brain is also dissociated from most muscular activity and ego/rational thought. It was this discovery that led Llinas and his colleagues to conclude that consciousness, or mind, is an intrinsic state of the brain rather than simply a by-product of sensory experience.

When we dream, the brain 'switches off' the outside world and attends to its own inner processes. Llinas suggests that the same is true of daydreaming and trance and hallucinatory states – the mind is attending to its own interior processes rather than to the outside world.

Where, then, does mind come from? How is it that we can have ideas and entertain meanings? How do the 40 Hz oscilla-tions arise in the brain? What causes them? To answer such questions we must look first at the role of the part of the brain called the thalamus, and its relation to the cerebral cortex.

The thalamus is part of the primitive forebrain. It deals mainly with incoming sensation, but some parts also deal with emotions and movement. It is present in lower vertebrates like fishes and reptiles. In humans the thalamus sits at the top of the spinal cord, now surrounded by the folds of the more recently evolved cerebral cortex. So it sits approximately dead centre in the brain and is a kind of main relay or switching centre. As recently as the late 1980s it was assumed that the function of the thalamus was to relay the signals of external sensory stimuli to the cortex, where they could be processed either serially or in parallel. Llinas and his colleagues have discovered otherwise. According to them, those specific pathways from the thalamus to the cortex that relay sensory stimuli account for only 20–28 per cent of the synapses connecting the thalamus to the cortex. Clearly, they conclude, the majority of connections between the thalamus and the cortex are devoted to some other purpose.

And that other purpose, in the view of Llinas and Pare, is to create a feedback circuit between the non-specific areas of the thalamus and the cortex through which intrinsically oscillating neurones can self-organize into across-the-brain 40 Hz oscillatory activity. This across-the-brain oscillatory activity, in turn, makes possible both the temporal binding and the content of our cognitive experiences, in other words the functioning of conscious mind: '. . . consciousness is not a by-product of sensory inputs but rather is generated intrinsically and is modulated (or contextualized) by sensory inputs'.[13] The brain, in short, was *designed* to be conscious, and *designed* to have a transcendent dimension.

Returning to our main theme of SQ, these 40Hz oscillations are what might be termed its neural substrate. Just as linear or serial neural tracts enable rational, logical data processing (IQ) to take place and parallel neural networks allow preconscious and unconscious associative data processing (EQ), the 40 Hz across-the-brain oscillations provide a means by which our experience can be bound together and placed in a frame of wider meaning (SQ).

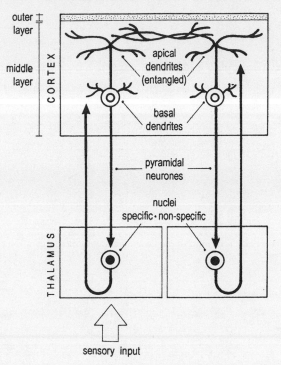

1. Sensory input via the thalamus goes to the mid-layers of the cortex in a localized fashion.
2. Wavelike activity in layer 1 of the cortex (the apical dendrites) is maintained via loops to the non-specific thalamic nuclei.

All very well, but we are still talking just about neurones and their oscillatory activity. Is that where mind comes from? Does it really begin with the vibration of single neurones and then become complex through coherent oscillations across the brain? If so, wouldn't a reductionist neuroscientist like Francis Crick be right? Wouldn't 'we' just be the activity of so many jangling neurones? Or do 'we' go deeper? What *causes* the neural oscillations that enable consciousness? Can we assume that conscious mind is something more primary, more fundamental, even than the neural machinery of brains? Philosophers, psychologists,

and scientists and theologians argue such questions end-
lessly.

In the wide range of books and research papers devoted to
them, four main points of view emerge. American philosopher David Chalmers has reviewed them and assessed the
weight of evidence that supports each.[14] Here is his presen-
tentation of the four possibilities, followed by my own
thoughts on which I think most likely, and how it could
work.

WHERE DOES CONSCIOUS MIND COME FROM?

The first possible explanation for where consciousness comes
from is known as the *dualist position*. Dualists argue that there
are two essentially distinct realities, or types of substance, in
the universe: one is material, and obeys the laws of known
physics; the other is consciousness, and is outside physics. The
seventeenth-century French philosopher René Descartes is
the best-known modern dualist. 'I know,' he said, 'that I have
a mind. I know that I have a body. And I know that the two
are utterly distinct.'[15] For Descartes, mind and body were
'accidentally' connected in the brain at the site of the pineal
gland. Were he alive today and aware of the work on 40 Hz
neural oscillations, he would no doubt say that mind and body
meet accidentally at the oscillations.

Descartes did not doubt the existence of the immortal
human soul, and its intelligence. The source of each was God.
Indeed, for Descartes *all* intelligence was 'spiritual intelligence', because he believed that our intelligence consists of
'clear and distinct ideas' planted in the mind by God.

There are many respected twentieth-century dualists, even
in scientific circles. The Nobel prize-winning neurobiologist
Sir John Eccles wrote jointly with the philosopher Karl

Popper *The Self and Its Brain*, which proposed that matter was made out of atoms and mind out of 'psychons', fundamental particles of consciousness. But the vast majority of scientifically inclined people today reject dualism as a scientific or philosophical fudge. The weight of opinion and evidence now suggests that, if there is such a thing as consciousness, it must somehow originate within those same fundamental physical laws that enable the existence of everything else.

Does such a thing as consciousness exist? Does anyone seriously doubt it? Yes, that is essentially the position of the people known as *eliminative materialists*. The best-known of these today is the philosopher Daniel Dennett who, in *Consciousness Explained*, essentially explains *away* consciousness. For Dennett and like thinkers there is just the brain with its neurones, their structure and function. As for Behaviourists of earlier decades such as J. B. Watson, nothing else is worth discussing – or indeed can be discussed. If there are 40 Hz oscillations across the brain, fine. We can ask what role they play in perception and other information processing. We can ask what behaviour they produce. And we can ask which neurones oscillate when we see what. But this concept called 'consciousness' is nothing but a chimera. The eliminative materialists regard discussion of such concepts as a waste of time.

Dennett's critics have said that, though he himself may not be conscious, he should allow for the possibility that other people might be. A great many neuroscientists experience themselves as conscious and wish to understand the phenomenon. Francis Crick, for instance, is among those who accept that there *is* a phenomenon called consciousness and that it needs to be explained, but at the same time his 'astonishing hypothesis' makes it clear that he and others like him think that mind can be fully accounted for within present materialist science. Such people are known as *'soft' materialists*. Whatever consciousness is, they say, it will one day be fully explained as nothing but a phenomenon arising from the structure and function of neurones. Those 40 Hz oscillations or something like them are the full story. There is no 'human spirit', so called, beyond brains and whatever they can do. Someone like Crick might concede the possibility of a 'unitive intelligence' enabled by coherent neural oscillations, and he might even connect it with 'meaning' in a limited sense,[16] but it seems highly unlikely that he would countenance calling this sense of meaning anything like 'spiritual intelligence'.

Then there are those who go well beyond current materialism in suggesting that matter actually has a *double aspect* – that mind and matter are two sides of the same coin. These people are sometimes called *property dualists*, since they hold that the same basic substance of the universe, whatever it is, has the dual properties of both mind and matter. Regarding the relationship between the 40 Hz neural oscillations and consciousness, they would say that the matter which makes up neurones acquires the property of consciousness when these neurones oscillate coherently. In this case, consciousness is viewed as an emergent property of neural oscillations. It is different from mere oscillations, a phenomenon in its own right, yet it has no antecedent. It is a property arising from the way neurones are sometimes combined.

In answer to the questions 'What *causes* the oscillations?' and 'Where does consciousness come from?', the double-aspect theorist would say that the oscillations just oscillate, but when they do, we get consciousness as a new property associated with that system. A bit like pulling a rabbit out of a hat, some critics say.

What then of transcendence and the 'human spirit'? Double-aspect accounts of consciousness, in our view, allow for a weak kind of transcendence, and for a human spirit, or soul, that is something akin to the psychologist C. G. Jung's 'collective unconscious': we share a dimension of our mental life with other creatures. On this view, consciousness is a property that emerges with brains, or even possibly with life, or at the very least with mammalian brains, in which 40 Hz oscillations are reliably found. We human beings, in that case, are at least the children of life on this planet, or at the very least of mammalian life, and therefore we are not just our neurones or even our limited ego selves. Our consciousness, or some aspects of our intelligence at least, belongs to a bigger story. The transcendent intelligence that we are calling 'spiritual intelligence' is in that case an intelligence that roots us outside ourselves in the wider stream of life.

David Chalmers comments that double-aspect theories make a lot of sense and yet leave him dissatisfied. Many others feel the same. In Chalmers' words, 'We expect a fundamental law to be about something fundamental.' If consciousness is a fundamental property of the 'primeval stuff', why does it emerge only with brains, or with collections of oscillating neurones? 'Why not with telephones?' he asks ironically.[17]

Chalmers, following the earlier lead of philosopher Bertrand Russell in 1927, proposes something more fundamental. Like Russell, he suggests that something called *proto-consciousness* is a fundamental property of all matter, just like mass, charge, spin and location. In this view, proto-consciousness is a natural part of the fundamental physical laws of the universe and has been present since the beginning of time. Everything that exists – fundamental particles like mesons and quarks, atoms, stones, stars, tree-trunks and so on – possesses proto-consciousness.

Other scientists have held the same view. The biologist Julian Huxley wrote, '. . . all reality then consists, as [the philosopher] Whitehead put it, of events. The events looked at from the outside are matter; experienced from inside they

81

are mind.'[18] A few years earlier, Jung had written, 'Since psyche and matter are contained in one and the same world, and moreover are in continuous contact with one another . . . it is not only possible, but fairly probable even, that psyche and matter are two different aspects of one and the same thing.'[19] Then some structures, like brains, have whatever is necessary to combine all these bits of proto-consciousness into full-blown consciousness. In line with the latest neural research, I would say that 40 Hz coherent neural oscillations must possess this necessary feature.

This view that proto-consciousness is a fundamental property of all matter is a weak form of *panpsychism*, the view held by Hindu and Buddhist philosophers, and by some Western philosophers such as Alfred North Whitehead, that consciousness pervades the universe and all its constituents. Any panpsychist theory of where consciousness comes from would lead to a strong form of transcendence for mind and its spiritual intelligence. If neural oscillations in the brain were a coherent version of a fundamental property pervading the whole universe, then our human SQ roots us not just in life but at the very heart of the universe. We become children not just of life, but, more strongly, of the cosmos.

Such strong transcendence as a property of SQ is naturally a very exciting prospect. It would mean that a fundamental aspect of human intelligence gives us access to the ground of being, to the fundamental laws and principles of existence, just as Hindu and Buddhist thinkers have always claimed. Mind, in this case, originates at the very centre of things. The aspect of our intelligence that is our SQ transcends the mere ego, the mere brain, the mere 'jangling of neurones', and becomes an expression of something that most Western people have usually called 'God'.

It is important to realize that this is not a materialist or reductionist view. In materialism, matter creates mind. In idealism, mind creates matter. In this present version of double-aspect theory, both mind and matter emerge from something still more fundamental, which is both or neither. To develop this view fully, it would be necessary to show that both the material and mental aspects of a system have causal properties. That would be outside the scope of this book, but the argument is developed in one of Ian Marshall's more specialist papers.[20]

I back this proto-consciousness view. It makes no sense to me that consciousness should appear just arbitrarily out of nowhere. Equally, it seems too strong to suggest that things like atoms and stones are conscious in the way that we are conscious. The notion that 'brute matter' possesses a weak form of proto-consciousness that becomes full-blown consciousness only in certain structures like brains seems to fit sensibly in between. It has a ring of credibility. Yet even a theory like this has a missing link. We still need to propose some sort of bridging phenomenon in the brain from proto-conscious brute matter to single neurones and then on to fully conscious coherent neural oscillations. To do this, I feel strongly that we must look at quantum phenomena in the brain. These may supply the necessary bridge and show why brains have what it takes to generate full-blown consciousness.

DOES THE BRAIN HAVE A QUANTUM DIMENSION?

Quantum theory was one of the four new sciences of the twentieth century. It was first formulated to describe the behaviour of the tiny micro-world within the atom, but today we know that the very different physical behaviour it describes applies to much larger structures. Laser beams and neutron stars are quantum devices. Silicon chips operate according to quantum principles. Indeed, much of the technology with which we are beginning the new millennium is quantum technology. People are even doing promising research into quantum computers that will be super-fast and able to 'think' in a different way from existing ones.

Quantum theory describes physical behaviour that is indeterminate and 'holistic'. It is quantum holism that interests us here. Holism in this context means that the many individual parts of a quantum system are so fully integrated that they behave as a single unified whole. The boundaries of the individual photons (particles of light) in a laser beam, for instance, are so overlapped that the beam behaves as though there is just one huge photon present. That is why laser light is so very focused.

There is a special class of quantum structures that have this property of extreme quantum holism. They are known as Bose-Einstein condensates, after Einstein and the Indian physicist Bose. Laser beams, superfluids and superconductors are almost perfect Bose-Einstein condensates. If a quantum structure of this kind were found in the brain it would allow all or a great number of our individual neurones to behave so synchronously as to become one. Such quantum activity would explain the special unity of consciousness.[21] It would also explain how many separate proto-conscious bits could combine to become one field of conscious experience.

Quantum theories of consciousness originated in the 1930s with the biologist J. B. S. Haldane.[22] In the 1950s the physicist David Bohm observed that there is a 'close analogy between quantum processes and our own inner experiences and thought processes'.[23] Most of the interesting modern theories have concentrated on looking for quantum unity (or quantum coherence) somewhere in neural structures – in the water within neural cells,[24] in neural microtubules,[25] or in special activity within the neural membrane.[26,27,28] But all these theories concentrate on micro-activity within the single neurone. Both the binding problem and recent MEG studies of the 40 Hz oscillations make it clear that the coherence relevant to consciousness is a coherence between very many different neurones. So the question now becomes: could there be large-scale quantum coherence at the level of the whole brain?

Let's begin with what it is that makes a single neurone oscillate. It is known that rhythmic electrical activity in the neural membrane is responsible, like the springs of a swing door. The whole neural membrane is permeated with channels that, when chemically or electrically stimulated, allow charged atomic particles (or ions) to pass through them. These channels are known as ion channels. Because ions are electrically charged they generate electrical fields as they pass along the channels, and this activity sets up electrical oscillations in the neurone itself. The electrical field across the whole brain in which the coherent 40 Hz oscillations are found is a collective phenomenon of these single neurone oscillations. The interesting question here is whether the across-the-brain electrical field is a *quantum* electric field, in which the 40 Hz oscillations are coherent quantum oscillations.

Michael Green at the City University of New York has very recently proposed that the activity in the neural ion channels is initiated by 'quantum tunnelling' phenomena.[29] (Quantum tunnelling is a process in which a particle 'tunnels through' an energy barrier by turning into a wave before exiting as a particle on the other side.) This explanation best fits the results of experiment. Thus there very probably is quantum activity in the single ion channel. Adjacent channels in the same dendrite are possibly close enough for the brain's electrical fields to pull their activity into quantum coherence.

On the next level up, cortical pyramidal neurones – 60–70 per cent of all cortical neurones – are a special and puzzling case.[30] They have not one, but two, sets of dendrites. The basal dendrites in the mid-layers of the cortex receive localized sensory input in the usual way. But there are also apical dendrites at the cortical surface, too far from the cell body to cause the neurone to fire unless they were all stimulated at once. The apical dendrites are closely intertwined, so that their electrical fields interact. This anatomical arrangement seems designed to create wavelike behaviour in the outermost layers of the cortex, so that the 'many voices' of separate neural oscillations are pulled into the one voice of a 'choir'. This is what Llinas and his colleagues observed, and nobody has been able to suggest any other good reason for the existence of the apical dendrites. Moreover, any drug which abolishes this wavelike activity also abolishes consciousness.

This is a strong argument for the conclusion that coherent oscillations in the outer layer of the cortex are necessary for consciousness. But are the oscillations quantum – do the individual quantum tunnellings through the myriad ion channels combine into one holistic quantum event? (An analogy is that electrons in Josephson Junctions, used in some very advanced electronic devices, tunnel through the barrier in pairs, rather than individually.) To prove this requires complex calculations and experiments that have not yet been carried out. For the electrical field across the brain to have the property of quantum holism, or quantum unity, only 1 per cent of all the electrical activity would have to be coherent. Superconductors display quantum characteristics, and yet in a superconductor only 1 in 10,000 electrons is coherent.[31]

WHAT DOES ALL THIS MEAN?

The notion that there is a third kind of thinking of which the brain is capable, and hence a third intelligence connected inherently to meaning, is radically new. It flies in the face of twentieth-century cognitive science, which sees mind essentially as a computation machine. There are no previous non-academic accounts of the research data that backs up this book's claim for the existence of SQ; indeed, there are no technical papers that combine all the relevant research. What, in plain words, are the wider implications of all this neurology and quantum physics? What can they tell us about the origins of SQ, about the extent of the transcendent dimension that it adds to our experience?

Experimental research presented here has shown that:

□ there are 40 Hz oscillations across the whole brain
□ these oscillations seem necessarily to be associated with the possibility of consciousness in the brain
□ these oscillations 'bind' individual perceptual and cognitive events in the brain into a larger, more meaningful whole, and
□ there may be a quantum dimension to the ion channel activity that generates the oscillations, as well as quantum coherence among the oscillations at multi-neurone level.

From all this I have concluded that the 40 Hz oscillations are the neural basis of SQ, a third intelligence that places our actions and experience in a larger context of meaning and value, thus rendering them more effective. Everything else discussed in this chapter boils down to two questions. Where does consciousness come from? And following on from that, where does meaning come from? Both are closely related to two further questions. Where do we conscious human beings belong in the universe? And how deep are our roots?

The first possible answer to where consciousness comes from is that it originates with brains, or at least with mammalian brains, all of which display 40 Hz oscillations. I reject this limited possibility, because it doesn't really explain very much. It says that consciousness just suddenly emerges with the mammals, as a new property of the universe.

The second possibility is that consciousness originates with brains because neurones possess proto-consciousness (pre-consciousness that in some combinations can become conscious). Here, I am assuming that the 40 Hz oscillations are the required factor for combining proto-conscious bits into consciousness. If this is the case, since neurones are single cells we human beings may be rooted in all other single-cell life on this planet. Our spiritual intelligence is rooted in life itself, and thus has biological and evolutionary origins, though life itself may still be just an accident in the universe, and thus without meaning or purpose beyond itself. I think this is possibly true, but unlikely. It presents the same problem as assuming that consciousness begins just with brains, only at a more primary, cellular level. *Why* should proto-consciousness begin just with neurones? Does it really have no roots in fundamental physics?

After considering all the main arguments, I have opted for the stronger view that proto-consciousness is a fundamental property of the material universe, just as mass, charge, spin and location are. Further, I have accepted the argument that everything possesses a degree of proto-consciousness but that only certain special structures, like brains, have what is needed to generate full-blown consciousness. In this case, we conscious human beings have our roots at the origin of the universe itself. Our spiritual intelligence grounds us in the wider cosmos, and life has purpose and meaning within the larger context of cosmic evolutionary processes.

So where does quantum physics enter the picture? And are there further implications if SQ is a faculty associated with quantum phenomena in the brain?

Quantum physics becomes necessary when we ask why it is that brains have the special capacity to turn proto-conscious bits into full-blown consciousness. Our consciousness is a particularly unified phenomenon. All the single neurones involved in a conscious experience oscillate coherently at 40 Hz. That is, they behave as many individual voices that have become one voice in a choir. No known classical phenomenon can generate this kind of coherence, but it is the rule in quantum processes. If the quantum tunnelling postulated in ion-channel activity can become coherent through close proximity in the brain's strong (at close range) electrical fields, then a mechanism exists for the coherent binding of single neurone proto-conscious bits into multi-neurone, across-the-brain, full-blown consciousness.

Nearly everything I have to say about spiritual intelligence in the rest of this book remains the same whether proto-consciousness begins with neurones or with elementary particles – that is, whether mind has a quantum dimension or not. In either case, our SQ gives mind a transcendent quality that roots us at the very least in the rest of life on this planet. The 'centre' of the self is rooted at least in something as deep as Jung's collective unconscious. We are not alone. Our intelligence does not isolate us within the narrow realm of ego experience, nor even within the experience of humankind. There is a wider context of meaning and value within which we can place the human experience. But the outlook becomes much more powerful and much more exciting if there *is* a quantum dimension to SQ.

At the beginning of this chapter I spoke of the quantum vacuum – the background energy state of the universe, the source of everything that exists. I pointed out that the vacuum is the ultimate transcendent reality describable within physics. It is the still, silent 'ocean' on which existence appears as 'waves' (oscillations of energy). The first thing to emerge from the vacuum is an energy field known as the Higgs Field.[32] This is filled with very fast, coherent energy oscillations that are the origin of all fields and fundamental particles in the

89

universe. It is in itself a huge Bose–Einstein condensate. If proto-consciousness *is* a fundamental property of the universe, then there is proto-consciousness in the Higgs Field, and the quantum vacuum becomes very like what mystics have called the 'immanent God', the God within all. In that case the 40 Hz neural oscillations that result in our human consciousness and our spiritual intelligence have their roots in nothing less than 'God'. 'God' is the true centre of the self. And meaning has its origins in the ultimate meaning of all existence.

5. THE 'GOD SPOT' IN THE BRAIN

In a back street of a poor district in Porto Alegre, Brazil, some sixty or seventy people crowd into a small, ramshackle wooden house with a tin roof. They are of various ages and races, children and old people, black, white, brown, mostly poor. Many of the men wear colourful cloaks or capes with layers of beads around their necks; the women are dressed as though for a wedding, in long taffeta or silk party dresses. As the people enter the main room of the house they prostrate themselves before an altar supporting a complex array of African and Indian totems, figures of the baby Jesus, Mother Marys of various colours, pictures and figures of saints, and fresh food of every description. The altar is lit with candles and blinking Christmas tree lights. A few of the women shake and have to be supported.

The people have gathered for an *um banga* ceremony, similar to a 'white' voodoo ritual. They have come to make contact with the spirits, to be possessed by them. A drummer appears, and begins to beat a regular, incessant, hypnotic rhythm. The people form a moving circle, their heads and bodies swaying back and forth to the beat of the drum. All through the night they dance and chant as, one by one, they are seized by a spirit. This is accompanied by violent shaking, an apparent loss of consciousness, the uttering of strange

91

sounds, and sometimes falling to the floor in what looks like an epileptic fit.

In a suburb of Minneapolis seventy or eighty young Americans, mostly middle-class, gather in what looks like a rock club. It is a Charismatic Christian ceremony. Loud music blares and strobe-lights fill the room with their eerie blinking light. 'Jesus lives! Jesus saves!' pounds out of huge speakers. Several people sway back and forth, their faces raised to the ceiling in ecstasy, their voices speaking in unknown tongues. A man shouts, 'I am filled with evil spirits!' and falls to the floor, writhing like a snake. Others stand around him shouting, 'Get out! You're not wanted here!' They are trying to exorcise the spirits within the man.

In remote northern Nepal, Tibetan monks gather at a monastery to perform the annual Mani Rimdu festival. They have come to invoke the spirit of Tanchi Panchan, the Lord of the Dance. The monks burn effigies of the evil deities who block their path and construct a mandala, a magic circle, in which the Lord of the Dance can dwell. They will enter the mandala themselves and become one with their god. 'Master,' they chant, 'affect my body, speech and mind. Let me dwell most earnestly in his magic mandala . . . My heart, the heart of this body, has become Lord of the Dance.'

In every culture, since the beginning of recorded time, human beings have communicated directly with their God or gods, and with spirits evil and benign. In the early 1990s, Canadian neuro-psychologist Michael Persinger experienced God directly for the first time. Dr Persinger is not a religious man, and he was working in his Laurentian University laboratory at the time of his experience. But there were exceptional forces at play. Dr Persinger had fitted his head with a transcranial magnetic stimulator, a device that beams a powerful and rapidly fluctuating magnetic field at selected small areas of brain tissue. If this device is used to stimulate various areas of the brain's motor cortex, certain muscles will twitch or limbs move involuntarily. If areas of the visual cortex are stimulated, even people blind from birth can experience what it is like to 'see'. In Dr Persinger's case, the device was set to stimulate tissue in his temporal lobes, that part of the brain located just under the temples. He saw 'God'.[1]

THE 'GOD MODULE'

It has been known for decades that people prone to epileptic seizures in the temporal lobes of the brain report a much greater than usual tendency to have profound spiritual experiences. Professor V. S. Ramachandran, Director of the Center for Brain and Cognition at the University of California, San Diego, has worked with epileptic patients all his professional life. Post-seizure patients regularly tell him, for instance, 'There is a divine light that illuminates all things', 'There is an ultimate truth that lies completely beyond the reach of ordinary minds, who are too immersed in the hustle and bustle of daily life to notice the beauty and grandeur of it all', or 'Doctor, suddenly it was all crystal-clear. There was no longer any doubt.' The patient who had the last-mentioned sensation reported that he 'experienced a rapture beside which everything else paled. In the rapture was a clarity, an apprehension of the divine – no categories, no boundaries, just a Oneness with the Creator.'[2]

Epilepsy is well known to be associated with higher than usual bursts of electrical activity in the relevant brain areas, and thus the intense spiritual experiences of temporal lobe epileptic patients have long been linked to increased temporal lobe activity. What Persinger's research has added is a kind of control condition. Having discovered that he can artificially stimulate the temporal lobes with magnetic field activity, he has been able to single out and investigate associated links with different kinds of mystical experience, out-of-the-body experiences, past-life experience, UFO (unidentified flying object) experiences, and so on – all under laboratory control. In the vast majority of cases, temporal lobe stimulation produces one or more of these experiences.[3,4]

One of Persinger's associates, Peggy Ann Wright at Lesley College in Cambridge, Massachusetts, has studied a similar link between heightened temporal lobe activity and so-called shamanistic experiences.[5] These are soul journeys to distant realms of experience in order to communicate with spirits of the living and the dead, and to bring back healing advice. Wright's work has also shown that rhythmic drumming of the sort used in a vast range of spiritual rituals excites the temporal lobes and associated areas of the limbic system.

Persinger's work, as we have seen, has focused on spiritual experiences 'created' by artificially stimulating the temporal lobes. In 1997, V. S. Ramachandran and his colleagues added a further step in linking heightened temporal lobe activity with spiritual experiences – this time in 'normal' people, under normal conditions. EEG electrodes were attached to the temples of normal people as well as epileptic patients. The researchers found that when normal people are exposed to evocatively religious or spiritual words or topics of conversation, their temporal lobe activity increases to something like that of epileptics during a seizure.[6] They concluded: 'There may be dedicated neural machinery in the temporal lobes [of quite normal people] concerned with religion. The phenomenon of religious belief may be "hard-wired" into the brain.'

The temporal lobes are closely linked to the limbic system, the brain's emotional and memory centre. Two crucial parts of the limbic system are the amygdala, a small almond-shaped structure in the middle of the limbic area, and the hippocampus, which is essential to recording experiences in memory. Persinger's work[7] has shown that, when these emotional centres in the brain are stimulated, heightened activity takes place in the temporal lobes. Conversely, heightened temporal lobe activity has strong emotional effects. The involvement of the memory-crucial hippocampus means that, even though most temporal lobe spiritual experiences last only seconds, they can have a strong and lasting emotional influence throughout the person's life – often described as 'life-transforming'. The involvement of the limbic system also demonstrates the importance of an emotional factor in religious or spiritual *experience*, as opposed to mere *belief*, which can be quite intellectual.

Neurobiologists like Persinger and Ramachandran have now dubbed the area of the temporal lobes concerned with religious or spiritual experience the 'God spot' or the 'God module'. Most suggest that this God spot has evolved in the brain to fulfil some evolutionary purpose, but they also hasten to add that it does not prove one way or the other whether God actually exists or whether human beings actually communicate with Him. So what does it prove?

Is the 'God spot' just some neurological trick played on us by nature because a human belief in God is in some way useful to nature or society? Have rituals and symbols evolved, poetry been written, lives dedicated, wars fought and cathedrals built for thousands of years just because of electrical activity in some parts of the brain? Is the force of St Paul's conversion on the road to Damascus no more than a side-effect of epileptic seizure? Or is the 'God spot' a crucial component of our larger spiritual intelligence, and temporal lobe activity just nature's way of allowing the brain to play its part in our deeper knowledge of ourselves and the universe around us?

When Harvard psychologist William James wrote his classic work *The Varieties of Religious Experience* at the beginning of the twentieth century he did not, of course, know about future

'God spot' research. But he did know that epileptic seizures and a proneness to certain forms of madness produced experiences very similar to other reported spiritual experiences, and felt that 'certain medical materialists', as he called them, might use this to discount the meaning of such experiences. James, though, thought the materialists were being 'simple-minded', failing to distinguish between two very important but very different questions. What is the nature and biological origin of spiritual experience? And what is its meaning or significance? The brain, he believed, was a crucial player in most psychological experience, but saying that was very different from saying that all such experience could be brushed aside as 'nothing but neurology'.[8] Scientists can, for instance, produce simulated 'visual experiences' by stimulating the optic cortex, but that does not prove that vision itself is hallucinatory.

It seems clear in the light of recent neurology that the 'God spot' does play an essential biological role in spiritual experience. The work of Persinger and Ramachandran, and that of other neurologists and psychologists who have studied 'God spot' activity in relation to madness and creativity, verifies the correlation of temporal lobe or limbic area stimulation with 'abnormal' or 'extraordinary' experience of many sorts. But to judge fully the role of the 'God spot', and the experiences it generates or mediates, we must look more closely at some of those experiences, at the madness and illness with which they are often associated, and at their positive role in problem-solving, the moral imagination and creativity.

THE VARIETIES
OF SPIRITUAL EXPERIENCE

In his classic book *Mysticism*, F. C. Happold reports how Christ came to him one evening while he was sitting alone in his college room in Peterhouse, Cambridge. Happold is not epileptic, and has never suffered a mental breakdown, so his experience is that of a 'normal' man.

> There was just the room, with its shabby furniture and the fire burning in the grate and the red-shaded lamp on the table. But the room was filled by a Presence, which in a strange way was both about me and within me, like light or warmth. I was overwhelmingly possessed by Someone who was not myself, and yet I felt I was more myself than I had ever been before. I was filled with an intense happiness, and almost unbearable joy, such as I had never known before and have never known since. And over all was a deep sense of peace and security and certainty . . . I realized that we are not lonely atoms in a cold, unfriendly, indifferent universe, but that each of us is linked up in a rhythm of which we may be unconscious, and which we can never know, but to which we can submit ourselves trustfully and unreservedly.[9]

In *The Varieties of Religious Experience*, William James reports a fellow psychologist's more tempestuous experience, though it has similarly peaceful consequences. The person had spent the evening dining and reading and discussing poetry and philosophy with close friends. Again, his mental health was perfectly normal.

> We parted at midnight. I had a long drive to my lodgings. My mind, deeply under the influence of the ideas, images and emotions called up by the reading and the talk, was calm and peaceful. I was in a state of quiet, even passive enjoyment, not actually thinking, but letting ideas, images and emotions flow of themselves through my mind. All at once, without warning of any kind, I found myself wrapped in a flame-coloured cloud. For an instant I thought of fire, an immense conflagration somewhere close

by; the next instant I knew that that fire was in myself. Directly afterwards there came upon me a sense of exaltation, of immense joyousness, accompanied by an intellectual illumination quite impossible to describe. Among other things, I did not merely come to believe, I *saw* that the universe is not composed of dead matter, but is, on the contrary, a living Presence; I became conscious in myself of eternal life.[10]

The experiences related by both Happold and James are religious, involving the sense of a Someone or a Presence. But personal spiritual experiences are often dissociated from religion, and based instead on love or some profound commitment or insight. For the German poet Rainer Maria Rilke (1872–1926), author of *Sonnets to Orpheus* and *The Duino Elegies*, such meaning and the deep peace it brought him were experienced through reading the words of an unknown poet. As we shall see in a few pages, all his adult life, Rilke feared for his sanity.

[I] was full of concentration and pure mental composure. Outside was the park; everything was in tune with me – one of those hours that are not fashioned at all, but only, as it were, held in reserve, as though things had drawn together and left space, a space as undisturbed as the interior of a rose, an angelical space, in which one keeps quite still . . . [The moment] is now present in me with a peculiar strength and survival, as though made of a higher degree of Being. I can think of two, three such moments during the last years . . . it's as though they sufficed to fill my inner life with a clear, serene splendour, they're such lamps within it, peaceful lamps – and the more I ponder them in recollection and attentive after-feeling, the more these, according to our present conceptions, content-less experiences seem to me to belong to some higher unity of events.[11]

Rilke drew on these experiences in later years when writing about the Whole that underlies daily existence, and when developing his vision that death is just another state of being.

Experiences like these, whether religious in content or more diffuse, are very common. In Western cultures, 30–40 per cent of the population are recorded as having had on at least one occasion feelings such as great euphoria and well-being accompanying deep insight that brings new perspective to life, the sense that everything around them is alive and aware, the sense of a guiding or comforting presence, or the feeling of being at one with the whole of existence. When more sensitive measuring techniques, such as personal interviewing, are used, this figure rises in some surveys to 60–70 per cent.[12]

In 1990, the Alastair Hardy Research Centre at Oxford University conducted a thorough survey of spiritual experience.[13] The team analyzed some five thousand research subjects who responded to a question placed in newspapers: 'Have you ever been aware of a presence or a power, whether you call it God or not, which is different from your everyday self?' In another questionnaire, they asked people to describe their experiences in their own words. Answers included descriptions like these:

> Feeling of mild elation not related to any particular event. Feeling that problems are minuscule and totally unimportant – different sense of perspective. Feel I have more understanding – more able to cope with life. Revitalises, rejuvenates and puts things into perspective.

> A feeling of being so very small and that all I experience and think is really so trivial in comparison. A feeling of being just on the circumference of some profound harmony and not knowing how to go any further. A sense of peace and calm but barely restrained raw emotion. Extreme emotion.

I have on several occasions seen, and also have just been aware of, my granddad since his death in 1977. He gives me a great feeling of comfort, security and confidence, especially as he only appears when I am unwell, anxious or worried.

Some of the responses described experiences of a more specifically religious sort, like Happold's; for instance:

I have experienced a sense of God's presence on many occasions. When I first experienced it (in a church service at the age of fifteen) I actually felt physically drunk (I wasn't!) and could hardly walk. On other occasions, I have just felt an overwhelming sense of peace and love, and often forgot the time.[14]

In this study nearly 70 per cent of the respondents answered affirmatively. From the detailed descriptions of these people's experiences the research team were able to discern two basic types of spiritual experience, the 'mystical' and the 'numinous'.

People who had had numinous experiences had a sense of a guiding supernatural presence, such as Jesus or the Virgin Mary, calling out to them and advising them to follow some particular path in life. Most of those people were from religious backgrounds. Those from agnostic or atheistic backgrounds tended to report experiences of extra-sensory perception, such as telepathy or precognition, or experiences of being in an altered state of consciousness, such as hovering above their own body during an operation or after an accident – so-called out-of-the-body experiences.

The mystical experiences described were more like that of Rilke: respondents reported feelings of profound meaning, deep insight, a sense of great well-being, euphoria, or an over-arching sense of unity in all things. Although this type of experience seldom has specific religious content, many studies link it to a greater capacity for creativity. Both types are a familiar accompaniment to increased temporal lobe or 'God spot' activity in the brain, but it is the numinous experiences that have a higher correlation with madness.[15]

MADNESS AND THE 'GOD SPOT'

Both schizophrenic and manic depressive patients see visions, hear voices, feel presences and receive instructions about tasks they are expected to carry out. Increased temporal lobe or 'God spot' activity is a feature of this kind of illness.

Some sceptics suggest that all such experiences are a sign of actual or incipient madness. But psychologists who specialize in studying links between spiritual experience and mental illness disagree. Ramachandran, for example, has shown that mentally healthy people show increased temporal lobe activity when exposed to spiritual words or topics.

However, other researchers assert that there are important differences between the experiences of normal people and those of the mentally ill. Michael Jackson did his doctoral research at Oxford University on this subject.[16] While concluding that there are similarities between the experiences of psychotic patients and normal people, he observes that, 'In general, the descriptions offered by the clinical group [the psychotic patients] were more disturbing, negative, and bizarre both in the way they were expressed, and in their content.'[17] He gives one powerful example of a typically negative schizophrenic experience. The patient reported:

I woke up one night and my curtains were slightly open. I could see the moonlight streaming in and I was aware of a supernatural presence. I quickly closed the curtains but the

awe-inspiring presence was still there. It was like a throb-
bing living being all around me. It pressurised me, I quickly
got out my canvas and painted the experience, the following day I was urged to protect my room from these rays and
influences by papering the inside with tinfoil.[18]

In many similar cases the experience of the psychotic patients
was disturbing rather than reassuring or inspirational. Psychotics also, Jackson reports, tend to be more overwhelmed by
their experiences than normal people, 'and had effectively lost
contact with consensual reality for longer periods of time,
during which they acted out their delusions in bizarre behaviour'.[19] Unlike the mentally healthy people, the psychotics
had difficulty integrating their spiritual experiences into their
everyday lives, and therefore found it hard to make lasting,
positive use of them.

There was also a distinction between the types of experience most common to psychotic patients and to normal
people. Psychotics were much more prone to have the
numinous kind, whereas mystical experiences occurred with
about the same frequency in both groups. If asked questions
about the following sorts of numinous experience:

□ A feeling of being controlled by something outside
  yourself
□ A feeling that you had entered another level of reality
□ A feeling that you were in the presence of a
  supernatural being
□ A feeling that you had lost your sense of time

nearly twice as many psychotics as mentally healthy people
answered positively.

By contrast, when asked about feelings of a more mystical
nature such as:

- Being surprised by the intensity of your emotions
- Having the impression that everything around you was alive and aware
- Feeling that you were in some kind of harmony with your surroundings
- A feeling of love or that you were loved
- Being in an unusually peaceful or serene state of mind

both groups answered positively with the same frequency – between 56 and 70 per cent of both groups had had such experiences. A study of 115 university students in Australia also found no correlation between mystical experience and introversion, neuroticism or psychoticism.[20]

Still, Jackson and many others noted enough similarity and correlation between experiences of madness and normal spiritual experience to inquire more deeply. As early as 1902, William James remarked that 'persons deep in the spiritual life' have a more ready access to the contents of their unconscious minds than others: 'The door to this region seems unusually wide open.'[21] Another student of mysticism observed in the early twentieth century that mystics have 'thresholds of extraordinary mobility. That is to say, a very slight effort, a very slight departure from normal conditions, will permit their latent or subliminal powers to emerge and occupy the mental field. A "mobile threshold" may make a man a genius, a lunatic, or a saint. All depends on the character of the emerging powers.'[22]

Newer psychological research from the 1970s has revealed much more about this 'mobile threshold' and explains why many non-psychotic people share some of the experiences common to schizophrenics and manic depressives. This research concerns the 'schizoid' or 'schizotypal' personality: people who show certain kinds of deviation from normal personality, or signs of incipient mental illness. Recognition of 'schizotypy', as it is most commonly called, has brought a subtlety to understanding the human mind and its deviations that was previously not possible.

Since the late nineteenth century, when psychiatry became established, the majority of leading thinkers in the field have accepted the view that mental disease is radically different from mental health, and that the insane are people with whom the rest of us have little in common. By contrast, the recent schizotypy research has shown that there is a scale of mental health from completely normal through schizotypal and finally to clinical madness. According to Professor Gordon Claridge of Oxford University, 60–70 per cent of the adult population of Western countries show some schizotypal features.[23]

But only 1 per cent are diagnosed schizophrenic, and a similarly small percentage clinically manic depressive. Most of the rest of us just have a few quirks.

Because several important research studies have now established a definite correlation between schizotypal personality and a propensity to have certain sorts of religious experience, and because, as we shall see, being somewhat schizotypal seems to confer a definite advantage on humanity, it is important that we recognize the features that define this state of mind. The degree of each depends upon where on the scale between normal and psychotic an individual is situated.

According to most assessments, a schizotypal person exhibits the following nine personality traits to varying degrees:

□ *Magical ideation*, which means a tendency to think that one's thoughts have a physical power or that they can come true (if I wish bad luck on someone and it happens, thinking it made it happen); also, a tendency to see significance in the correlation of supposedly unrelated events (like black cats and bad luck), or in mundane objects such as crystals, bones or anything that might serve as a talisman. Whether such magical ideation is considered schizotypal or normal is, of course, culture-dependent; in many societies such associations are regarded as mainstream.

☐ *Easy distraction*. The highly schizotypal poet Rilke expressed his easy distractibility as, 'If there is noise, I give myself up and am that noise.'[24] A more seriously schizophrenic patient commented, 'I attend to everything at once and thus I do not attend to anything.'[25]

☐ *A tendency to fantasize or daydream*, and sometimes not to know the difference between fantasy and reality.

☐ *Looseness of thought*, or 'thought slippage'. The individual's thoughts don't have the usual logical restrictions and boundaries, so he or she makes connections between things that others might not make.

☐ *Impulsive non-conformity*, in other words just acting on impulse; sometimes odd speech, odd behaviour or eccentric dress.

☐ *Unusual experiences*, such as the visual and auditory kind associated with spiritual experiences of the type described in this chapter.

☐ *Introversion*: liking one's own company and preferring solitary pursuits.

☐ *Social anhedonia*, also known as 'integrative pleasure deficiency': a diminished ability to enjoy social encounters, usually accompanied by a tendency to withdraw from them. Physical anhedonia is a diminished pleasure in sensory experience.

☐ *Ambivalence*: not being able to make up one's mind, because the individual can see the value or possibility of both or many alternatives.

Most of these are everyday features of the mental life of children, but in adults they are usually associated with eccentricity, and can be a sign of incipient madness. There is firm evidence that they are associated with conditions like epilepsy and dyslexia.[26] Yet they are also associated with higher than usual levels of temporal lobe or 'God spot' activity and thus seem to be hard-wired into our brains. Why? Why is brain activity that can in many cases cause suffering and dysfunction a normal part of our neurobiological inheritance? That question must be addressed before we can assess whether the temporal lobe activity commonly associated with spiritual *experience* plays any useful role in our overall spiritual *intelligence*.

WHY DO WE HAVE THE 'GOD SPOT'?

In 1994, Felix Post published for *The British Journal of Psychiatry* a personality survey of 291 men who had achieved world fame within the past 150 years. They included statesmen, intellectuals, scientists, artists, writers and composers, and most were household names: Einstein, Faraday, Darwin; Lenin, Roosevelt, Hitler, Ben-Gurion, Woodrow Wilson; Ravel, Dvorak, Gershwin, Wagner; Klee, Monet, Matisse, Van Gogh; Freud, Jung, Emerson, Buber, Heidegger; Chekhov, Dickens, Faulkner, Dostoyevsky, Tolstoy; and so on. The point of the survey was to see what correlations existed between creative greatness and mental instability.[27] Post's results were striking.

Using reliable sources that included medical records and first- or second-hand accounts, Post came up with the following statistics:

Occupation	Percentage who suffered mental instability
Scientist	42.2%
Composer	61.6%
Statesman	63%
Intellectual	74%
Artist	75%
Writer	90%

The degrees of instability ranged from occasional, isolated episodes to major ongoing problems that could disrupt work and severe incidents that required professional treatment in hospital. The problems included alcoholism, depression, manic depression, psychosexual problems, obsessive-compulsive behaviour, antisocial or histrionic behaviour, and borderline schizophrenia.

American psychiatrist Kay Redfield Jamison, herself a lifelong sufferer from manic-depressive illness, has conducted a similar survey of associations between manic depression and the artistic personality.[28] Her long list of those affected to some degree includes William Blake, Lord Byron, Rupert Brooke, Dylan Thomas, Gerard Manley Hopkins, Sylvia Plath, Virginia Woolf, Joseph Conrad, F. Scott Fitzgerald, Ernest Hemingway and Hermann Hesse. Many spent long periods in mental asylums or psychiatric hospitals, and a large number, particularly among the poets, committed suicide.[29] Jamison opens her book with a salute to these tempestuous colleagues by one poet, Stephen Spender, who does not appear on her list:

I think continually of those who were truly great.
Who, from the womb, remembered the soul's history
Through corridors of light, where the hours are suns,
Endless and singing. Whose lovely ambition
Was that their lips, still touched with fire,
Should tell of the Spirit, clothed from head to foot in
    song.
And who hoarded from the Spring branches
The desires falling across their bodies like blossoms.

Near the snow, near the sun, in the highest fields,
See how these names are feted by the waving grass
And by streamers of white cloud

107

And whispers of wind in the listening sky.
The names of those who in their lives fought for life,
Who wore at their hearts the fire's centre.
Born of the sun, they travelled a short while towards the
    sun
And left the vivid air signed with their honour.

Such 'fine madness', as Spender's poem makes clear, has resulted in great suffering as well as great creativity. Yet many of these creative, artistic types have not regretted the price, and some have even felt grateful for their unusual temperaments. Early in his career, just after he had broken with Freud, Jung suffered something like a schizophrenic breakdown that troubled him for seven years; yet decades later he wrote, 'Today I can say that I have never lost touch with my original experiences. All my works, all my creative ability, has come from these initial fantasies and dreams which began in 1912, almost fifty years ago. Everything that I accomplished in later life was already contained in them.'[30]

In the same vein, Rilke wrote of his borderline schizophrenic episodes, 'It might be necessary for every meaning to dissolve like a cloud and fall down like rain, necessary, that is, to endure something like mental disintegration or dying to be able to see everything differently.'[31]

Much of R. D. Laing's work in the 1960s was devoted to stressing the positive side-effects of his own patients' schizophrenic breakdowns. But as Post's study makes clear, there is very little correlation between creativity or high achievement and full-blown, long-term madness. Many of those who were borderline mad, or merely schizotypal when they did their best work, ceased all useful output once their madness had engulfed them. Madness itself can be sterile, constricting and stifling, its experience a nightmare. And though most creative people can be regarded as somewhat mad, it is not similarly true that most mad people are creative.

British psychologist J. H. Brod looked in detail at which particular schizotypal, as opposed to purely psychotic, qualities were likely to be useful for creativity.[32] Most of his findings, relating to the personality traits listed on pp. 104–5, follow common sense. For instance, schizotypal looseness of thought correlates with high test performance rates for fluency, flexibility of thought, and an originality in making associative or allusive links between ideas or between events. This 'over-inclusiveness' gives the schizotypal person a broader and more unusual range of thinking. Similarly, a tendency towards magical ideation and towards fantasy and daydreaming correlates very highly with being able to imagine things that don't exist, to create characters who have never lived, to have visual images that lead to new concepts, or to see things from an unconventional angle. Being prone to unusual experiences can expose the individual to more vivid colours and emotions, or to aspects of reality that are not common in daily experience. Both St Paul and St Teresa made full use of their spiritual visions in their careers. A tendency to be easily distracted can be disabling, but it also can lead one to pay attention to a wider range of things. And ambivalence, though it crippled Hamlet, is correlated with a high ability to see the benefits of many different options or possibilities at once.

SCHIZOTYPY AND PROBLEM-SOLVING ABILITY

We have seen that one of the criteria for intelligence is that it helps us to solve problems. This ability is also a feature of creativity, particularly scientific or political, so it is not surprising that some researchers connect the possession of schizotypal personality traits with special problem-solving abilities.

Michael Jackson points out that such experiences can play an especially creative role in dealing with existential problems – 'life problems' such as bereavement or serious illness, where what is needed is less a change of fact than a change of perspective or of attitude:

> A common spiritual experience in the context of bereavement is a period of awareness of the deceased person's presence, through a direct sensory perception or, less tangibly, simply the feeling that they are present. Through such experiences, people gain comfort in the face of bereavement in a more emotionally direct sense than would be available through relatively 'cold' cognitive processing.[33]

Jackson cites the case of Sean, a young family man who had been told by his doctor that he might have multiple sclerosis. This tentative diagnosis threw the man into despair and generally disabled his life and relationships. He was from a stable, middle-class, non-religious family, and declared himself a militant atheist. Yet one day, some weeks after his crisis began, he was walking through some fields when he heard a voice calling his name. 'Sean,' the voice said, 'none of this matters. You will always have what you need.' The voice then 'instructed' him on the ephemeral nature of existence and on how to cultivate a peaceful attitude of acceptance towards events rather than fighting them. When Sean reached the road some minutes later, 'My own thoughts started to come back, and all worry lifted.' The voice spoke to him several times over the next nine months, transforming his perspective and allowing him to deal with his problems in an effective and peaceful way.[34]

Such shifts of perspective are not limited to the solution of existential problems. Consider the story of the chemist Kekulé's dream of a snake biting its own tail, which led to his discovery of the benzene ring. And Einstein famously re-marked that we cannot solve problems from within the mind-frame that created the problems in the first place; his relativity theory was one of the great perspective shifts of the twentieth century. Some commentators think that schizotypy's problem-solving associations may confer an evolutionary advantage on the human species, making us more flexible, adaptive and creative. If this is so, the very low incidence of schizophrenia or manic-depressive illness may just be the price humanity pays for the far greater incidence of schizotypy.

'GOD SPOT' EXPERIENCES AND SQ

The big question so far as this book is concerned is whether 'God spot' activity contributes to our spiritual intelligence. The answer has to be both Yes and No. The 'God spot' certainly contributes to our spiritual *experience*, and to asso-ciated myth-making and mentally broadening experiences. Like dreams, and the mind of the child, it gives us access to the preconscious or unconscious mind and to symbolically rich associative trains of thought. But 60–70 per cent of us experience some noticeably raised 'God spot' activity (we have schizotypal personality traits), while only a very few of us create, for instance, great works of art or literature or solve paradigm-breaking problems.

A mere sense of the spiritual does not guarantee that we can use it creatively in our lives. To have high SQ is to be able to use the spiritual to bring greater context and meaning to living a richer and more meaningful life, to achieve a sense of personal wholeness, purpose and direction. A mere sense or experience of the spiritual may give rise to no more than confusion, disorientation or some indefinable longing. It can result in madness, or a craving that leads into self-destructive behaviour such as drug abuse, alcoholism or senseless consumerism. In other words a merely ephemeral experience of the spiritual can lead to an actual loss of perspective. Its sudden richness can make our ordinary lives feel so dull by comparison that we withdraw rather than evolve.

The 'God spot' is an isolated module of neural networks in the temporal lobes. Like other isolated modules in the brain – our speech centre, our rhythm centre and so on – it confers a special ability, but it has to be integrated. We may 'see' God, but that doesn't bring Him into our lives. Spiritual intelligence, by contrast, rests on the integrating whole-brain phenomena of our 40 Hz oscillations.

From this, it must be concluded that the 'God spot' may be a necessary condition for SQ, but it cannot be a sufficient condition. Those who score highly on SQ would be expected to score highly on 'God spot' activity, or on schizotypy, but it doesn't follow that high 'God spot' activity guarantees high SQ. For that to be achieved, as we shall see in the following chapters, the whole brain, the whole self, the whole life must be integrated. The special insights and abilities conferred by the 'God spot' must be woven into the general fabric of our emotions, motivations and potential, and brought into dialogue with the centre of the self and its special way of knowing.

Part III

A NEW MODEL OF THE SELF

INTERLUDE: A BRIEF
HISTORY OF HUMANITY

Where do we come from? What is our origin in time? How big is the story of which we are a part? What are we rooted in? How long do we last? Where are the ultimate boundaries of our human existence? What is the source of our intelligence? Of our penchant for asking questions such as these? It is surely impossible to think deeply about spiritual intelligence without considering such issues. In Chapters 6–9 I shall propose a model of the self that is intended to be both broader and deeper than any postulated before. But it is not possible to do so without considering the place of self within the unfolding history of creation. What I present here consists of some brief mythological and scientific vignettes that set human being and human intelligence in a larger context.

Every civilization in recorded history has had its own version of a creation story, a story that addresses questions like those above. These stories are an implicit part of how we know ourselves and how we value our existence. Many anthropologists have noted powerful common themes in the stories that different peoples have told, as though human consciousness itself has told its story through the different voices of many civilizations. Ian Marshall has gathered four of these voices in a narrative that has been performed in public, and it is given here as a prelude to the Lotus of the Self.

IN THE BEGINNING
A NARRATIVE FOR FOUR VOICES

The Voices

J.C.   Judeo–Christian/Esoteric
P.   Physicist
G.   Ancient Greek
E.   Eastern: Taoist, Hindu, Buddhist

1. Chaos

J.C.: 'In the beginning the earth was without form, and
        void. And darkness was over the face of the abyss.'
        So says our holy book of Genesis.

> Genesis 1: 1–2

G.:   'In the beginning was chaos, vast and dark . . .',
        the void from which all forms arise, and to which
        they may return. Thus we said in ancient Greece.

> Hesiod, *Theogony*

E.:   In Buddhist lands we call it Shunyata, the Void.
        'To say that it exists is wrong. To say that it does
        not exist is equally wrong. It is best to say
        nothing at all about it.'

> Zen Scripture

P.:   Before there was anything tangible, there was the
        quantum vacuum – a sea of all potential but
        nothing actual. No matter, no space, no time, but
        something we cannot describe. Possible worlds
        flickered around the margins of existence. But none
        had the energy needed to survive. Thus the story
        we scientists tell.

E.:   'The Tao that can be expressed in words is not the
        eternal Tao. The name that can be named is not

116

the eternal name. The nameless is the beginning of
heaven and earth.'

Tao Te Ching, 1

2. Gaia

P.:   Then something irreversible happened. One
possible world, a random mass of borrowed
energy, seized its brief moment and evolved a
structure. In the twinkling of an eye it had escaped
from its origins. Before space and time, the
structure was yet circular, closed, without
beginning or end. In our uncouth way we called
the structure 'superstring'.

G.:   You speak of full-breasted Gaia, the mother of
all things. She was complete in herself, a
uroboros, a snake biting its own tail, alpha and
omega.

J.C.:   'God said, "Let there be light," and there was
light. And he separated the light from the
darkness.'

Genesis 1: 2–3

E.:   'Something mysteriously formed. Born before
heaven and earth, in the silence and the void,
standing alone and unchanging . . . Perhaps it is the
mother of ten thousand things.'

Tao Te Ching, 25

3. Polarity

G.:   Gaia was mother to Uranus, the great arch of sky,
'whom she made her equal in grandeur, so that he
entirely covered her'.

Hesiod, *Theogony*

J.C.: 'On the second day, God divided the world into two — the wide earth beneath and the curving vault of heaven above.'

Genesis 1: 6–8

P.: The primal universe divided its being in two. One remained as mass and energy. The other became space/time and gravity, as Einstein showed us. The two entities were balanced, coupled, and now beyond the reach of Chaos. Now the universe began to grow.

E.: 'The Tao begot one. One begot two. Two begot three. And three begot the ten thousand things.'

Tao Te Ching, 42

4. Matter and Forces

G.: Uranus and Gaia had many sons and daughters. But Uranus was a tyrant who imprisoned his children. Cronus, the youngest, castrated his father and ruled in his place. His sister Rhea became his consort, and they in their turn had children.

P.: The crushing power of gravity was too strong. Nothing could escape its grip. The universe would soon have collapsed back into Chaos and ended. But the first manifestation of the quantum vacuum, the Higgs Field, had a subtle power. In a flash, the world inflated hugely, and the power of gravity became much weaker. The Higgs Field, Cronus as you have called it, was the foundation for all that now evolved.

G.: We recall especially Zeus and Aphrodite, rulers of forces: and Ares and Hermes, rulers of forms.

P.: We named these forms and forces after members of our own company, Bose and Fermi. The principles were the same.

J.C.:   We saw their symbols later in the seven visible
        planets: Jupiter and Venus, Mars and Mercury, Sun,
        Moon and Saturn. In our own occult tradition we
        placed them on the Tree of Life.

E.:   We saw the same energies reflected in the human
        body, in the seven chakras.

5. Stars

G.:   As the world grew older, the children of Cronus
        overthrew him in turn. Zeus with his thunderbolts
        now ruled the sky.

P.:   The Universe was dominated by the thunder of
        cosmic radiation. No solid matter could form. All
        was fiery plasma, as it is again in the stars today.

E.:   In ancient India we called this the epoch of Agni,
        the fire god. Recall that matter has four states: solid
        earth, liquid water, gaseous air and fiery plasma.
        Agni is the oldest of the elemental gods.

P.:   As the world cooled further, after three hundred
        thousand years, matter was no longer harried by the
        cosmic radiation. Other principles had their day.
        Galaxies and stars could form in peace. But a faint
        whisper of that fiery early time can still be heard
        today.

J.C.:   The constellations formed, patterns of glowing fire
        against the dark arch of sky. As we see them now,
        there is a circle of twelve: Aries, Taurus, and the others
        round to Pisces. The sun god visits each of his domains
        in turn. The cycle of the year is like any life cycle.
        Stars, like us, are born, live and die. Time had begun.

E.:   In India we honoured the cycle of birth, life and
        death with three gods: Brahma, Vishnu and Shiva.
        Everything that lives is subject to their rule.

6. Elements

P.:   The first stars were made entirely of fire; the cooler gas clouds between them, of air. But within the stars heavier elements were incubated. When a star died, these elements were scattered into space. From these ashes were made new stars, which now could have solid planets made from all four ancient elements.

All: Earth my body
Water my blood
Air my breath and
Fire my spirit

Findhorn Community Anthem

J.C.:   All the seven planes of existence between Uranus and Gaia, spirit and matter, were now created. A different phase of evolution could begin.

7. Life

P.:   This was the turning point. Solid earth had emerged. Until now, the Universe had little by little become more solid, inert, and divided into parts. But out of this cooler, deader matter more complex and delicate structures could be formed. First rocks, water, crystals, and chemical compounds. Then living creatures, and finally creatures with soul. The long, slow climb of existence back to its Source had begun.

All: Each new life is a new star, a sun in its own kingdom. The elements flow round it and through it. They follow its pattern like planets and comets. It creates new substances, food for future generations. Therefore we honour all life and its rhythms.

8. Soul

G.:   In our mental and cultural revolution, we began
        to understand and to express, not only the visible
        world around us but also the stages of the past.
        For all the past stages still live. The principles we
        called Uranus and Gaia, Saturn and Jupiter, are
        still here. We are still mass and energies in space
        and time. Evolution has not replaced but has
        built upon what went before. In our arts and
        sciences, in our religions and mythologies, in our
        efforts at right living, the still active spirit of the
        sky god is incarnated within the earth goddess in
        a new way.

E.:   Between the Tao of Heaven and the Tao of Earth
        there has arisen another bridge: the Tao of
        Humanity, a way of living in harmony with both.
        'The space between heaven and earth is like a
        bellows. The shape changes, but not the structure.'

        Tao Te Ching, 5

J.C.:   On the sixth day God created Man and made him
        in His own image. The work of heaven has begun
        to be done on earth by conscious beings. As above,
        so below. We have found analogies everywhere.
        Uranus and Gaia, our own male and female
        energies. The seven wandering planets in our sky,
        the seven chakras in our bodies, the seven forms
        and forces from Cronus' time.

P.:   The forces and particles that made the stars, and
        then made the planets, made our bodies too. Some
        think our minds and souls follow the selfsame
        rhythms. We are microcosms.

All: We are made of stardust. Those who understand
        and are of good heart can evoke these transforming

121

energies in our daily lives. In our end is our beginning.

End

In this simple, unfolding pattern of cosmic evolution, which is the true history of humanity, we see the first emerging outlines of the Lotus of the Self.

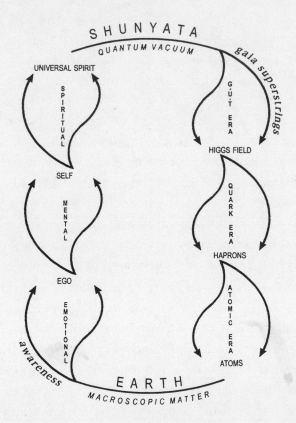

The cosmic spiral: a representation of the complete history of the universe from the Big Bang to the evolution of human higher consciousness. The stages of evolving consciousness are seen as analogous to the stages of evolving matter and force.

6. THE LOTUS OF THE SELF I: THE EGO LAYER

> The lotus might be called the first of all flowers, generally
> blossoming on stagnant and murky waters with so sensual
> and imperious a perfection that it is possible to imagine it
> as the very first sign of life upon the undifferentiated
> vastness of the primeval waters.
>
> Jean Chevalier and Alain Gheerbrant (eds),
> *The Dictionary of Symbols*

Originating in darkness and mud and blossoming towards the sunlight, the lotus spans heaven and earth. For Hindu philosophers, the lotus is the ultimate symbol of spiritual fulfilment, retracing the journey of self from darkness to light. For Buddhists it is the symbol of Buddha-nature that lies at the heart of every human being. The lotus represents the purity and excellence that are the essence of the human enterprise, the origin of all manifestation that lies coiled within human being. In some early Taoist secret societies it symbolized an 'inward alchemy',[1] the path to inner transformation. It represents the Tao of Man sitting between the Tao of Heaven and the Tao of Earth. In this book, I use the lotus as the symbol of the self that could be spiritually intelligent.

To describe our spiritual intelligence needs a deeper and

123

more detailed model of the self than has been available in previous thought systems. Spiritual intelligence, in essence, represents a dynamic wholeness of self in which the self is at one with itself and with the whole of creation. I believe this fuller model of the self can be described only by combining the insights of modern Western psychology, those of the Eastern philosophies, and many from twentieth-century science.

The lotus is itself a powerful symbol of such integration. In Asian philosophies, the lotus is the ultimate symbol of wholeness. The goal of all great Western spirituality has been the achievement of a kind of wholeness. Psychology calls it 'integrity'. The best science of the twentieth century is all about wholeness ('holism'), whether the deeply inter-related wholeness of physical reality, the closer integration of mind and body, or the holistic nature of neural oscillations that underpin human consciousness. To use the lotus as the ultimate symbol of the spiritually intelligent self seems the obvious way to combine the great Eastern and Western traditions of the self with the latest insights from science.

The lotus is also an appropriate symbol of the spiritually intelligent self because of its physical structure. In previous chapters we have seen that there are three basic human intelligences (rational, emotional and spiritual), three kinds of thinking (serial, associative and unitive), three basic ways of knowing (primary, secondary and tertiary) and three levels of the self (a centre – transpersonal; a middle – associative and interpersonal; and a periphery – personal ego). The spiritually intelligent self integrates all three. The lotus has a centre, its bud. Eastern philosophies call it 'The Jewel at the Heart of the Lotus' (*Om mani padme hum*). The petals of the flower itself have full, rounded centres and more pointed peripheries. And each lotus has a number of distinguishable petals, whether four, six, eight or 'one thousand' as in the crown chakra of Hinduism.

The self also, we assume, has a source, an origin in the history and development of the universe and a starting point in its own history. Physically, we begin as stardust that has itself evolved out of the quantum vacuum. Spiritually, too, we may begin as proto-consciousness associated with that stardust. As infants, we begin as innocent, undifferentiated consciousness. The stem of the lotus originates in the primeval, undifferentiated mud of original being, mirroring this origin of the human in some primal, undifferentiated wholeness. The self also *is* a source – the source of further developing meaning and value; even, according to quantum physics, the co-source of manifest physical reality. In Asian spiritual mythology, the lotus is the source of all manifestation.

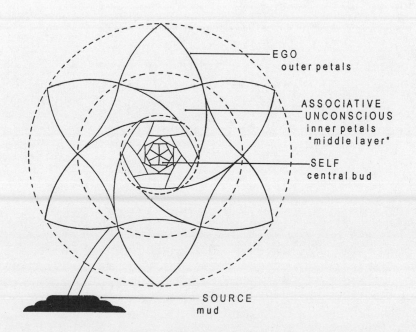

EGO
outer petals

ASSOCIATIVE
UNCONSCIOUS
inner petals
"middle layer"

SELF
central bud

SOURCE
mud

The basic Lotus of the Self.

In the Lotus of the Self as I develop it here, we go from outer to inner, from last to first, since that is the way of self-understanding in modern Western culture. Today we know ourselves first from the perspective of the conscious ego, from the periphery of the self. This ego self is essentially rational in its approach to experience, and is associated with the serial neural tracts and programs in the brain. I place the ego personality on the outermost edge of the lotus petals.

Next we become aware of the personal and collective unconscious, that vast pool of motives, energies, images, associations and archetypes that influence thought, personality and behaviour from 'within'. This is the associative 'middle' of the self, the part of our mind that is associated with parallel neural networks in the brain. This middle functions mainly through the body and through emotion. I place the associative unconscious on the inner edge of the lotus petals.

Those Westerners who are among the 50 per cent or so who have had a mystical experience of unification – a deep sense of being at one with reality – may have had a brief awareness of the self's centre. In fact all of us, whether aware or not, are in touch with the self's centre when we experience some new insight, see life in some larger context, or ask ultimate questions. This centre is associated with the synchronous 40 Hz neural oscillations across the brain, and is essentially unitive or integrative in its function. I place the centre of the self on the centre of the lotus, the bud.

And finally, according to all Eastern traditions and to the great mystical traditions of the West, there is that aspect of the self that is beyond all form. This is the Source, God, Being – it bears different names in different traditions. But in all traditions, the source of self that is beyond awareness is both the ground of being itself, the source of all manifestation, and the ultimate source of the energy which becomes conscious and unconscious mind. In twentieth-century science, this source of both existence and self is associated with the quantum vacuum, the still, ground energy state of the universe. In the Lotus of the Self, I depict it as the primal mud out of which the lotus's roots and stem grow.

The Lotus of the Self looks like, and is even intended to be used as, a kind of mandala, those Hindu/Buddhist maps of psyche and cosmos that guide meditators through the many levels of being and experience towards enlightenment in contact with the centre. With our 'mandala', the purpose is to achieve greater knowledge of the self at all three levels and to integrate them into a psychic wholeness that I call spiritual intelligence. In Chapters 7–9 I shall present the map itself, placing upon it the chief ego-level personality types; some of the main unconscious motives, energies and archetypes of the middle self; and then the centre.

The Lotus described here can accommodate a great deal of detail from a broad range of traditions – the many schools of Western psychology, material from the cabalistic Tree of Life, the deities of Greek mythology, the astrological and alchemical traditions, the Tibetan bardos, the Hindu chakras, the sacraments of Christianity and so on. Readers who are interested in these correlations should look at the Appendix on p. 297.

THE SIX PETALS

Ego is the most recently developed, most rational layer of the self. It is associated with the serial neural tracts and programs in the brain, the neural system responsible for logical, rational thought and conscious, goal-oriented or strategic thinking. In effect, it is a set of coping mechanisms and strategies with which self meets its world. If I have had damaging emotional experiences in childhood, my ego will protect me from further damage by developing strategies for adult relationships that avoid repeating the childhood pain. If a great deal was expected of me as a child, my ego will form strategies to meet these high expectations or, alternatively, to rebel against such demands. My ego is the mask I present to the world (and very often to myself), the role I play on life's stage. Ego is the part of myself that I most easily and most readily identify with: the person I believe myself to be.

Western culture is ego-dominated. Its emphasis is on public personas and formal relationships, and its extreme emphasis is on the isolated individual who must constantly make rational decisions. This is why most of us in the West live from the periphery of ourselves, wrongly believing ego to be the whole story of the self.

Each of us is unique. No two brains, no two sets of fingerprints, are alike. Each of us carves out our own destiny in dialogue with our unique experience. And yet it is almost universal in Western psychology, at the ego level of the self, to divide people into anything from four to sixteen personality types. These types – introvert, extrovert, realist, neurotic, artist, entrepreneur and so on – can be differentiated through tests, and so appeal to the objective, scientific bias of Western psychology.

For the ego periphery of our lotus petals I have chosen to use the six personality types identified by American psychologist J. L. Holland. First published in 1958, and described at length in his classic text *Making Vocational Choices: A Theory of Vocational Personalities and Work Environments*, the Holland test is the most widely used vocational guidance test in the world. Its basic tenet is that there are six personality types, each of which can be linked with a range of jobs best suited to it.

Holland's types are based on individuals' interests and abilities. Over the years, millions of people in many cultures have taken the Holland test as students or job applicants, and it has been the subject of hundreds of research papers. Though differing slightly in its description of the six personality types from other well-known tests, like that of Myers-Briggs based on Jung's work, the Holland categories can easily be rejigged to correlate with almost any other.

Holland asks questions such as, 'Would you enjoy being a nurse, a teacher, a mechanic, etc.?' Wide-ranging research has repeatedly yielded these six personality types:

□ the conventional
□ the social
□ the investigative
□ the artistic
□ the realistic
□ the enterprising

The personality types are paired in opposites so that an artistic person displays very different interests, preferences and abilities from those of a conventional person, a realistic person different qualities from a social person, and so on. But unlike some other personality tests, Holland's is sufficiently flexible to allow any one individual to score highly in two, three or four different traits, some of them even opposite to one another. As an artist I may be impractical and impulsive, yet in my more conventional role as a professional business lecturer I may be efficient and methodical. A scientist might be cautious and precise (an investigative trait) yet enjoy mountain climbing (an enterprising trait) and going to parties (a social trait).

In fact, we will see that a tendency to display traits from differing categories (identified with different petals of the lotus) is a sign of personal maturity and high SQ. A very immature person might have developed only one ego style (one lotus petal), whereas a fully enlightened (highly spiritually intelligent) person would show more balanced characteristics of all six. The lotus itself, as presented here, is a 'map' with which we can work our way round the different ego traits towards a more balanced personality. It is in that respect, especially, that the Lotus of the Self is similar to an Eastern mandala.

In Chapter 13 readers can take a test to determine which personality type or types they most closely resemble. Below is a summary of the salient qualities associated with each type (with each outer petal of the lotus). The petals and their personality equivalents are described in an order that corresponds to the ascending order of the Hindu chakras, energy patterns found in the unconscious middle layer of the self that, if used properly, can help to shift ego level personality traits. I shall discuss the chakras in Chapter 8.

FIRST PETAL:
THE CONVENTIONAL PERSONALITY

Only 10–15 per cent of people[2] satisfy Holland's criteria for the predominantly conventional type, though for many others it is their second or third string. These are people who are careful, conforming and methodical. They are efficient and conscientious, but can also be defensive and inflexible. Conventional people tend to be inhibited, never wanting to shock or stand out from the crowd. They are obedient, orderly, persistent, practical and thrifty, but they can also be prudish and unimaginative. Those who like to follow convention are the exact opposite of the more artistic personality type. Some of the occupations that Holland suggests would suit the conventional personality type are receptionists, secretaries, clerks, computer operators and accountants.

SECOND PETAL:
THE SOCIAL PERSONALITY

Social personalities form the largest of these groups: 30 per cent fall into this category, more of them women than men. Social types, as would be expected, like people and enjoy mixing with them. They are friendly, generous, helpful and kind. Social types find it easy to empathize with others, and can also be very persuasive. They are patient and find it natural to cooperate. Holland also describes them as idealistic, responsible, tactful and warm. They make very good teachers at every level. Therapists and counsellors are usually drawn from this personality type, as are many management consultants. They are also natural and loving home-makers.

THIRD PETAL:
THE INVESTIGATIVE PERSONALITY

Investigative types make up another 10–15 per cent of the population. They are passionate about ideas and, as the name suggests, love investigating them deeply. They are the most rational of the personality types, the archetypal intellectual. Analytical, complex, curious and precise, they can be as deeply critical of people as of ideas. Whereas the social personality type loves a crowd, investigative types usually require periods of their own company. They are introspective, retiring and unassuming. Cautious and reserved, they try not to be swayed by emotion. Deeply independent, they can also make themselves unpopular. The occupations where investigative types congregate include scientists, doctors, translators, surveyors and researchers. Most professional intellectuals have a substantial element of the investigative type in their personalities. University teachers, particularly those specializing in research, are good representatives of the type.

FOURTH PETAL:
THE ARTISTIC PERSONALITY

The very opposite of conventional types, and often at odds with the investigative type (sometimes inside the same personality!), artistic types make up another 10–15 per cent of the population. These complicated people are often untidy, emotional, impulsive and impractical. The artistic types' idealism can carry them away, as with Don Quixote and his windmills. Like the investigative type, the artistic type is independent and introspective, but has no difficulty expressing bold strokes of imagination. Deeply nonconformist and original, the artistic type is intuitive, sensitive and open, therefore often highly popular. These people are found obviously among writers, musicians and artists, but they also make good journalists, designers, arts critics and actors.

FIFTH PETAL:
THE REALISTIC PERSONALITY

The realistic personality is down-to-earth and no-nonsense and doesn't waste words. These hard-headed, materialistic, very practical types make up some 20 per cent of the population, far more of them men than women. They don't like very intimate relationships, shy away from social groups and put on few airs. These people are natural and genuine. When they speak they do so frankly, but they tend to be conformist and can be inflexible. They are not known for their original insights, but are persistent and thrifty. They are the only Holland personality types described as 'normal'. These realistic personalities prefer hands-on vocations, often where their workmate is a machine. They are frequently found among drivers, pilots, mechanics, cooks, farmers and engineers. Though the exact opposite of the social personality type, realistic personalities often make good marriages with them – each complements the other.

SIXTH PETAL:
THE ENTERPRISING PERSONALITY

These very self-confident and out-going types make up the remaining 10–15 per cent of the population. They are acquisitive, agreeable and ambitious, but can be domineering. Adventurous and full of energy, they seek excitement. They like to flirt, and can take things to exhibitionist extremes. Enterprising personality types are usually very optimistic, ready to try anything, and often inspire as much confidence as they feel. They are very sociable, and love to talk. Not surprisingly, a high percentage of politicians come from this type. So do salesmen, executives, managers and small businessmen. Enterprising types are also found among the police and armed forces.

GROWING AND
BALANCING OUR PERSONALITIES

For the most part, Holland's personality typology fits well with the scheme I suggest for the Lotus of the Self. But it is important to emphasize that, as Holland himself recognized, the average person is a blend of two or more of these types.

Ideally, in the course of a spiritually intelligent life, our personalities will grow to include a balance of all six. When the average person takes the Holland test first as a young adult and then later as a fully mature adult, the results tend to be the same. In other words, most people don't change very much at the ego level over their adult years. But in this book I want to concentrate on the few who *do* change, and on the notion that, if the spiritual intelligence in the general population were raised, more could change. Most adult personality traits are about half inherited and half acquired. We cannot become whatever we like, but there is quite a lot we can change if we really want to.

In early adulthood most of us are preoccupied with finding strategies that match environment and relationships to our existing ego personality. But later, classically during the midlife crisis, many people seek further growth and greater balance to their personalities. Jung referred to this further growth process as 'individuation' and associated it with life's spiritual dimension. It is, of course, the goal of SQ.

THE MYERS-BRIGGS SYSTEM

Holland's group of six personality types can be compared with another very popular system. In 1921 Jung described six styles of ego activity as three pairs of opposites: introversion vs. extroversion, thinking vs. feeling, and sensation vs. intuition. Some combination of these usually becomes habitual, so that I might, for example, be an extroverted feeling type with introverted intuition as my second string. Jung's work became the basis for the very popular Myers-Briggs Type Indicator test, now taken by over one million people per year, often in a business or educational context.

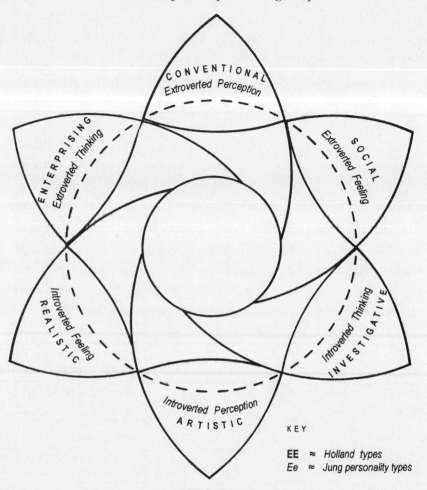

CONVENTIONAL
Extroverted Perception

ENTERPRISING
Extroverted Thinking

SOCIAL
Extroverted Feeling

Introverted Feeling
REALISTIC

Introverted Thinking
INVESTIGATIVE

Introverted Perception
ARTISTIC

KEY

EE ≈ *Holland types*
Ee ≈ *Jung personality types*

The Lotus of the Self I.

The overall relations that Jung suggested between his types have been challenged. For example, people may be capable of either thinking or feeling, or both, or neither – depending on the context. But the basic concepts remain very useful. Certain combinations of them map on to the Lotus of the Self very closely. For example, Jung's extroverted feeling corresponds to Holland's social type. Holland's artistic type corresponds to introverted perception (introverted sensation plus introverted intuition).

135

7. THE LOTUS OF THE SELF II:
THE ASSOCIATIVE MIDDLE

The large middle layer of the lotus is the associative unconscious, that vast store of images, relationships, patterns, symbols and archetypes that sway our behaviour and body
language, shape our dreams, bind our families and communities together, and give a sense of meaning to our lives
without reference to rational thought. This is the part of the
self where skills and patterns are embedded in our bodies and
in the neural networks of the brain. As Freud rightly saw
when he described his id, the unconscious seethes with energy
that has a logic of its own. The conscious ego, by contrast, is
more precisely formed.

How do the conscious and the unconscious meet? How do
they communicate information and negotiate strategies? What
happens at the border between the two, and how does this
bear on spiritual intelligence?

MOTIVATION – THE
BOUNDARY BETWEEN
CONSCIOUS AND UNCONSCIOUS

A crucial link between the conscious and the unconscious is
motivation. In the Lotus of the Self I place motives, and the
attitudes behind them, between the ego periphery of the

lotus's petals and the associative middle, and extending into both territories. The ego periphery is about IQ and how we perceive situations. The associative middle is about EQ and how and what we feel about situations. Where they meet lie motives – what we want to *do* about situations. Since an important aspect of SQ is about asking whether we want to change situations, and if so how, our motives for doing things may be linked to exercising our SQ. Indeed, the existence of half a dozen separate motives is a main reason why the ego has half a dozen ways of relating to the world (the six petals of the lotus).

Why does the artist want to create something that doesn't exist? Why does the enterprising type want to climb a high mountain or communicate some bold idea? Why does the investigative type so deeply need to *know*? Motives are what move us, what send the energy latent in emotion into ego personality channels and their consequent actions. Motives, emotion, movement – all these words come from the same linguistic root, and all are about channelling our deeper psychic energy or libido, as Freud called it. Understanding what motives exist and how they work is crucial to understanding how we can change or broaden the way we channel the basic, deep energy of the self – in other words, understanding motives is crucial to exercising our SQ.

Most Western psychologists accept that motives are a blend of the conscious and the unconscious. An artist is partially conscious of why he has to paint a given picture, but does not fully know the deep forces within his unconscious that impel him to create a vision that has never been seen before. A politician is partially aware why he promotes a certain cause, but does not fully know where the passion of his commitment springs from. We are always partly strangers to ourselves because we are always more than our conscious selves.

Again, psychologists discriminate motives from drives – forces that move us mainly through instinct. Reproduction is an instinct shared with all lower animals, but intimacy is a motive that requires higher evolutionary faculties. Defence of one's territory is another instinct found in most animals, but self-assertion is a motive found chiefly among humans and the higher apes. Motives are more *psychological*, more global, they imply some sort of exercise of free will, have more to do with real choice because they can be satisfied in a variety of ways. I can defend my territory only by pushing others off, but I can satisfy my motive for self-assertion by speaking up, by elbowing others out of the way, by issuing commands to subordinates and so on. In human beings, motives probably replace our lost instincts.

According to personality theorists, certain motives congregate around certain personality types. Opinions differ about how many basic motives there are, and about which ones correlate with which personality types. The American motivational psychologist R. B. Cattell is one of the great names in Western psychology, and a pillar of the personality testing tradition. His work is perhaps the most comprehensive, the most empirically based and the most widely tested. Like Holland's work on vocational guidance, Cattell's on motivation[1] is used throughout the world. He reached his conclusions through a variety of means for testing both conscious and unconscious motives – statements of conscious preference, 'lie-detector' type responses, measurements of the amount of time and energy vested in given activities and so on.

Whereas Freud thought there were only two basic human motives, sex and aggression, Cattell outlines about twelve. But I think some of these, like hunger, are better regarded as drives or instincts; others, like narcissism, are negative forms of a more positive motive; and yet others, like loyalty to one's profession, could be described as learnt behaviour. So I have taken just six of Cattell's motivational categories as basic ones, in some cases renaming and recategorizing them. These correlate with five of Holland's six personality types, and thus with five of the six petals of the lotus and its centre. The motives left are:

- □ gregariousness
- □ intimacy (parental)
- □ curiosity
- □ creativity
- □ construction
- □ self–assertion

I have indicated which features Cattell lists as components of these motives.

Gregariousness is associated with the conventional person-ality type and the first petal of the lotus. It means being moved by an interest in socializing, in fitting in with the group, in participating in or watching sporting activities, in enjoying group activities of almost any sort. Those whose chief motive is gregariousness have little interest either in rebelling or in being alone. Negative, or shadow, forms of this motive include withdrawal and narcissism – a preoccupation with self and an inability to relate (Cattell).

Intimacy of the parental kind is associated with the social personality type and the second petal of the lotus. A motive to find intimacy means being moved by a need to give love or to feel that one is loved. In Cattell's scheme, this motive is associated with feelings of parental protectiveness. In its more developed forms it is also linked with helping the distressed and wanting to do good works on a wider scale. Negative or shadow forms of intimacy include anger (Cattell) and hate.

Curiosity is associated with the investigative personality

type and the third petal of the lotus. It means being motivated to explore (Cattell), being interested in literature, music, the arts in general, science, ideas, travel, the study of nature and so on. Negative or shadow expressions include fear (Cattell), retreat and apathy.

Creativity is clearly associated with the artistic personality type and the fourth petal of the lotus. It means being moved to make something that has never existed, to say something in a way that has never been said, to live differently from the norm, to long for the unseen or the unexpressed, to dream of the impossible. Negative or shadow forms of creativity are destructiveness or nihilism. The creativity motive is named in Cattell's scheme only as 'sex', but it has been found in his and many other psychological studies as creativity, the life instinct, or romantic feelings. It is the dominant motive in 10–15 per cent of the population and is present in all human beings by virtue of the nature of our consciousness and the way we grow our brains.

Construction is associated with the realistic personality type and the fifth petal of the lotus. It means deriving enjoyment from playing with mechanical gadgets, building or fixing things. People driven by this motive often have a rich inner life of feelings, but have difficulty expressing then in words. Before the days of mass production, such people could express their feelings in pottery, furniture-making and other crafts. When more developed, realistic types follow the learnt motivation pattern that Cattell calls the 'self-sentiment'. This emphasizes self-control, self-respect, good citizenship and community interests.

Self-assertion is associated with the enterprising personality type and the sixth petal of the lotus. It implies being moved by an interest in high earnings, reputation, competitiveness, providing well for one's family, success at work, and politics (for one's own betterment). When more developed, this personality type still enjoys independence and leadership but is motivated more by serving the community or even by transpersonal interests. Shadow forms of self-assertion are abdication of responsibility, putting oneself down or the abuse of power for personal motives.

Cattell found a further motive that he calls 'religious'. I accept this as a central motive, but prefer to call it 'unification' because of the experiences with which it is associated. Cattell associated it with 'feeling in touch with God, or with some principle that will give meaning and help to my struggles' and with an interest in organized religion. This motive, however, seems not to be associated with a single personality type or activity but rather to be a potential driving force in the lives of all personality types, a motive clearly associated with finding meaning and value in whatever we do. So I place it not on a petal of the lotus, but at the centre.

THE ASSOCIATIVE UNCONSCIOUS: THE MIDDLE LAYER OF THE LOTUS

At the middle of the self are the habits, associations and traditions of daily life, the personal unconscious, Freud's id. Here also are the narratives and images of our religions and mythologies, and the internal rhythms of our culture. The dramas played out in our night-time dreams and the psychic models for our daytime behaviour are found here. Here is the place where each of us dips into wisdom and madness from beyond the ego, where each of us knows the nightmare world of the schizophrenic and the sublime ecstasy of the seer. Here is the place where we converse with the gods, goddesses and heroes of the race, with all the demons of the underworld, and where the energies that result in motivation first take root in the deep unfolding processes of the self.

The middle is the area of self exposed first by Freud in his study of neuroses and dreams, and expanded greatly by Jung and others who, in order to chronicle the unconscious, combined the study of psychotic mental patients and primitive peoples, the narratives of great mythologies, and images and symbols of mankind throughout recorded history. Among this mass of material are recurring patterns, images and symbols that suggest a universal structure for the unconscious psyche that Jung called the collective unconscious.

What are these deep patterns and archetypes that recur in different civilizations? How do they relate to the ego layers of our personalities? Which archetypes match which personality types? Which deep energies link with the set of basic personal motives outlined above? And what is the structure of these deep psychic energies? Why are they so universal?

At the external, ego layer of self I am out on a limb. The ego cannot repair or transform itself: these are resources of the deeper layers of the unconscious. But even here in the deep unconscious, the symbols and images of the Western tradition frequently have a static quality. What moves them? How does contact with them energize the self? How, in short, does transformation happen?

These questions bring us to the point on the lotus where the chakras of Hindu Kundalini yoga need to be introduced. There is no Western equivalent of this 'lotus ladder' of serpent-like, transforming energy, a set of seven vital locations within the body that represent stages of psychic development in the process of being and becoming. By incorporating the chakras in our lotus, we find a dynamic energy that represents a more primary stage of more familiar personal motivation. I said earlier that motives, because they can become conscious and change and can therefore contribute to personal transformation, are an important element in raising our spiritual

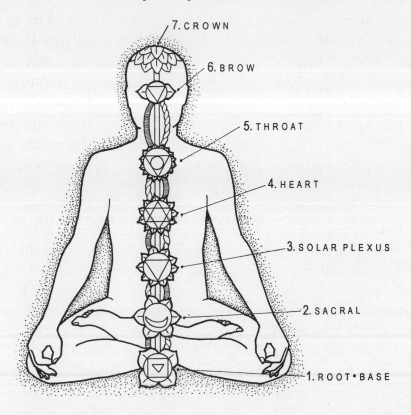

The chakras.

intelligence. This is even more true of the chakras: in Hindu tradition, working one's way up the chakras is the key to personal transformation.

These Hindu energy points correspond almost exactly to the psychic content of the more static Western structures adapted from Cattell, and the various archetypes and planetary gods (see diagram on p. 150) which I describe as shaping the unconscious. That they do so reinforces my belief that the self contains universal structures and energies that are definitive of human being, and which must be worked with when we come to the challenge of increasing our spiritual intelligence.

143

At this point, I want to work my way round the middle layer of the lotus with a summary of the psychic material and energy that shape the sector of the unconscious that is associated with each ego-level personality type. The vast wealth of images and symbols from many cultures can be distilled into certain basic patterns which recur under different names and in different forms. A summary of the recurrence of these patterns in different symbol systems can be found in the chart in the Appendix on p. 298.

THE DEEPER ROOTS OF THE CONVENTIONAL PERSONALITY

Ancient Western science, Greek and Roman mythology and earlier Babylonian and Egyptian mythology used a seven-fold psychological structure derived from a result of the seven 'planets' which were then observable. Since according to ancient physics physical bodies would eventually come to rest unless pushed by a living being, these seven 'wanderers' were thought to be gods, or the homes of gods. In the ancient and classical mind, gods were associated with human psychological traits and personality types. This association persists today in our fascination with astrology and in expressions like moonstruck lovers (Moon), martial music (from Mars) and venereal disease (from Venus). Similarly, Jung's archetypes of the collective unconscious correlate almost exactly with the traits of the planetary gods. Further correlation is found, though not consciously intended by those who devised the systems, between these planetary gods, Cattell's human motivational scheme and the Hindu chakras.

The conventional personality type and its associated motivation of gregariousness draws its unconscious roots from qualities associated with Saturn. Older than the Olympian gods and a very slowly moving planet, Saturn represents steadiness, form, structure, balance – all that is sane, normal and predictable. The conventional personality type is the glue of society. For Jung, the associated archetype of the collective unconscious is the Tribe, bound together by what he called 'participation mystique', primitive identification and fusion with the group. Some of this is needed even by the most independent adults; otherwise we could not feel we belonged to any group.

For its deepest source of energy, the conventional type is associated with the first of the Hindu chakras, the root chakra, located between the anus and the genitals. Appearing as a lotus with four petals, this chakra is associated with the elephant, which symbolizes strength, firmness and the solidity of the earth. But, as the twentieth-century authority on myth and mythology Joseph Campbell says, the elephant 'is also a cloud condemned to walk upon the earth, so that if it could be released from this condition it would rise'.[2] The root chakra represents spiritual energy in its lowest form, uninspired, reactive, with no explicit impulse to expand. Consciousness at this level must be awakened in order to rise to higher things. Some writers associate the root chakra with infancy and its need for security and support, both of which are the basis for stable further development. Caroline Myss[3] associates it with the Christian sacrament of baptism, a child's introduction into the human community.

THE DEEPER ROOTS
OF THE SOCIAL PERSONALITY

The social personality type, and its chief motive of intimacy, is associated with Venus. She is the Roman goddess of love, equivalent to the Greek Aphrodite, but derives from earlier

Great Mother goddesses such as Astarte. Venus nourishes and protects as well as firing couples' passions. Jung's archetype of the Great Mother also represents these nurturing and protecting qualities.

For its deepest source of energy the social personality type is associated with the second or sacral chakra, just above the genitals. A vermilion lotus of six petals, this chakra is linked with water. The primal energy here is sex and parenthood, either expressed directly in intercourse, fertility and marriage rites or sublimated into wider helping activities. Some writers associate this chakra with all gut-level feelings towards sexual partners and close family members, including empathy and nurturing. Distortions of this chakra energy can result in a pathological obsession with sex. Freudian psychoanalysis tends to treat the whole psyche as though it were caught at this level of psychic energy evolution.

THE DEEPER ROOTS
OF THE INVESTIGATIVE PERSONALITY

The investigative personality, with its chief motive of curiosity, is associated with the Roman Mercury (Greek Hermes), youthful herald of the gods who brought messages to the people from Jupiter (Zeus). Mercury also guided souls to the Underworld (source of deeper knowledge), and occasionally back again. He was a childlike and changeable god, easily associated with Jung's archetype of the Eternal Child who is also a guide of the soul.

For its deep source of psychic energy the investigative personality draws from the third or solar plexus chakra. Depicted as a lotus with ten petals, this chakra is associated with fiery heat and light, with the aim of mastering and turning the world into oneself, and with power. Its symbol is a white triangle containing fire and bearing swastika symbols on its sides. Energy here is connected to our attempts to become independent and self-assured. As in Freud's latency period, emotional and sexual issues take second place here to more intellectual and assertive activities, to achievement and conquest.

THE DEEPER ROOTS
OF THE ARTISTIC PERSONALITY

The artistic personality type, with its deep motive of creativity and its need to transform existing reality, is associated with the ever-changing Moon (Diana in Roman mythology, Artemis in Greek). The Moon shining in darkness symbolizes intuition and knowledge within the deep unconscious. It represents the powers of darkness, themselves always associated with creativity, the treasures found in the Underworld, magic and transformation. The artistic type draws creativity from deep within himself, from beyond his own conscious ego, from a source of knowing that is beyond rationality and logic. In ancient Greece the Moon was associated with rites of creativity and ecstasy, with wild dancing and insight through free play of the emotions. The associated Jungian archetype is the Priestess or wise woman who is part sorceress, part witch, the guardian of death and rebirth (the phases of the Moon) and hence of transformation. Jung and others have also associated this archetype with the shaman, the wise man or woman who journeys between the different worlds of consciousness to bring back healing and transformation to troubled souls.

The deep psychic energy source of the artistic personality is associated with the fourth or heart chakra. According to Joseph Campbell and his Hindu sources, the first three chakras are concerned with life in this everyday world – belonging to the community, sex and parenting, and the acquisition of personal knowledge and power. But with the energy of the heart chakra we make the transition to a concern with higher things. Depicted as a lotus of twelve red petals and associated with the element air, the heart chakra is where thought and feeling meet, where we experience an openness to others and to new things, an expanding sense of beauty and a deep idealism. The writer Caroline Myss associates the Christian sacrament of marriage with this chakra.

THE DEEPER ROOTS
OF THE REALISTIC PERSONALITY

The realistic personality, with its attraction to struggle and material achievement, can be associated with Roman Mars (Greek Ares), god of war. Like the realistic type, Mars is not particularly intellectual or empathetic, but shows great perseverance and courage. The accompanying Jungian archetype is that of the hero, who struggles against the forces of darkness (the shadow) to win a treasure for himself and others.

The deeper psychic energy of the realistic type is grounded in the fifth or throat chakra. This chakra is concerned with the struggle to marshal the forces and energies of the first four chakras for the higher purpose of contemplating enlightenment. Shown as a lotus with sixteen smoky purple petals, the throat chakra is associated with the Hindu god Shiva in his hermaphroditic form, clothed in a tiger skin and waving his trident, battle-axe, sword and thunderbolt. Some writers associate the fifth chakra with the harsher realities of adult life and the will to persevere through difficulties.

THE DEEPER ROOTS OF THE ENTERPRISING PERSONALITY

The enterprising personality, with its chief motive of self-assertion and its love of big schemes and political games, can be associated with Roman Jupiter (Greek Zeus), great father king of the gods and of humanity. Jupiter was god of the sky, storms and fertilizing rain. He was powerful and resourceful, but bad-tempered and sometimes tyrannical. Like any politician he loved to hatch grandiose plans, often with disastrous consequences. The equivalent Jungian archetype is the Great Father, symbol of leadership and authority.

The basic psychic energy from which the enterprising type draws is that of the sixth or brow chakra. Situated above and between the brows, it is described as a lotus of two pure white petals. Seated on the white lotus is the six-headed goddess Hakini, who offers fear-dispelling and boon-bestowing signs. Joseph Campbell refers to Hindu scholars who see those at the stage of this chakra being totally consumed by visions of the divine. But other scholars associated the brow chakra with wisdom and maturity, whose challenges often become apparent during the mid-life crisis. At this stage the individual, having achieved worldly success, seeks through involvement with the deeper symbols and meanings of his culture to find and express the meaning of life. Caroline Myss associates this chakra with the Christian sacrament of ordination into the priesthood.

As we go deeper towards the centre of the self, distinctions and boundaries begin to merge and fall away. Each personality type begins to draw on more of our common psychic inheritance – the deeper layer symbolized by Jung as the collective unconscious, the shared unconscious memory of our species. Here we find all the planetary gods, all the archetypes and all the chakras welling up into our

149

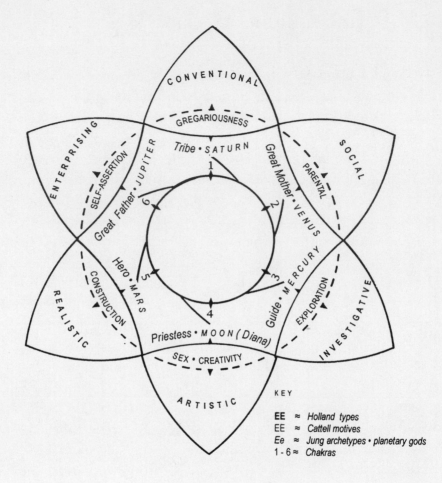

The Lotus of the Self II.

personalities and actions through our dreams and unconscious associations. The chakras themselves I place as forces of energy linking this deepest middle layer of the unconscious with the source and centre of the deepest self, the heart or bud of the lotus. Let's look now at that centre, at the place within self where all the many forces, energies, symbols and structures of the self begin.

8. THE LOTUS OF THE SELF III:
THE CENTRE

Thirty spokes on a cartwheel
Go towards the hub that is the centre
– but look, there is nothing at the centre
and that is precisely why it works!

If you mould a cup, you have to make a hollow:
it is the emptiness within that makes it useful.

In a house or room, it is the empty spaces
– the doors, the windows – that make it usable.

They all use what they are made of
to do what they do,
but without their nothingness they would be
nothing.

Tao Te Ching, 11

We could almost describe modern Western culture as a
culture of the 'absent centre'. There is no particular centre
of the cosmos in Newton's physics. Gravity just is, a force
present between material bodies wherever they are found. In
Western medicine the body has no vital centre or unifying
integrity. It is just a collection of parts – heart, lungs, kidneys,

brain and so on, each of which is studied in isolation. In Western education we have no deep sense of the educated human being or of education *per se*. We just teach our children 'subjects' – mathematics, geography, English, chemistry. In our traditional Western religions God is something 'out there' with respect to which we orient ourselves 'in here'.

Likewise in Western psychology the self, or personality, has no centre. We are just a combination of personality traits and unconscious motives, a set of behavioural characteristics, a set of genetic tendencies, a collection of neural operations. When psychology sets out to help us know ourselves, it does so in terms of these superficial characteristics. It offers us no inner focus from which we can unify and transform ourselves and our experience. In the language of this book, modern psychology has no concept of a spiritual intelligence.

The quotation from the *Tao Te Ching* on p. 151 illustrates the different philosophy of Eastern traditions. In the East, as in the quantum field theory of twentieth-century physics, emptiness has a kind of pregnant fullness, stillness is witness to truth. Things, existence, the self, the body are held together by a permeating centre that cannot itself be seen or expressed. The self cannot be lived or understood except in terms of its centre, which is the whole of creation expressed through this psychic reality that I experience as 'I'. 'I am the cosmos and the Buddhas are in myself,' say the Eastern texts. 'In me is the cosmic light, a mysterious presence, even if obscured by error.'[1] The Hindus speak of 'that indwelling Self which shines not forth, though It is hidden in all things',[2] and of 'the divine light which is mysteriously present and shining in each one of us'.[3]

In Western Christian mysticism, too, there is a sense of an indwelling centre that is linked to the source of all things and is also the key to true knowledge. In the biblical Book of Job we read, 'It is the Spirit in a man, the breath of the almighty, that makes him understand.' (32:8). St Luke tells us in his Gospel, 'The Kingdom of God is within you', and in other passages of St Luke's and St John's Gospels this 'kingdom within' is compared to a tiny seed which can grow into a great tree.

The great Christian mystic St John of the Cross defined the centre of the soul as God, '. . . and when the soul has attained to Him according to the whole capacity of its being, and according to the force of its operation, it will have reached the last and deep centre of the soul'.[4] In similar vein, the modern American mystic monk Thomas Merton believed the soul was not some independent, individual essence, 'but a point of nothingness at the centre of our being that belongs entirely to God'.[5] This point of nothingness is a point of deep solitude, and it is in our deepest solitude that we meet God: 'This inner "I", who is always alone, is always universal; for in this innermost "I" my own solitude meets that of every other man and the solitude of God.'[6]

Jewish mystical texts of the seventeenth and eighteenth centuries express similar ideas: 'Knowledge of the self is a means to knowledge of God the Creator and also to knowledge of the created universe,' wrote Rabbi Schneur Zalman. The pillar of Socrates' philosophy was, 'Know thyself.' His knowledge of the self led to knowledge of truth, goodness and beauty. And finally, knowledge of a deep self and of a deep centre is not restricted to mystics or philosophers. Contemporary British sculptor Anish Kapoor, whose life's work depicts a pregnant Void within both self and reality, describes the centre of the self as 'a place of quietness and singularity'. And in P. W. Martin's account of a First World War soldier experiencing warfare and the terror of death, we read an account of the soldier realizing, during the heat of battle, that there is a deep centre within himself which is 'completely indestructible':

In the summer of 1916, I was moving up with my battalion to the line. We were eager and rather nervous. It was our first active experience of war. The last march before the trenches had to be made in the late afternoon and at night. We started, heavily laden, stumbling over cobbled roads. The rain pelted down, soaking us. We went on till midnight, and came, in the black, to a half-ruined village. Everything was quiet, almost peaceful. We quartered in such barns and farm buildings as still had roof and walls; struggled out of our equipment and were asleep at once, as our bodies touched the ground.

I awoke with a start; a shrieking in my ears and a crash like the crack of doom. For a few seconds, silence, broken only by the sound of falling fragments. Again the ghastly drawn-out shriek and another, more shattering explosion. As I lay there on the floor, torn from the depths of sleep, I felt such extremity of fear as I have never known. From the waist downwards I shook in an uncontrollable trembling, horrible to experience. In the same fraction of time, the upper part of me reached out instinctively, with deep gasping breath, to something beyond my knowledge.

I had the experience of being caught, as neatly and cleanly as a good fielder catches a ball. A sense of indescribable relief flowed through my whole being. I knew with a certainty, such as no other certainty could be, that I was secure. There was no assurance that I should not be blown to pieces in the next instant. I expected to be. But I knew that, though such might be my fate, it was not of great account. There was something in me that was indestructible. The trembling ceased and I was completely collected and calm. Another shell came and burst, but it had lost its terror.[7]

In modern psychological terms we might best associate the centre of the self with the source of human imagination, with that deep place within the self from which we dream, or conceive the impossible or the not-yet-existent. In Zen Buddhism the centre is deeper still, a place beyond all imagining:

> We can actually penetrate beyond the depths of the collective unconscious of human nature and there come to the bottomless sea of Buddha-nature. If we go beyond the collective unconscious, thereby breaking through the final barrier of the self's unconscious layers, we experience true birth completely anew in the ocean of emptiness. This is infinite freedom of no-self, no-mind, no-idea; this is life itself, completely unconditioned. Here in the infinite no-mind we find flowers, the moon, our friends and families, and all things just as they are; we appreciate our everyday lives as miracles.[8]

The centre is a source within ourselves that is replete and inexhaustible and is itself the heart of some wider, perhaps sacred or divine reality. It is at once that which nourishes us and that through which we nourish our own creativity.

The more sensitive modern scientists speak of a deep source within the self from which their creativity springs. In *Faith of a Physicist* D. H. Huntley writes:

> The physicist is driven by his own experience to conclude that his personality has depths and resources beyond the analyzing conscious mind, wherein lie powers of synthesis, appreciation, and understanding, a latent skill and wisdom superior to that to which his consciousness is routinely accustomed. This suggests that the framework of physics, filled with a host of facts, has been fabricated in mental regions where reality is secondary to synthesis.[9]

Huntley's closing words are as good an approximation as any to the dynamics of the brain's unifying 40 Hz neural oscillations and the synthesis of thoughts, emotions, symbols, associations and perceptions with which they are linked. The recent research into the role of these oscillations in our conscious and unconscious mental life is science's own depiction of a centre for the self.

This centre is of course the main focus of this book. It is from the centre's unifying activities in the brain and from the centre's place within both self and cosmic reality that our spiritual intelligence emerges. Knowing the centre, knowing what can and cannot be said about it, knowing how it can be experienced and suffused throughout the personality, is the key to raising and using our SQ.

Conversely, ignorance of the centre, a failure even to know that our selves have a centre, is the principal cause of spiritual dumbness. Today we often speak of 'finding ourselves'. But if we have no relationship to the centre we 'find' ourselves out on some far petal of the lotus, at a more superficial ego level.

So what is this centre of the self, this Deep Self which is the source of all that we know and are, of all personal synthesis and transformation? What attempts have been made to speak of it in mythology and Jung's archetypes? With what motives and chakra energies is it associated? Can twentieth-century science add to our knowledge of the centre?

SYMBOLS OF THE CENTRE

The Sun is the source of light, heat and life energy. It is the centre round which all the other planets revolve. Like the centre of the lotus, it is a metaphor for the centre of the personality. But this metaphor fails to express the formless, indescribable quality of some mystical experiences. Empty space, or the quantum vacuum, comes nearer.

Jung's archetype of the Self is the closest Western equivalent to our centre of the lotus. Unlike Freud, who considered ego the dominant organizing principle of personality and thus waking consciousness the key to personal integration, Jung described the Self as embracing both conscious and unconscious mind, 'both centre and circumference' of the person. Yet in other writings Jung described Self as the centre of the personality, the central archetype and the centre of the personality's energy field.[10]

This apparent paradox resolves itself when we see that Jung used the term in three different senses. The original self, present at birth according to some analysts, later gives rise to the ego and other complexes and to the central self of the adult. This image is like the original cloud of dilute gas which, contracting, gave rise to the present-day Sun and its planets; or the lotus bulb which gives rise to the flower with its centre and petals. Jung's third, and most important, reference to Self is as an integrating or transforming aspect of the personality.

Jung often thought the Self only became accessible to people after the mid-life crisis. At that point, in conjunction with his 'transcendent function', the Self archetype synthesized opposites in the personality, such as thinking and feeling. The Self archetype and the transcendent function were the symbol and process of self-transformation. But Jung thought self-transformation most appropriate to later life, whereas I associate it with spiritual intelligence and think it potentially active throughout life.

In terms very similar to what I have been saying about SQ, Jung felt the Self archetype could not be dissociated from the psychologically integrating role played by the pursuit of meaning and purpose in life. As Jungian scholar Andrew Samuels points out, words such as 'unity', 'order', 'organization', 'wholeness', 'balance', 'integration' and 'to-

157

tality' keep appearing in Jung's discussion of the Self. 'Such a variety of terms would have little weight were it not for the fundamental connection of the self to questions of meaning.'[11]

Among existing symbol systems, the deep psychic energy of the centre is associated with the seventh of the Hindu chakras, the crown chakra. Located outside the body, above the head, it is often depicted in religious paintings of the Western tradition as a halo. It is pure, luminous energy, 'sheer light, one light, beyond names and forms, beyond thought and experience, beyond even concepts of "being" and "non-being" '.[12] Represented by a thousand-petalled lotus shedding rays of lunar light, the crown chakra realizes the pure union of the human soul with whatever we call 'God'. 'While at its centre, brilliant as a lightning flash, is the ultimate yoni-triangle [symbol of creation], within which, well concealed and very difficult to approach, is the great shining void in secret served by all gods.'

Though the energies of the crown chakra can *create* new symbols and forms, this chakra itself is beyond all existing symbol and form. We can experience this pure energy in spontaneous mystical experience of Unity, and it is very commonly reported in near-death experiences. Dante describes such an experience in his *Paradiso*:

One single moment is for me greater than oblivion
    Than five and twenty centuries to the emprise
    That made Neptune wonder at the shadow of Argo.
Thus my mind, wholly rapt,
    Was gazing fixed, motionless, and intent
    And ever with gazing grew enkindled.
In that Light one becomes such
    That it is impossible he should ever
    Consent to turn himself from it for other sight.[13]

THE NEUROLOGY
AND PHYSICS OF THE CENTRE

In the *Surangama Sutra*, the Buddha's chief disciple Ananda poses the question, 'Lord Buddha, you have spoken about the exclusive unity and oneness of the pure, mysterious and eternal Essence, but I do not fully understand. As soon as my six sense organs perceive this reality, it appears as so very many emanations. How can the One appear as so many?' In reply, the Buddha takes out a handkerchief. 'You see,' he says, 'that this is one handkerchief. Now I will tie it into six knots. Then we have here six knots, but it is still one handkerchief.'[14]

Until the late twentieth century only this kind of language described the unitive energy found at the centre of the self and of existence. But such accounts don't speak to the modern mind. Today such questions demand 'scientific' answers, brain phenomena that we can 'weigh and measure', experiments that we can read about.

Neurologically, we saw in Chapter 4 that the brain's unitive experience emanates from synchronous 40 Hz neural oscillations that travel across the whole brain. They provide a 'pond' or 'background' on which more excited brain waves can 'ripple', to generate the rich panoply of our conscious and unconscious mental experience. These oscillations are the 'centre' of the self, the neurological source from which 'I' emerge. They are the neurological ground of our unifying, contextualizing, transforming spiritual intelligence. It is through these oscillations that we place our experience within a framework of meaning and value, and determine a purpose for our lives. They are a unifying source of psychic energy running through all our disparate mental experience.

For the physics that best describes the centre of the cosmos we must turn to quantum field theory, the late twentieth-century adaptation of quantum physics. Quantum field theory describes all existing things as being states or patterns of dynamic, oscillating energy. You and I, the chairs on which we sit, the food we eat are all patterns of this energy. And what does this energy oscillate *on*? We saw in Chapter 4 that the ground state of all being is a still 'ocean' or background state of unexcited energy called the quantum vacuum.

This vacuum is the scientific version of the Buddha's handkerchief, the One Thing which, when tied into many knots (excited into many different energy states), appears as many manifestations. All things that exist are excitations of the quantum vacuum, and the vacuum therefore exists as the centre within all things. Vacuum energy both underlies and permeates the cosmos. Because we ourselves are a part of this cosmos, vacuum energy ultimately underlies and permeates the self. We are 'waves' on the 'ocean' of the vacuum; the vacuum is the ultimate centre and source of the self. When the self is truly centred, it is centred in the ground of all being. On our Lotus of the Self diagram, the quantum vacuum is the 'mud' out of which the stem of the lotus grows.

HOW DO WE USE
THE LOTUS OF THE SELF?

The Lotus of the Self is a map or mandala, an image of the layers of the human psyche from the outermost rational ego through the unconscious associative middle to the centre with its transforming psychic energy. Each petal, each ego-level personality type, can exist in isolation from the other ego qualities, from the personal or mythical levels of the associative unconscious, and from the centre. But this, as we shall see in Chapter 10, results in a spiritually stunted person. In the spiritually intelligent self, more integration is required. Being a doctor, for instance, requires both intellectual and interpersonal qualities. Leading scientists move beyond their field of

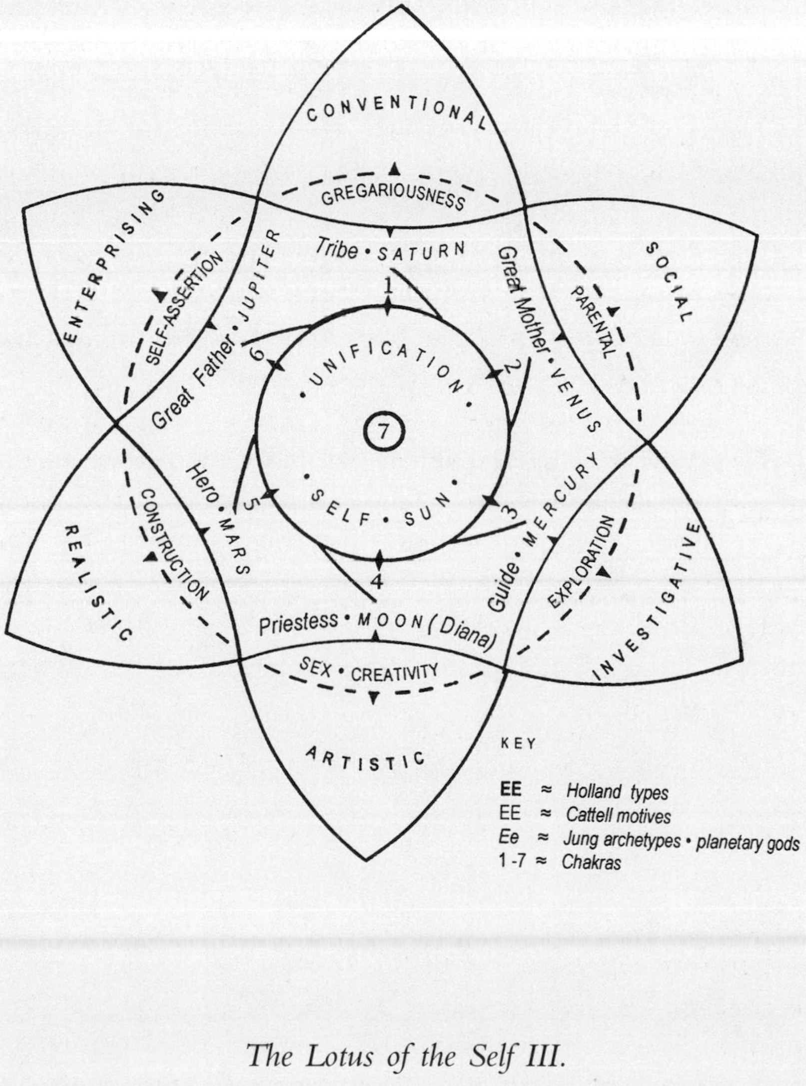
CONVENTIONAL
GREGARIOUSNESS
ENTERPRISING
SELF-ASSERTION
SOCIAL
PARENTAL
Tribe • SATURN
Great Father • JUPITER
Great Mother • VENUS
UNIFICATION
7
SELF • SUN
1
2
3
4
5
6
Hero • MARS
Guide • MERCURY
Priestess • MOON (Diana)
REALISTIC
CONSTRUCTION
INVESTIGATIVE
EXPLORATION
SEX • CREATIVITY
ARTISTIC
KEY
EE ≈ Holland types
EE ≈ Cattell motives
Ee ≈ Jung archetypes • planetary gods
1-7 ≈ Chakras

The Lotus of the Self III.

strict scientific expertise and use their knowledge to contribute philosophical or spiritual wisdom about the wider context of human life. Great artists reach beyond ego to the mythical, unconscious level, and today are required to make contact with the centre itself if their creations are to have real vitality. Indeed, all of us, if we are to be spiritually intelligent and to make vital creations of our own lives, must today make contact with that centre. This will be discussed at length in Chapters 10 and 11.

Here, I want to finish with some words from the twentieth-century American monk Thomas Merton on the purpose of the mandala. I cannot think of a better expression for the purpose of using the Lotus of the Self map:

> What is the purpose of the mandala? . . . One meditates on the mandala in order to be in control of what goes on within oneself instead of 'being controlled by it'. In meditation on the mandala one is able to construct and dissolve the interior configurations at will. One meditates not to 'learn' . . . a religious doctrine but to become the Buddha enthroned in one's own centre.[15]

Part IV

USING SQ

9. HOW WE BECOME
SPIRITUALLY STUNTED

Everything real is at the centre of the earth.
But if the centre of the earth meets the surface of
the earth, I might break.

Richard, a schizophrenic patient

In this chapter I want to define the key ways in which we become psychologically fragmented or broken through being spiritually stunted or spiritually ill. First, therefore, I must explain what I mean by spiritual illness.

Freudian psychology is about psycho-pathology – ways in which the psyche can get out of balance or damaged through anger, fear, obsession, repression, compulsion and so forth. Freud felt that such pathologies resulted from a dynamic imbalance between id, ego and superego, an imbalance between the rational, conscious ego and the demands of the generally unconscious realm. Causes included our parents not loving us enough, expecting too much of us or teaching us to repress our instincts and thus giving us sexual problems; and the moral codes of our society crippling our natural instincts.

Spiritual illness and reduction in SQ result from problems in relating to the deep centre of the self. These are caused by being cut off from the nurturing roots of the self that transcend

165

both personal ego and associative culture, and extend into the ground of being itself. Some people might call it 'existential illness'. Jung was very concerned with such spiritual or existential illnesses, and said that any psychoneurosis 'must be understood, ultimately, as a suffering soul which has not discovered its meaning'.[1] Irish medical consultant Dr Michael Kearney calls this kind of suffering 'soul pain': '[It] arises when an individual becomes cut off from or is at odds with the deepest parts of him or herself. And just as connectedness with soul may bring wholeness and a sense of significance, soul pain describes an experience of fragmentation, alienation, and meaninglessness.'[2] Kearney, who works with the dying at a hospice in Dublin, argues that soul pain is both at the root of, and a cause of pain associated with, many physical diseases.

There are three main ways in which one can be spiritually stunted:

□ not to have developed some side of the self at all
□ to have developed some side out of all proportion, or in a negative or destructive way
□ to have a conflicting or absent relationship between different sides

In the language of our Lotus of the Self map, spiritual stuntedness is on some far petal of the lotus, cut off from the other petals (aspects of personality), cut off from or engulfed by the middle (common symbols and mythologies of the appropriate culture) and, crucially, cut off from the integrating forces of the vitalizing centre.

In a spiritual pathology we have to deal with the same illnesses as mainstream Western psychology and psychiatry – manic depression, addiction, paranoia and so on – but the difference is that we attribute these conditions to problems of meaning and value and to a consequent inability to integrate and balance the personality. A spiritual pathology also takes us into areas not normally touched on by mainstream psychology and psychiatry – despair, the rejected or 'dark side' of the self, possession and evil.

Schizophrenia is one classic illness that I would describe as originating in problems with the centre and with chronically low spiritual intelligence. The schizophrenic cannot integrate himself or his world. His experiences, emotions and perceptions appear out of context. What psychiatrists recognize as the psychological component of schizophrenia – the effects of environment, relationships, personal reaction and personal choice – is, I think, better described as a spiritual component – an inability of the schizophrenic patient to contact and use the vitalizing and integrating energies of the centre. Richard, quoted on p. 165, is fascinated by the centre but terrified of allowing it to meet his 'surface', his conscious ego. I want to tell Richard's story here because it illustrates what I mean by the spiritual quality of a human life and how that life can be stunted by a lack of spiritual intelligence.

Richard is thirty-five and for the past ten years has had sporadic schizophrenic breakdowns which leave him largely unable to deal with the demands of daily life. He becomes dreamy and lost in conversations with himself, he sleeps very little, loses or gives away his money and possessions, acquires bizarre and sometimes dangerous companions, and speaks in a stream of far-flung though deeply meaningful associations.

His early life put a severe strain on his emotional development. Abandoned by his mother, he was placed with working-class foster parents in a home that offered inadequate intellectual stimulation for his high IQ. By fourteen, Richard was exhibiting behaviour problems and was expelled from school. He went to live with his father and a new stepmother, where the environment was intellectually rich but still emotionally inadequate. He took refuge in books and intellectual problems.

After a brilliant university career he was faced with the challenge of entering the real world, and had his first breakdown. Since then he has lived alone, does a menial job and has few friends.

The aspect of Richard's story that interests me most is the profound difference in his personality and abilities according to whether he is well or ill. When well, he is dry and unemotional, his conversation about abstract intellectual topics. He is perceptive about others, but in a cold and clinical way. He seems almost devoid of personality. Although highly attractive he exudes no sexual energy and seems not to belong to his body. He never discusses feelings.

When he is ill, Richard's high IQ is of little use because his breakdowns dissociate him from logical, rational and practical thought. But the rest of his personality bursts into life, and with it a striking emotional intelligence. He exudes warmth and charisma. All his thoughts have a profound archetypal layer and are impregnated with wider meaning, his intuition is sharp, and he freely expresses his emotions and vulnerability. He radiates sexual energy and seems at home with his body. He relates well to others, becoming open, deeply empathetic and good-humoured.

If we think of the soul as a channel between our outer personality and an inner world of deeper meaning, we would say that Richard's soul is broken. He is, in R. D. Laing's sense, a 'divided self' – divided into a brittle, sane outer ego and a warm, intuitive and deeply meaningful inner life which he can access only through madness. We would say he is in touch with his spirit only when mad.

Richard's story illustrates two opposed pathologies of the spiritual, two extreme ways in which we can be made ill through problems of meaning. When he is sane, Richard is wholly out of touch with his spiritual core. He can't make contact with existential meaning. When he is ill, he is wholly engulfed by it. What he needs is a blend of the two.

OUR SCHIZOID SOCIETY

Many of us are a little like Richard's 'sane' side, isolated from meaning by what can feel like a glass cage. We look at the world as if we are actors following a script we don't fully recognize, going through the motions of playing a role we don't understand, we can't really *feel*. As one former alcoholic described her addictive condition to me, 'It was like being in a vacuum, a void, like being in a dead place, a dead field. I felt cut off from myself, from others around me, and from God.'

The characters in Kafka's novels all have these qualities. In their somewhat petrified lives they are sleepwalkers in a social landscape, and their inability to make sense of the world and events is of almost nightmarish proportion. The literature of the twentieth century is rife with such reports – Sartre's 'nausea', 'alienation' and 'bad faith', Kierkegaard's 'sickness unto death', Heidegger's 'fallenness', Camus' 'outsider', even Marx's 'false consciousness of the bourgeoisie'. All describe a kind of disconnection from self and others. In mentally healthy people this is regarded as a common symptom of the condition known as 'schizoid' or 'schizotypal'. We saw in Chapter 5 that this is associated with raised activity in the brain's temporal lobes. The other, less common, symptom of the condition is like Richard's mad side. It is seen in people who are so open to wide trains of association that they appear dreamy and indecisive, unable to commit themselves to a definite path in life, quirky or eccentric in their thinking and behaviour, somewhat engulfed by their inner life, impulsive, unrealistic. As we have seen, these traits are often linked to creativity.

I describe our society as schizoid because the condition is so common, and because it is so closely linked to problems of meaning and of dealing intelligently with meaning. Most psychiatrists and psychologists who write about schizoid personality traits remark that they are much more common in the twentieth century than previously, indeed, that they are *characteristic* of life in this century.

The mid-twentieth-century psychologist Rollo May wrote years ago that most patients coming to him for treatment were suffering schizoid personality disorders. It was, he said, the illness of our times. Viktor Frankl, describing the state as an 'existential vacuum', links it to the pervasive sense of boredom in our culture, particularly among the young. 'A statistical survey,' he writes, 'recently revealed that among my European students, 25 per cent showed a more or less marked degree of existential vacuum. Among my American students it was not 25 but 60 per cent.'[3]

The Frankl survey was conducted in the late 1950s. In Chapter 5 we saw that late 1990s psychiatric surveys indicate that 60–70 per cent of the population in developed countries are thought to suffer some degree of schizoid disorientation. They include the vast number who see their family doctor for depression, fatigue, eating disorders, stress and addiction – the 'diseases of meaning'. In other cases these complaints are signs of still further mental illness. If we include links between stress and diseases like cancer and heart disease, mental/emotional illness makes up the largest body of reasons for which modern Western people consult doctors today. Collectively, they are also prominent among people who are in prison for crimes associated with personality disorder.

As a culture, we are going mad. Why? It is the argument of this book that the reasons are mainly spiritual, that our personal and collective mental instability follows from the peculiar form of alienation associated with alienation from the centre – alienation from meaning, value, purpose and vision, alienation from the roots of and reasons for our humanity.

THE THREE LEVELS
OF SPIRITUAL ALIENATION

From the Lotus of the Self we have seen that there are three basic levels of the self. All three play their role in psychic wholeness. Equally, some form of alienation from the integrating centre can occur at each of the levels, leaving us spiritually stunted in different ways.

In modern, Westernized culture the most common form of spiritual stuntedness results because our vastly overgrown ego layer has been cut off from the middle and/or the centre. We are too rational, too self-conscious, too prone to games and posturings. We are too cut off from the body and its energies, too cut off from our own dreams and deeper sources of imagination. Usually this leads to a noticeable drop in our emotional intelligence. We can be carried away by anger, fear, greed or envy. We become unbalanced and can't handle the imbalance in others. But we lose contact with our spiritual intelligence, too. Games and posturing usually mean that we are caught up in playing roles, and thus caught up in living out of some small part of ourselves. While we have the potential to realize something of all six personality types within ourselves, we become stuck instead within the script of just one type: we become too consumed with power, too reliant on convention, too obsessed with detail, too given over to rebellion, or whatever.

When our SQ is high and we are in touch with our wholeness our personalities express a little of the leader, a little of the artist, a little of the intellectual, a little of the mountaineer, a little of the nurturing parent, and so on. Our imaginations are fired by both Mars and Venus, by both

171

Mercury and Saturn. We contain some of the masculine and some of the feminine, some of the child and some of the wise man or wise woman. When our SQ is low, we become caricatures of ourselves and our emotions and our emotional patterns become caricatures of healthy human response. Our responses themselves are limited and fragmented.

Personality type	Normal responses	Disturbed or fragmented responses
Conventional	Kinship with group	Blind loyalty to group (fanaticism)
	Estrangement from group	Split from group (narcissism)
Social	Empathy with people	Addiction, masochism
	Antipathy to people	Sociopathic inability to feel for others, sadism
Investigative	Exploration of problems or situations	Obsession
	Retreat from problems or situations	Hysteria or phobic reaction, repression
Artistic	Joy in creation or achievement, celebration	Mania or misplaced euphoria
	Sadness at not having accomplished one's goal, mourning	Depression
Realistic	Wholeness, spontaneity, centredness	Self-indulgence
	Shame, inferiority complex	Degraded sense of inferiority, self-hatred
Enterprising	Taking responsibility, assuming leadership, loyalty to an ideal	Misuse of power, grandiosity
	Feelings of demoralization, betrayal of responsibility, denial of the situation	Self-destructiveness, paranoia, projection

For each of the six main personality types that we looked at in the ego layer of the Lotus of the Self (see p. 161) there are two healthy or normal emotional responses to people, situations or events, and two disturbed or fragmented responses.

The conventional personality type (secretary, accountant, clerk, computer operator and so on) is pulled between the normal responses of kinship with his or her group and estrangement from it. But when the ego is detached from the deeper layers of the middle and the centre, these responses can become blind loyalty to the group on the one hand, or a narcissistic withdrawal of interest on the other. Both fanaticism in the former case and narcissism in the latter are spiritually stunted responses.

The social personality type (teacher, therapist, counsellor, management and so on) is pulled between the normal responses of empathy, or affection for people, and feelings of some antipathy. Both are normal, and quite healthy in appropriate circumstances. But when the ego is detached from deeper layers of the self, empathy can turn to masochistic self-sacrifice, and simple antipathy can turn to sadism or a sociopathic inability to feel for others. Both addiction and the sociopathic are spiritually stunted responses.

The investigative personality type (professional intellectual, academic, scientist, doctor and so on) experiences either the healthy response of engagement with problems/situations, or its opposite, retreat from problems/situations. But in more disturbed form engagement can become obsession, and simple retreat can become hysteria, complete repression or a phobic reaction to something. Both obsession and hysteria (or phobia) are spiritually stunted responses – in other words, they are split-off responses.

The artistic personality type (writer, poet, musician, painter, interior decorator and so on) may move between the normal responses of celebration, a joyful feeling of achievement or creation, and mourning, a sad feeling of not having accomplished one's goal. But when these normal responses become split off from the middle and the centre of the self, celebration can become mania, a misplaced sense of euphoria, an unrealistic 'high' or false sense of accomplishment. Mourning, on the other hand, can give way to depression, an exaggerated and sometimes tragic failure to find any pleasure or good in a situation, relationship or project. Manic depression, the two sides of these disturbed responses, is present at abnormally high levels in creative types. It is a spiritually stunted condition because it deprives its sufferers of perspective, context and therefore wholeness.

The realistic personality type (driver, pilot, engineer, farmer and so on) ranges normally between the positive response of spontaneity and the negative response of shame. But when these responses become split off, spontaneity can turn into self-indulgence, whereas shame can degenerate into self-loathing. Both cripple the individual's sense of perspective and wholeness. They are spiritually stunted.

The enterprising personality type (politician, business executive, policeman, soldier and so on) experiences the positive emotional response of taking responsibility, loyalty to his ideal, assuming leadership. If his response is more negative, but still within the normal range, he may feel demoralized and betray responsibility. But when the egos of these power-oriented types become split off from their deeper layers, all the positive qualities of leadership can degenerate into grandiosity and misuse of power. Equally, the sense of betrayal can degenerate into an unhealthy paranoia and feeling that others have betrayed oneself.

The key factor in unhealthy responses is alienation from a part of myself, like two quarrelling friends. 'Myself' in fact contains a number of sub-personalities, as nearly all therapists have recognized – Freud's ego, superego, and id, Jung's complexes and archetypes, and so on.

174

None of us is exactly the same person at work, with close friends or at a social gathering, nor would there be any point in being so. Our dreams are a countless stream of further sub-personalities. The healthy state is to be on friendly terms with all sides of myself, so that they don't undermine each other and I can move easily from one to another as circumstances require. But some of my sub-personalities may be implacable enemies. And others are hard to find at all, creating 'holes' in my personality. These raise more challenges to personal growth and unity.

POSSESSION, EVIL AND DESPAIR

As we have seen, alienation can take many forms and can result in many categories of mental or psychic illness. The ones I have described so far are familiar to Western psychiatry, even if it doesn't attribute them to spiritual causes. This is because they arise mainly from problems of the split-off ego, and Western psychology and psychiatry are very ego-oriented.

There are, however, three states of alienation that can only be spiritual, and have always been outside the brief of mainstream psychiatry and psychology. Possession, evil and despair are far more often the subjects of literature or religious writings, though twentieth-century psychologists such as Jung, Viktor Frankl and R. D. Laing have attempted to engage with them. Anyone trying to come to terms with the greater atrocities and ills of the twentieth century has had to confront them, though with difficulty. They are conditions off the scale of the normal and fly in the face of all meaning. Without question they are conditions that exist in that grey area where psychology and the spiritual meet.

Towards the end of Joseph Conrad's *Heart of Darkness* the anti-hero Kurtz utters the chilling words, 'The horror! The horror!' Kurtz is a European trader who went into the African jungle and eventually went more native than the natives. When found by the expedition sent to rescue him from fever and from himself, he is presiding over bestial scenes of sadism and death. He sits in the midst of drumming natives waving skeleton heads on poles around blazing fires in the jungle night. Eerie cries fill the air. Kurtz is a man possessed. A demi-god to the natives, he has become a stranger to himself. Kurtz's eyes are glazed, his body almost rigid, his attention fixed on some unseen distant point, his psyche in thrall to a call from beyond himself. No longer just a man who attends a primitive ritual, Kurtz has been taken over by an inner drama from which he cannot escape. The ritual has taken on a life of its own inside him, and in consequence taken over his life.

Human history is filled with tales of possession, tales of shamans and medicine men who allow themselves to absorb the sorrows or sicknesses of their people and are then trans-ported into other realms of being, tales of religious zealots who hear voices in the desert or who fall down before burning bushes. And there are darker tales of young girls possessed by witches, of Jewish bodies inhabited by souls of the dead, Christians possessed by devils and Tibetan Buddhists by demons. In all these cases the person possessed is 'carried away' by something beyond his or her control.

Many twentieth-century tales of possession are like those of Kurtz, people carried away into sadistic or Satanic rituals. Others are more mundane: the alcoholic who simply cannot control his need for a drink because he is moved by some deep psychological pain or calling, a pain that hurts more than any physical pain, a pain that wrongly promises, 'Assuage me and you'll feel better'; the person who is 'called', impelled, uncontrollably moved to engage in dark or strange or for-bidden sex rituals that are almost beyond the reach of his own conscious awareness and well outside the scale of his normal behaviour or character; the person who must on occasion venture out to meet 'the shadow', who must frequent brothels or 'dives' or consort with unsavoury companions or engage in illicit deals and take risks with possibly self-destructive consequences.

Possession is like addiction, but more so. Addiction is to a substance or a behaviour – alcohol, drugs, sex, gambling, spending. Possession is by a force that impels a person, against his conscious control, to heed some call that comes from beyond himself. Possession seems archetypal, but in thrall to an archetype that itself has come loose from its moorings in the centre. To say that one possessed is haunted by demons is to say that he or she is in the grip of psychic forces that have become anarchic.

In the person of the religious believer who seeks his God, the voice crying in the wilderness is that of an angel. The voice comes from the centre. It is rooted in contact with the divine, with something that makes positive sense of the believer's life. In the person of the schizophrenic who has lost all contact with the centre, the voice crying out in the kitchen to raise a knife is that of a demon. The voice is disconnected, uncentred, anarchic psychic energy. The voice that cries out to the alcoholic to take that drink or to the otherwise normal person to engage in self-destructive sexual acts, or even to a culture to follow an evil leader like Hitler, is the voice of a demon that haunts a psyche which has lost its moorings.

In the language of twentieth-century physics, archetypes are probably patterns of psychic energy of the kind known as 'strange attractors' – patterns of energy that pull us into their field. When that field is itself rooted in the centre, the archetype makes us larger than our ego selves and gives us a pattern to live by. When the archetype is anarchic it causes us to spin out of control, to be possessed by forces larger than ourselves.

Jung did not say so, but I think that any archetype – the Great Father, the Great Mother, the Lover, the Warrior, the Child, the Priestess, and so on – that has come loose from its moorings in the centre falls under the sway of the Shadow archetype. The shadow is the dark, unloved, unacceptable side of any personality, the rejected sides of ourselves. The Shadow archetype consists of those rejected things raised to the force of an archetypal energy, and it can be the anarchic expression of any archetype. When they hold us in their grip we are possessed: we are pulled, 'called', carried away by an energy larger than ourselves which we cannot control and which is itself out of control.

The 'call' of possession is in fact a misguided call to wholeness. The split-off archetypal energy that calls to us when we are possessed represents split-off, rejected sides of ourselves. Possession is a pain-filled quest for those lost or broken or damaged pieces of ourselves. But it is a misguided call because possession is archetypal energy that is not rooted, energy that is split off from the centre. And only energies grounded in the centre can truly make us whole.

Evil is archetypal energy which is out of control. The ultimate archetype here is the Devil. The most loved of all God's angels, who out of pride rejects heaven (the centre), the Devil rules the kingdom of all that we call evil. The Devil is negative, disconnected archetypal energy *par excellence*. But is he evil *in himself*? Can anyone really *be* evil, or are some people just in the grip of evil? Is anyone born evil, does anyone become evil, or is evil just the strongest form of possession?

In the late 1990s I visited a maximum security prison to write a newspaper article about a dialogue group experiment being conducted amongst violent male sex offenders.

When I first entered the prison meeting room holding forty-five sex offenders, I experienced a violent personal reaction that left me nauseous and with a blinding headache.

The group included serial rapists and child killers. I recognized one notorious serial killer from his photographs in the newspapers. On first impression, all my worst assumptions about men who commit such crimes seemed justified. Most seemed of very low IQ, their facial features twisted and distorted, and a few had misshapen skulls. There were only two prison guards present and the dialogue facilitator; I was the only woman. The palpable feeling of evil and its threat in the room made me want to flee. Yet it was these apparently sub-human monsters who taught me most about what it means to be human.

The concept of the dialogue group is a way for people to learn to talk together, to get to know themselves and each other. Reinvented by the group psychology movement in the 1940s, its origin goes back to ancient Athens and to Socrates' use of incessant questions and discussion to break down his companions' assumptions and stereotypes. He believed the technique could lead us 'to find knowledge latent even in the most ignorant and to discover the good in every man'.

The prisoners were angry and frustrated, and their vocabulary was limited mostly to four-letter words. Yet in the three-hour session many of them found their voice. They spoke of their total isolation. 'Everyone thinks we're just scum. We *are* scum, but not *just* scum.' Some spoke of their guilt and of their shattered self-esteem when made to confront their victims' suffering. Others seemed bewildered, not fully understanding what they were supposed to have done nor why they were in prison. The collective pain in the room was intense. Many had been abused and/or abandoned as children, and they spoke of this. Their anger was a cry to be recognized as human, and in being given voice some basic human quality did shine through, something irresistibly likeable.

One of the guards commented that previously he would

not have wanted anything to do with these men. 'But now, after sitting in on this group, I would be happy to talk with any of them.' My own feelings were even stronger. Many of the prisoners had addressed their comments to me. Most of their crimes were against women or children, and they seemed especially to need me to see beyond their crimes to what they considered themselves. The experience was one of the most powerful of my life and has left me with a haunting perception: there are no evil people as such, but any one of us might be capable of evil. It is a human potential – an extreme potential of the fragmented, decentred, spiritually stunted self.

The vital, integrating force of the centre is present in every living being, and particularly in human beings due to the nature of our consciousness. Many of us are ignorant of our relation to the centre, ignorant that the whole of universal reality wells up within us. Many of us are estranged from it. But it is always there, even if unreachable.

Each of us is a cacophony of sub-selves relating like the members of a dysfunctional family. We have a dominant 'I' that we identify as 'me', but the repressed presence of the others haunts us and sometimes overwhelms us. Evil is a real thing, a force that can act within us and can overwhelm us. There are evil acts with horribly evil consequences. But evil itself is a form of possession, a lack of response to the deeper reality within us. There are no evil people, but rather people who are possessed by evil.

In the Hebrew language, the word for Devil is *Shitan*. Literally, it means 'no response', 'he who cannot respond'. In the biblical mythology of the Devil, his pride was so great that he could not respond to God – he could not love God – and thus he could not live as part of God's kingdom. The striking thing about both possession in general and evil in particular is the inability of the possessed person to respond to wider reality and to the people around him. The psychotic sadist feels no response to his victim's pleas or suffering; he does not identify with the victim as a fellow being. The Nazis called the Jews 'pigs', the artists they murdered 'degenerates'. American soldiers in Vietnam responsible for mass killings called their victims 'gooks'. Evil only becomes possible when it is perpetrated against 'the other', against those to whom we feel no response.

The Latin origin of the English word 'response' is the same as for 'spontaneity'. In everyday usage, being spontaneous is not distinguished from being impulsive or acting on a whim. But that is not its original meaning. If we think of spontaneity as a response to the centre – in ourselves, in others, and of universal existence itself – then being spontaneous is equivalent to being in a state of grace, a state of deep connectedness. The spontaneous human being is linked to others like waves on the sea. He is linked to that sea itself as the wave to the water of which it is the form. The twentieth-century Jewish mystic Rabbi Abraham Heschel defined spontaneity as 'those moments of immediacy in the communion of the self with reality'.[4]

Spiritual stuntedness is essentially a state of lacking spontaneity, and therefore of being low in response to the centre. Our egos become trapped in games and postures and pretences. We carry around too much self-consciousness, become too much concerned with form and appearances, too little open to what matters deeply. We get 'stuck on a petal of the lotus'. When our archetypal energies become disconnected from the centre, our lack of spontaneity leaves us open to the forces of possession and evil. And when our spontaneity is so lacking that we can no longer respond even to trapped or distorted psychic energy, we fall into despair.

It was despair that the Danish philosopher Soren Kierkegaard called 'the sickness unto death'. Despair is the ultimate abdication from life, a kind of ongoing act of quasi-suicide. The despairing person has given up, he can find no meaning, no thing or person of value to which he can respond. His days are a succession of grey sameness, his nights often occasions of dull terror. Death, the lack of life, the lack of response to anything living, haunts him. He fears it, feels panic in the face of it and yet, like a person standing giddy on the edge of a precipice, he feels drawn to it, drawn to jump. Suicide itself is the ultimate act of ultimate despair, the ultimate surrender to meaninglessness. It is the total loss of spontaneity.

In modern society suicides, or suicide attempts, are something of an epidemic, particularly among the young. A London *Sunday Times* article of the late 1990s reported that some 22 per cent of young women aged between sixteen and twenty-five attempt suicide, and 16 per cent of young men in the same age group. The male statistics were lower simply because men tended to succeed more often than women. Some of these young people try to kill themselves because they can find no meaning in life. Others do so because they have lost all perspective: a broken relationship or a bad set of exam results feels like the end of the world. Both are signs of low SQ – an inability to see beyond the moment or to place things in a wider framework of meaning and value.

Despair that drives us to suicide is the deepest form of spiritual stuntedness. It is the denial of spirit itself. But all levels and forms of being spiritually stunted bring us pain and often cause us to give pain to others. All mean that we have lost some degree of the spontaneity that makes us human, and that we have in consequence lost some of our ability to respond to life and to others around us. Ultimately, this loss of spontaneity and response cripples our ability to take responsibility for our lives and actions. Low IQ leaves us unable to solve rational problems, low EQ causes us to behave like strangers in the situations in which we find ourselves, but low SQ cripples our very being.

How can we heal ourselves? If high SQ is a potential of every human being, how can we access it? What does it mean to live from the centre, to live with total spontaneity and thus with deep response? How can our SQ help us to drop our games and pretences, free us from our compulsions and take us beyond our negative potential for evil and despair? These are the questions we will look at next when we ask how we can heal ourselves with spiritual intelligence.

10. HEALING OURSELVES WITH SQ

Recollection makes me present to myself by bringing together two aspects, or activities, of my being as if they were two lenses of a telescope. One lens is the basic semblance of my spiritual being, the inward soul, the deep will, the spiritual intelligence. The other is my outward soul, the will engaged in the activities of life.

Father Thomas Merton[1]

Recollection is one of the three key elements of Christian monastic prayer. As Thomas Merton describes it, recollection is the bringing together of our world inside and our world outside, the meeting of the deep, inner self and its innate wisdom or spiritual intelligence with the outer ego and its worldly concerns, strategies and activities. The soul itself, we saw earlier, is nothing but this channel or, better still, this dialogue, from the inner to the outer, the spontaneous communion of the rational, conscious mind with its centre and with the centre of all being.

When this channel or dialogue is broken, as in the case of Richard, the schizophrenic patient in Chapter 9, the soul is broken. We are fragmented and spiritually ill. When insight and energy flow freely through the channel from inner to outer, as in the case of the Georgian tenor in Chapter 2, the soul can heal us and perhaps those with whom we come into contact. We become centred, whole. Our SQ (the brain's coherent 40 Hz neural oscillations) is working to unite all the levels of being.

Spiritual illness is a condition of being fragmented, especially from the centre of the self. Spiritual health is a condition of centred wholeness. Spiritual intelligence, SQ, is the means by which we can move from one to the other, the means by which we can heal ourselves. In their Old English derivations, 'health', 'wholeness' and 'healing' all come from the same root. And recollection, the vehicle of spiritual intelligence, literally means to 're-collect', to 'pick up' or 'gather' the fragmented pieces of ourselves.

In *The Soul's Code*, Jungian psychologist James Hillman presents his 'acorn theory' of our origins. We are not, he says, simply the combined result of our genetics, environment and upbringing. Each of us has a unique fate which we bring into the world through being born. 'Each person bears a uniqueness that asks to be lived and that is already preset before it can be lived.'[2] This original uniqueness is an original wholeness and, according to Hillman, it is our destiny to recollect it and to live it.

As infants we begin life's journey in a state of fused wholeness with our environment. As family systems psychologists and psychotherapists argue, the human infant and young child forms its world and its self in relation especially to its mother and the family environment. This environment is the infant's framework. He has spiritual intelligence, a need to seek larger context, but at this stage he has nothing against which to test any given situation that might provide such a context. If the mother is a fragmented person, or if the family is a fragmented system, the child grows into this state of fragmentation. His own spontaneity ('innocence') works against him and against his original wholeness as it works

185

to adapt him to the fragmented family. A young child with a violent and sadistic father will identify violent sadism as love. He will seek it out in later life, and probably abuse his own children. A child with a cold and rejecting mother will identify these qualities as love and, again, will seek to reinforce them in his relationships in adult life.

When we recollect our experience later in life, we do so from the perspective of a wider framework. We can now place childhood experience in the larger context of adolescent or adult life and experience. And if it is the experience of our cultural conditioning, we now have the maturity to distance ourselves from the culture. SQ allows us to see that certain patterns of response, relationship or behaviour have consequences that we don't want. This is how both individuals and cultures evolve and transform. It is one of the dynamics that drive good psychotherapy. It is also an essential ingredient of meditation and prayer.

Recollection is not mere remembering. It is remembering from the viewpoint of a fresh framework. It is an opportunity to rewrite the family history by giving it a different outcome, to recapture the original self (the acorn) and to reinvent the mature self and its culture. Recollection is SQ in action.

RECOLLECTION
IN TIMES OF SPIRITUAL CRISIS

How do we come to the point of recollection? Why or when does our SQ 'kick in'? Many of us are spiritually stunted to some extent – some degree of personal fragmentation is almost inevitable in our modern ego-dominated society. Yet the deep self is always there. SQ is an innate capacity of the human brain, and we don't have to be spiritual heroes to hear its call. The soul is always capable of recollection. As Rabbi Heschel says, 'There is a loneliness in us that hears.

When the soul parts from the company of the ego and its retinue of petty conceits; when we cease to exploit all things but instead pray the world's cry, the world's sigh, our loneliness may hear the living grace beyond all power.'[3] That loneliness may be called forth by such experiences as our dreams, the creative use of our suffering or the death of a loved one. It may be evoked because the lifelong ego strategies with which we have coped cease to work – the psychic glue binding our fragmented selves together suddenly gives way. When we do hear its call, a spiritual crisis results.

In a spiritual crisis the whole meaning and perhaps the value of our lives is called into question. We may become stressed or depressed, turn to drugs or alcohol for temporary relief, become lethargic or dysfunctional, or even break down into madness. Such crises are always painful, but if faced courageously and *used* they offer an opportunity for recollection and the consequent mending and transformation of self.

There is a personal story behind this book that may help to give a concrete example of what I mean by such spiritual crisis, and of the search for and saving grace of recollection and spiritual intelligence for healing and growth. Though it can be painful, and sometimes risky, for an author to share personal material from which her work is drawn, I offer my experience here for whatever light it may shed on the processes I am trying to describe.

I conceived the idea for this book a full year before I was able to begin writing it. My 'annus horribilis' began just after my family and I left for a pre-writing holiday in Kathmandu. I had been travelling and lecturing for months and felt burnt out both mentally and emotionally. At night, while my family slept peacefully, I lay awake seized by dreadful stomach burning and pain. When I did eventually fall asleep, I experienced night after night disturbing dreams about being trapped in my childhood family situation. Soon I developed insomnia that was to last for months. When we returned to England, I tried in vain to get down to the task of writing.

The next months saw more of the same: night-time insomnia and disturbing dreams, always about childhood. During the day I slept twelve to sixteen hours. Whenever I was awake, I sat in our darkened sitting room with the curtains drawn, drinking heavily.

While I sat immobile in my house, our publishers kept selling more international contracts for the new book. Their own and other publishers' expectations were growing daily. 'How is the writing going?' they asked. I felt desperate, and in the end decided to consult a therapist. Together we looked at what the childhood dreams and the feeling of total burn-out were trying to say.

My father, as I mentioned earlier, was an uneducated Irish–Polish railroad worker and an alcoholic; my mother a highly educated classics teacher who abused drugs. There was a lot of violence in the marriage and they were divorced by the time I was five. From then on I was discouraged from seeing my father. He was the family 'shadow', to be repressed and forgotten. When I received good grades at school, won awards, did well at university, I was my mother's good child. 'I love you because you are a winner,' she repeated many times. When I did anything bad, failed at anything, became physically awkward as an adolescent, I was 'little Logan-insky', a derogatory bastardization of my father's name and a reminder of his Polish roots. I tried very hard always to be the good child. I never saw my father; I seldom consciously thought of him.

As a mature adult I began to succeed as a writer. After publication of *The Quantum Self* and its successors I became an international figure on a small scale, constantly invited to lecture and give interviews. Like my mother, I became a 'teacher'. Yet as the praise and the demands increased, so did a negative feeling of being a fraud, of being 'bad' inside, of concealing a putrid, rotting black baby at the centre of my being. The more brilliant the response to my lectures, the greater the depression I felt afterwards. After my mother committed suicide, no praise could lift the depression. It was all this that came to a head in Kathmandu, when something in me broke and all I could say was, 'I don't want to play my mother's game any more.' I came to hate my 'teacher' role and, now beyond the power of my conscious will, openly flirted with self-destruction.

After months of such immobility we went on holiday to Greece, where I had a crucial dream. In that dream I, as an adult, decided to call on my father. He lived with three old harpies who tried to turn me away, saying my visit was inconvenient. It was clear that the harpies had an alcohol problem and that my father was upstairs sleeping off the effects of the night before. I said, 'This is OK, because I have a drink problem, too. I understand.' My father came down the stairs to greet me, his face swollen with alcohol and sleep. I liked him at once and he was glad to see me. We agreed to meet from time to time, and he saw me to the door. But at the door of my father's house, two policemen said to me, 'What are you doing with this pimp and drug pusher?' I realized that my father led a life of vice.

My father and I met often during the day, but he would never let me see him at night. I knew that he spent his nights in the city's vice centre, and I decided to find him there. I went down into the bowels of the city, but my father had two lieutenants put me off his trail: 'He says we cannot allow you to find him here.' I realized then that my father was the King of the Underworld.

I awoke from this dream smiling, with a sense of exhilaration and release. 'So,' I said, 'my father is "the Devil". I am the Devil's daughter. Yet he wants to protect me.' I experienced a great feeling of warmth for my father and felt that he (the Devil) had a certain nobility of spirit. My mind followed all the associations about the Devil as a fallen angel, the most loved of God's angels, now condemned to rule over the Underworld, and I saw him as a tragic figure.

My dream was what might be called in this book a 'spiritually intelligent' dream. To be 'spiritual' is to be in touch with wholeness, literally to have a sense of one's own integrity. The dream put me in touch with a lost, 'dark' side of myself and made me want to own it. It made me want to re-collect myself and make myself whole. The dream also added a 'mythological' dimension to childhood events that had simply been too painful to recall and live with.

But wanting to recollect and to become whole is only the first step in what can be a long and painful healing process. For months after the dream I longed to know my father, and mourned dreadfully that this was impossible because he had died years before. I ignored the message of the dream that my father did not want me to find him in the 'bowels of the city', and sometimes I became obsessed with trying to find him there, with going through an inner ritual of what I called 'going down'. I drank more heavily and visited dark night clubs in strange cities wherever I was lecturing. In looking for my father, in 'going down', I was not yet aware that I was trying to recapture my own lost side. This only became obvious in a dream that I had months later during a return to Kathmandu.

In the earlier dream my father had specifically forbidden me to find him in the dark bowels of the city. I had to meet him somewhere in the light of day. I now took that to mean I had to find him within myself. In the new dream I was a dancer moving with a grace beyond the power of my own will. At first I thought my arms and legs were being pulled by strings, like those of a puppet. But then I realized that I was being moved from inside, that some force resident within my body, within my being, was orchestrating the graceful movements.

The dream left me with a visceral sense of deep spontaneity, a deep sense that there was an active centre within that bestowed grace (symbolized in the gracefulness of my movements). It was a spontaneity that I could not just admire in the people of Nepal, but take home with me as well. It was, of course, the healing call of my own SQ.

LETTING OUR SQ SHINE THROUGH

When we are cut off from the deep centre of ourselves – through fragmentation, one-sidedness, pain or distraction – it is as though we are walking on a muddy path in the dark with only a small torch to guide us. We move along warily from one pot-hole to the next, our perspective limited to one faltering step at a time. When we walk the same path in the daylight we can see it in a much larger perspective. We see the pot-holes in context and can avoid them with confident ease. The inner light of SQ has that effect with life's 'pot-holes'.

When we are using our spiritual intelligence we are seeing things from the centre. We are putting feelings and events in an ever wider context, relating things that had seemed separate, seeing and creating relationships and patterns. We are living the whole Lotus of the Self. But how do we come to see by this inner light? Must we always get there on our own, or is help available?

We have seen from both the neurology and the physics of consciousness that SQ is an innate ability of our brains and of the way they are related to larger reality. We don't have to be given the light of SQ by anybody else, we don't have to learn it, we don't have to inherit it. The deep self is with us as our human birthright, and is always there bearing witness to our unfolding lives. It is there whenever we strive for or act on meaning. But our conscious ego selves may not always be aware of this companion. Our SQ is never absent, but our sight of it, and thus our ability to use it, may be blocked. What blocks us may be the act of looking for SQ as though it were some object outside ourselves. But SQ is in the seer as much as in the seen (a wave looking for the ocean). What we first find may be a painful emptiness, but if we can weather this Dark Night of the Soul attentively, we can always find something real and fresh.

Sometimes, as in the case of my own spiritual crisis, the sheer strain of living an inner split may become so great that we cannot go on until this inner light breaks through. I simply could not go on living as though one half of me did not exist. That loneliness within, that 'loneliness that hears', as Rabbi Heschel puts it, finally demands to be heard. The very experience of spiritual crisis is itself a form of hearing.

We are not alone. Each of us is a part of the long human quest for meaning and of the traditions, symbols, associations, holy places and images that have given expression to this quest. Even our language is, as the German philosopher Martin Heidegger said, 'a house of Being', and we all dwell within that house. We carry the whole history of the universe itself within our deep unconscious, which is part of the collective unconscious of humanity. Each of us is a part of the larger human community, and most of us are also part of a smaller, personal community of friends and family. We can draw on all these things.

We can be helped in our quest to heal ourselves in many ways, for instance by the compassion of loved ones, by a good priest or rabbi, by a wise therapist or counsellor, by being close to nature, by drawing on a personal interpretation of spiritual symbols that mean something to us, such as the Cross, the Star of David, the *Shema Israel*, the Tree of Life, a Buddha statue, a candle flame, by reading or recalling a poem that stirs our unconscious, by reciting a chant that has meaning for us, through the inspiration of others' lives and actions, by a close attention to our dreams and a courageous willingness to confront our demons. As a Tibetan lama once said, we can even find the meaning of life through drinking a glass of water if we do it in the right spirit.

SPIRITUAL EMERGENCY IS NOT THE ONLY WAY

So far I have spoken about finding the light of SQ and thus one's personal centre through spiritual crisis, or what the psychologists Christina and Stanislav Grof call, in the most extreme cases, spiritual emergencies.[4] Such moments undoubtedly provide an opportunity for growth towards wholeness if handled wisely, but they are not the only means to experience and use our SQ. A great many well-balanced people have experiences when the light of SQ shines through, and many others long for it so strongly that their search itself becomes one of spiritual intelligence.

Children, for example, according to the definition offered in this book, show a high degree of spiritual intelligence. They are always asking, 'Why?', always seeking the meaning of their own and others' actions, always struggling to put feelings and events in a larger, meaning-giving context. Children are not yet locked into a set of assumptions or a set way of seeing things. Everything is fresh for them.

The natural spirituality of children that people like America's Robert Coles write about[5] is due to their high SQ. At their young age, and with their penchant for asking how and why, children naturally want to construct what adults would call a metaphysical framework for their lives. They want to know who they are, why they were born, where they came from, where the world comes from, why people behave as they do. When my own son was aged five, he asked me one night at bedtime, 'Mummy, why do I have a life?' That was a spiritually intelligent question. But too often parents and teachers brush their questions aside or patronize them with answers we would not accept ourselves. This can lead to cynicism, despair or mere conformity in later life, any of which is damaging to a child's originally high SQ.

Equally, we cynical or spiritually stunted adults can some-times find the light of SQ within ourselves by recapturing the inner child, by seeing some event or relationship with the wonder and freshness of the child's eye within us. That is one of the well-known joys of parenthood. This childlike vision is also commonly associated with creativity in adults. Isaac Newton described his relationship to physics as being like that of a small boy standing on a beach and discovering beautiful pebbles and shells. The painter Henri Matisse said, 'We must learn to see the world again, as through the eyes of a child.'

Any time that we step outside our assumptions or habitual way of seeing things, any time that we break through into some new insight that places our behaviour in a larger, meaning-giving context, any time that we transcend ego and act from our centre, any time that we experience the thrill of beauty or truth larger than ourselves, hear the sublimity in a piece of music, see the majesty in a mountain sunrise, feel the profound simplicity of a new idea, feel the depths of meditation or the wonder of prayer, we are experiencing our SQ and to some small extent, at least, using it to heal ourselves.

Joseph Campbell tells the story of two young policemen driving through a mountain pass in Hawaii. There was a bridge popular with both sightseers and suicides, and as the policemen approached they saw a young man about to throw himself into the canyon below. One of them jumped from his car, grabbed the young man and would have been dragged over the edge with him had not his colleague come to the rescue.

'Do you realize,' Campbell asks, 'what had happened to that policeman who had given himself to death with that unknown youth? Everything else in his life had dropped off – his duty to his family, his duty to his job, his duty to his own life – all his wishes and hopes for his lifetime had just disappeared. He was about to die. Why?' He refers to the German philosopher Schopenhauer, who says that in such crises a kind of metaphysical truth can break through – the truth that you and the other are one, that there is no separateness, that you and the 'stranger' are two aspects of one life. Our true reality is our identity and unity with all life.

'The hero,' says Campbell, 'is the one who has given his physical life to some order of realization of that truth.'[6] In doing so his physical, or ego, life becomes larger and somehow healed.

There are experiences of death, or near-death, that also cause the light to shine through. In the face of his apparently imminent death in the Auschwitz concentration camp, Victor Frankl says he found the meaning of life:

> In this critical situation my concern was different from that of most of my comrades. Their question was, 'Will we survive the camp? For if not, all this suffering has no meaning.' The question which beset me was, 'Has all this suffering, this dying around us, a meaning? For, if not, then ultimately there is no meaning to survival; for a life whose meaning depends upon such a happenstance – as whether one escapes or not – ultimately would not be worth living at all.[7]

195

Marie de Hennezel, a psychologist who works with the terminally ill at a hospital in Paris, says:

> [The awareness that I must die] is, paradoxically, what binds me to every other human being. It's why every man's death touches me. It allows me to penetrate to the heart of the only true question: So what does my life mean? . . . Death, which we will live to the end one day, which will strike our loved ones and our friends, is perhaps what pushes us not to be content with living on the surface of things and people, pushes us to enter into the heart and depth of them.[8]

Death brings to life a larger context of meaning and value.

And finally, I think of Neale Donald Walsch's best-selling *Conversations with God*. At one level, we can take these literally and say that Walsch has a hot-line to some Supreme Being outside our worldly scheme of things, a hot-line to the Judaeo-Christian God who created the world and us. But at a much more subtle, and to me more credible, level we can say that Walsch is really conversing with his own SQ. In Walsch's scheme of things, God represents the ultimate framework of meaning and value, the ultimate context-giver. God can give Walsch the 'big picture'. That is precisely what our SQ does for us — it recontextualizes and places things in the largest frame of meaning available to us at any given stage of our spiritual growth. When we 'talk' or pray to God, we are doing the best we can to reach that innate wisdom within the heart of our own deepest being, which puts us in touch with the whole of reality. When He answers, it is from our own deepest selves that we are hearing. But for that reason 'God's word', or the healing power of our own SQ, can never be final. It is an ongoing process of communication, a dialogue. 'God' is always changing.

THERE IS NO GRAND REDEMPTION

The Western mind is given to belief in grand finales, in Days of Judgement, Millennial Catastrophes and Redemption. Even the more subtle Eastern philosophies direct us towards a final Nirvana when the cycle of rebirth and suffering will cease. But both the processes of evolution and the integrating powers of our own brains argue that life is more a series of small redemptions than of one grand salvation.

The ground state of the universe, the quantum vacuum, is in constant dialogue with the excitations of energy which are existence. Things arise from the vacuum and pass back into it, to be born again as something else. We can see this process happening very clearly in a simple Wilson cloud chamber, a device for watching the tracks of small, charged sub-atomic particles. The particles emerge suddenly from the vapour of the cloud chamber, traverse the space of a few inches, and then just as suddenly disappear again into the vapour. Then new particles reemerge. This process of creation, annihilation and rebirth of particles will go on so long as the universe lasts. So it is with the birth and death of stars, of galaxies and planets.

In biology, there is no end of evolution. So long as our planet continues to support life, that life will change and evolve, constantly giving rise to new forms.

So it is with our brains. The brain itself, we have seen, is constantly 'rewiring' itself as a result of experience. My brain of today is not the same as my brain of yesterday. The 40 Hz neural oscillations that enable my SQ are constantly having to integrate new experience, constantly having to reframe and recontextualize meaning, constantly having to grow beyond problems and crises as they arise. Even a spiritually intelligent life can only offer us at best a series of mini-redemptions, a healing for now with the mature knowledge that other challenges will arise in the future. I may find one missing part of myself today; other parts of my fragmented self are still waiting to make their appearance. But that insight itself can bring a form of healing, giving us a sense of accepting peace rather than of impatience with the deep and ongoing processes of life and the psyche. As Bilbo Baggins says as he sets forth for his great adventure in J.R.R. Tolkien's *The Lord of the Rings*:

> The Road goes ever on and on
> Down from the door where it began.
> Now far ahead the Road has gone,
> And I must follow, if I can,
> Pursuing it with eager feet.
> Until it joins some larger way
> Where many paths and errands meet.
> And whither then? I cannot say.[9]

As we shall see next when we look at SQ and our deep spontaneity, spiritual intelligence allows us to relate to ongoing experience with a deeply peaceful, balancing trust. We needn't ask, because we can respond to and accept responsibility for whatever comes.

11. OUR COMPASS AT THE EDGE: USING SQ TO BUILD A NEW ETHICS

How can I go forward when I don't know
which way I'm facing?

John Lennon

You have to get beyond what you want to do, and
beyond what you think you *ought* to do, and only then
can you see the clear light that shows you what *to* do.

Man at a Quaker Meeting

Recently, my fifteen-year-old daughter complained to me, 'It's very difficult to be my age today. You and Dad are always changing what you say is right or OK, and nobody else knows what they're doing either. I just have to keep figuring everything out for myself.' More bleak still was the conclusion of a woman I met at a local church meeting for 'religious doubters'. 'Now that science has shown that God doesn't exist any more,' she said, 'it doesn't matter how we behave. It's just up to us.'

We are under stress today about questions of right and wrong, about how to keep ourselves on a straight path and how to guide our children. Formal religion and its ethics no longer hold sway, family structures are fluid and constantly changing, and our sense of community and tradition has

199

broken down. Somebody has moved all the moral goalposts and we don't know any longer what game we are playing, never mind what constitutes its rules. The historian Eric Hobsbawm claims that there has been more change in the last fifty years than since the Stone Age. Speaking of our times, he writes, 'Uncertainty and unpredictability impeded, compass needles no longer had a North, maps became useless.'[1]

As a result, many people today feel lost, disoriented, even terrified. Yet, as the early twentieth-century German poet Rilke wrote, sometimes our deepest fears are like dragons guarding our deepest treasure.[2] In the words of the Tibetan teacher Sogyal Rinpoche:

> The fear that impermanence awakens in us, that nothing is real and nothing lasts, is, we come to discover, our greatest friend because it drives us to ask: If everything dies and changes, then what is really true? Is there something behind the appearances, something boundless and infinitely spacious, something in which the dance of change and impermanence can take place?[3]

Perhaps the death of the old ethics and the whole frame of mind on which it was based, gives us a precious opportunity to forge a new ethics based on our own innate spiritual intelligence. Using our SQ, we can live with uncertainty and find an inner poise with respect to it. We can live creatively, not despite the uncertainty but because of it. Uncertainty can inspire us because it creates conditions in which we must make a choice. It gives us our freedom and sets the conditions for our responsibility.

THE OLD ETHICS

Somewhere in our evolutionary history, we human beings lost those instinctive moorings that make life so much more certain for the simpler animals. We were then able to break nature's absolute rules and restraints, to carve out a new, more complex way of life based on free will and its expression in culture. Yet having thrown off the shackles of instinct, the West at least sought to replace them with rules and certainties imposed by our gods or reason.

Moses came down from Mount Sinai carrying the Law written on tablets of stone. Christianity and Islam honoured these laws and added more of their own. In the philosophical tradition of ancient Greece, objective, universal principles of goodness and justice seemed essential to any system of genuine ethics.[4] Indeed universalism, the belief in objective truths and standards applicable to everything and everyone, can be seen as the foundation of Western culture. In the seventeenth-century Enlightenment tradition, reason became Western humanity's unfailing guide to what was right and good. The science of Isaac Newton followed the same principle, with laws of nature that governed every event in the physical universe. Newtonian science was a science of absolutes – absolute space and time, absolute laws, absolute certainty, predictability and control.

While formal religion kept alive the certainties of Moses, and philosophers and logicians the certainties of ancient Greece, the social sciences of the seventeenth, eighteenth and nineteenth centuries reinforced the certainties of Newtonian absolutism. Freud's psychology, Locke's democracy, Adam Smith's economics, Marx's iron laws of history, Darwin's laws of evolution, and Frederick Taylor's scientific management theory all attempted to apply analogues of the three laws of motion. In everyday life, certainties were further held in place by custom and tradition, by the family and the community.

THE UNCERTAINTY PRINCIPLE

The twentieth-century physicist Werner Heisenberg's Uncertainty Principle is the main tenet of quantum theory. More even than Einstein's Theory of Relativity, which simply questions our position in or perception of space-time, Uncertainty questions our ability ever to know anything absolutely. Knowledge, Heisenberg says, is always limited. If we know 'x' about a fact or a situation, then we can't know 'y' and vice versa. The quantum reality that Heisenberg describes has an infinite number of possible expressions, all of them necessary, each of them in some way valid. But we can only know the aspect of reality that we are looking for. Our answers will always be answers only to the questions that we ask. And if we ask different questions, we shall get different answers.

In 1997, the London *Sunday Times* ran two different Gallup polls on the state of religious belief in Britain. In the first, people were asked whether they went to church on Sunday. Only 10 per cent answered in the affirmative, so the poll concluded that Britain is not a very religious nation. But the second poll, conducted six months later, asked, 'Do you believe in God?' To this question, 80 per cent answered in the affirmative and the pollsters concluded that Britain *is* a very religious nation. This is the Uncertainty Principle at work.

Einstein and Heisenberg helped to bring about a fundamental change in our relationship to truth and ethics. The old way was top-down, an attempt to replace the lost certainties of our biological past with reference to an externally imposed set of truths. But both Heisenberg and Einstein are saying that it all depends in some crucial way upon *us*. Truth depends upon our point of view, upon the questions that we choose to ask. This is bottom-up truth, which in some fundamental sense comes from within. It is, I contend, ultimately a truth that we can access only with our spiritual intelligence.

The spin-offs of scientific discovery, technology and the general spirit of scientific inquiry affect us all. But even more revolutionary than the discoveries of science has been the spirit of science. Top-down truth is based on faith: ethical systems are based on acquiescence, on belief in an outside authority. But creative science is bottom-up, based on observation, on testing the theories, on questioning the facts. If I am a scientist schooled in the Uncertainty Principle, I'm not interested only in answers. I want to know more about *questions*, about what further realities can be observed by asking further and deeper questions. Is it any wonder that a twentieth-century teenager insists on reinventing the wheel, or that almost anyone now asks, 'What is possible?' before going on to wonder, 'What is right?' The spirit of science has become the guiding spirit of our times.

There have always been religious or spiritual movements that have honoured bottom-up truth. The mystics of all the Abrahamic religions, Taoists, Hindus, Buddhists and, more recently, Quakers have always stressed the importance of inner experience and an inner path to the sacred. Rejecting the sufficiency of mere belief or obedience as a path to truth, they stress that we must work on ourselves to find some inner light. Mainstream Western religions have rejected, often persecuted, those who hold this attitude, but perhaps their time has now come.

UNCERTAINTY IS NOT RELATIVISM

Moral relativism is the view that, because there are no absolute standards or truths, truth itself is relative. The truth is just what

I happen to believe or what I find it comfortable to assert. There is no objectivity, only subjectivity.

This kind of scepticism was originally expressed in ancient Greece by Sophist philosophers. It is implicit in Nietzsche's and Freud's views that people believe what they find most convenient in pursuit of their individual impulses. Twentieth-century anthropologists have reported conflicting beliefs about right and wrong in different tribes and cultures, though nearly all cultures prohibit cheating and murder. Many twentieth-century philosophers relied on the work of Einstein and Heisenberg to give moral relativism its strongest argument. Einstein, they contended, demonstrated that we are always locked inside some individual space-time framework and that therefore there is no God's-eye view on reality. Heisenberg's Uncertainty Principle, they asserted, demonstrates that truth is just a matter of how we look at things and what questions we happen to ask. Both these conclusions misunderstand what twentieth-century science has to say about truth and reality, and miss the exciting and subtle new perspective that this science gives to truth.

Einstein's work does not support the view that 'everything is relative'. It *does* contain objective descriptions. He supplies a unique four-dimensional space-time description of the *real* world in abstract terms, and this contains the perspectives of all possible observers as *aspects* of the truth. The individual perspectives are related to each other by the abstract description of the whole. There is a God's-eye view, but it is available only to God. The best that we can do is gain knowledge of as many perspectives as we can, and acknowledge a whole that is greater than we can perceive.

Similarly, Heisenberg is saying that quantum reality itself is filled with infinite potential (infinite truth), but that we can only know some aspects of it. As observers, we are involved in a co-creative dialogue with this infinite background reality, and what we see depends upon the questions that we ask. Truth is not limited or uncertain, but our view of it always is. Again, the best thing a Heisenbergian observer can do is capture as many faces of the underlying truth as possible by asking as many questions as possible.

Twentieth-century science invites us to appreciate that reality and truth are beyond our finite grasp. Yet it also invites us to celebrate this multi-facetedness of truth and to accept responsibility for our role in its unfolding. We can never know its full extent, but we are each playing a part in a universal drama. Each of my finite actions may seem small and isolated to me, but each contributes to the future of the whole.

BEING AT THE EDGE

Many people speak of being 'at the edge' today, but don't often know what it really means. 'The edge' is an expression from chaos theory, a relatively new science which describes the unpredictable behaviour of things like the weather, the human heartbeat, beehives and stock markets. In chaos theory, the edge is the meeting point between order and chaos, between the known and the unknown. In nature, it is where creativity and self-organization happen. It is where new information is created.

We can get a strong, concrete image of the edge of chaos by imagining ourselves standing on a bridge, looking down on a stream below. Upstream, the water is flowing smoothly, still, quiet and mirror-like. That is order. Information is nothing but non-random order, so the smooth flow of the stream contains some finite information. If we know the stream's 'code' we can access this information. It is the same with the rules of a top-down ethical code. As adherents of the code, we can read its rules and behave accordingly.

Just as the water flows beneath the bridge it hits some twigs or rocks and forms itself into whirlpools. Then, beyond the whirlpools, further downstream, the water breaks into white turbulence. That white turbulence is chaos. Chaos may contain information, but its code is so complex that we could never hope to access it. We are 'all at sea', like people who have no sense of what game they are playing.

It is at that point where the water is forming itself into whirlpools that the stream has come to the edge of chaos. It is forming a new code, creating new information. It is at this point of self-organization that we find ourselves in uncharted but none the less navigable territory. There is good science that studies order, and good science that studies chaos, but science that wishes to study creativity focuses on the edge of chaos. This is where living systems like ourselves 'happen'.

All biological systems are poised at the edge of chaos. That is what makes us open and adaptive, what makes living systems so miraculously flexible. For instance, the human immune system puts up every conceivable defence against viruses and bacteria, so that when one of them proves effective it can settle into an ordered pattern of producing just that and no more. The human mind, when it is using SQ, is also poised at the edge.

Being at the edge makes our lives and creativity possible, but it can also add an element of fear – the goalposts of life are less certain. Today, we all have to live at the edge whether we like it or not. We can't just paper over the cracks in the old tradition and its traditional ethics. Nor can we give way to nihilistic relativism, denying the reality of any truth at all. We have to devise new concepts and redefine our categories of judgement. An ethics by which we can live creatively today will of necessity be an ethics poised at the edge.

In Nietzsche's *Thus Spake Zarathustra*, in which he announced the death of the old order, he wrote, 'One must have chaos in one to give birth to a dancing star. I tell you, you do have chaos in you.' What Nietzsche meant by 'chaos' was the ability to self-organize, to re-invent, going beyond the traditional categories of good and evil that had been imposed by top-down religions. Nietzsche's central image for this is a tightrope walker who has to walk between the towers of certainty. He doesn't make it: he falls off and is killed. Zarathustra remarks that he wasn't ready yet. But Nietzsche wrote at the end of the nineteenth century. At the birth of the twenty-first century we are still walking that tightrope, but can we know better what is required of us? If we learn to rely on our SQ we shall become less fearful, more accustomed to relying on ourselves, more willing to face the difficult and the uncomfortable and more ready to live at the edge.

SQ AND THE 'EYE OF THE HEART'

I like the image of Nietzsche's tightrope walker because such artistes have an inner poise, just as SQ is a sense of inner balance. Unlike IQ, which orients itself with respect to rules, and EQ, which is guided by the situation in which it finds itself, SQ lights our way through what mystics have called the 'eye of the heart'. A person who knows God, says Bahya Ibn Paquda, 'will see without eyes, hear without ears, perceive things which his sense cannot perceive, and comprehend without reasoning'. 'My heart saw Thee and believed Thee. I have seen Thee with the eye of the heart,' was how Yehuda Halevi expressed it.[5]

The heart of the spiritually intelligent self is, ultimately, the quantum vacuum, the ground of being itself. It is a still and changing ground, and the heart that knows it is the still and changing heart.

For the medieval Jewish and Christian mystics, the 'eye of the heart' was a metaphor for intuition. In many traditions, the right eye represents the Sun's perception of the active and the future, the light of reason, whilst the left eye represents the Moon's perception of the passive and the past, or the sight which comes from emotion. But there is also a 'third eye' which synthesizes the two and gives us wisdom. In Hinduism, this third eye sits in the middle of the god Shiva's forehead: 'This third eye corresponds to fire. It reduces everything to ashes.' In Buddhism it is the All-seeing Eye of the Buddha which sits 'at the edge' between unity and multiplicity, between emptiness and non-emptiness. Travellers to Nepal or Tibet can see this eye painted vividly on the spires that crown the great temples or stupas.

On the album cover of his CD *The Eyes of the Heart*, the modern jazz composer Keith Jarrett describes musical improvisation as a thing which 'is at its best when everyone involved in the music is aware of an intent greater than his own; therefore more his own'.[6] Using our SQ to forge a new ethics requires similar improvisation, and that in turn requires a deeper sense of 'my own' or 'my self' that takes me beyond the petty constraints of my ego and beyond the dangerous waters of relativism. The modern Western concept of self does not do this. We who were born in the twentieth-century Western world have little sense of a deeper self to which that eye of the heart can belong.

The concept of the self that we have inherited from Freud is isolated and shallow. But the spiritually intelligent self is a fuller self, possessing a deep sense of the interconnectedness of life and all its enterprises. This fuller self is aware that human endeavours are part of the larger, richer fabric of the whole universe. It has a sense of humility and gratitude before the Source from which it and all other things arise. And it has a deep sense of engagement and responsibility. It recognizes that the individual cannot be whole without affirming the larger Whole of which each of us is an inseparable part.

The spiritually stunted self cannot give us an ethics based on SQ, or on the eye of the heart. It has no deep source from which to draw its wisdom or intuition. But the deeper self which I have described as the spiritually intelligent self will enable us to walk the tightrope between the towers of certainty. We can access something within ourselves which makes our questions more valid than any partial answers, and which guides our values and our conduct more truly than any imposed dogma. We may still fall off the tightrope, but there is a deep recollectedness and joy from which even this possibility is not the most important thing.

USING OUR DEEP SPONTANEITY

In Hebrew, the words for 'compass' (*matzpen*), 'conscience' (*matzpoon*), and 'the hidden inner truth of the soul' (*tsaffoon*) all come from the same root. To have a conscience is to be in touch with the hidden, inner truth of the soul and, if we are so in touch, we have an internal compass to guide us in our behaviour. In ancient Greek, both the word for 'intelligence' (*euphyia*) and the word for 'nature' (*physis*) come from the root *phyiame*. *Euphyia* means literally 'he who grows well', and *Physis* literally 'that which comes to emerge'. We grow well, are intelligent, by allowing something from within to emerge. The Greek word for 'truth' (*alithia*) means literally 'not forgetting' – not forgetting what we have always known. Both these ancient languages are telling us that there is a source of true knowing within us.

In Plato's dialogue *The Meno*, Socrates takes an ignorant slave boy and, by asking him a series of questions, extracts all the fundamental principles of geometry. 'You see,' says Socrates, 'he knew the foundations of geometry all along. He had just forgotten them.' In Plato's doctrine of knowledge, human beings are born knowing everything. Knowledge is innate, including a knowledge of good and bad, right and wrong. A baby lives very close to the truth, but as he grows he forgets and falls into ignorance.

Socrates and Plato exaggerate because of their conviction that all truth that is always has been and was thus always there to be known. The lesson of twentieth-century science, by contrast, is that truth is an infinite, never-ending, unfolding *process*. But science agrees with Socrates to the extent of saying that we are born and continue to live with a *potential* for knowledge, in engagement with truth. We fall into ignorance because of our tendency to lock ourselves into habits, assumptions, rules and belief systems as we grow older. As R. D. Laing describes it, 'To adapt to this world, the child abdicates its ecstasy.'[7]

As adults, most of us have forgotten our original deep selves and the profound wisdom they possess. Except in rare moments of childlike spontaneity when we are exposed to something that touches us deeply, we forget that our selves have a knowing centre. We forget how to respond to what is within. We lose faith in ourselves and turn to external rules for guidance. The challenge is to regain that lost childlike spontaneity, tempered with an adult's discipline, experience and wisdom – and constant humility. We must always be willing to test our 'inner truth' against its consequences in the outside world.

Both spontaneity and discipline are difficult concepts for Western people. We tend to trivialize spontaneity and to exteriorize discipline. The Freudian influence on Western psychology pictures the conscious ego as a hapless victim caught between the whim, irresponsibility and instincts of the id (our spontaneity) and the domineering voice of the super-ego with its expectations from parents and society (our discipline). The assumed spontaneity of the id is placed in sharp opposition to the top-down discipline of the superego. We are caught between 'mere feeling' and rational control. As the Quaker quoted on p. 199 said, we are caught between what we want to do and what we think we ought to do. We thus come to suspect our instincts, to distrust our spontaneity, to feel guilty, and to rely on imposed discipline for self-control. This diminished, Freudian concept of spontaneity is not the same as the deep spontaneity that would allow us to use our SQ as an inner compass.

Since the words 'spontaneity', 'response' and 'responsibility' all have the same Latin origin, it tells us something important about the true meaning of spontaneity. Spontaneity is a response to something for which we must take responsibility. It is initially a response to our engagement with the unfolding drama of fundamental reality. As Heisenberg's Uncertainty Principle shows us, it is our engagement with, our response to, reality that makes reality happen. We thus become responsible for unfolding reality. In this sense, spontaneity cannot be mere whim or impulsiveness. It is not the response to a chocolate bar or a new car. It is the response to something I know without being told, to something I know from within, a response to my own inner compass. It is SQ that gives me this capacity to respond.

SQ is a deep form of spontaneity, a response to the deepest core of the self and to the core of being in which that deep self is grounded. When I am deeply spontaneous, I am naturally in connection with my own inner self, with all others who are a part of that self, with all of nature and its processes that are a part of that self, with the whole of universal reality that is a part of that self. When I am deeply spontaneous I know my self and know that I am the world, and thus I take responsibility for the world. I take responsibility for others because I respond to others and know they are a part of me. I don't need rules or certainties or codes of practice to know how to treat others. Such things can only get in the way of my truly spontaneous knowing. Of course, uncertainty and risk are involved. I shall make mistakes, but I hope to learn from them.

In Chapter 10 I spoke of a dream in which I was a dancer being moved from within, a dancer whose movements were being orchestrated by some inner music. I explained that it gave me a deep sense of what true spontaneity means, and how it is related to spiritual intelligence. Just before his Crucifixion, Jesus spoke to his disciples of something like this.

The Acts of John, one of the early Gnostic Gospels (the Gnostics were a sect who combined early Christianity with mysticism and other philosophies), tells how in Gethsemane, the night before the Crucifixion, Jesus called his disciples to him and asked them to form a circle, holding one another's hands. He then stepped into the middle of the circle and began to chant:

> To the Universe belongs the dancer. Amen
> He who does not dance does not know what happens.
>   Amen.
> Now if you follow my dance, see yourself in Me who
>   am speaking . . .
> You who dance, consider what I do, for yours is
> The passion of Man which I am to suffer. For you
>   could by no means have understood what you suffer
> Unless to you as Logos I had been sent by the
>   Father . . .
> Learn how to suffer and you shall be able not to suffer.[8]

In another of the Gnostic Gospels, *The Gospel of Thomas*, Jesus said to his disciples, 'If you know who you are, you will become as I am.' According to this, he did not see himself as divine, but rather as someone who had awakened to a divine force within himself. He felt that that divine force was within us all. To dance with Jesus is to feel that force. To dance spontaneously with existence is to feel the active force of our spiritual intelligence, and to know what it knows.

DISCIPLINE AND COMPASSION

Spontaneity that is linked to response and responsibility is also related to discipline and compassion. The spontaneity with which I contact my inner self is achieved by making myself strong at the centre. I learn to control my whims and easy desires through disciplines like meditation or prayer, through the constant practice of my skill or my art, through deep reflection and constant awareness. My discipline becomes inner. It is a form of poise that the ancient Chinese called the *Tao*, the Way – the deep, inner law of being. One of the greatest commentators on Lao Tzu's *Tao Te Ching*, Chuang Tzu, tells us of the inner discipline of a master butcher:

> Cook Ting was cutting up an ox for Lord Wen-hui. At every touch of his hand, every heave of his shoulder, every move of his feet, every thrust of his knee – zip! zoop! He slithered the knife along with a zing, and all was in perfect rhythm, as though he were performing the dance of the Mulberry Grove or keeping time to the Ching-shou music.
>
> 'Ah, this is marvelous!' said Lord Wen-hui. 'Imagine skill reaching such heights!'
>
> Cook Ting laid down his knife and replied, 'What I care about is The Way, which goes beyond skill. When I first began cutting up oxen, all I could see was the ox itself. After three years I no longer saw the whole ox. And now – now I go at it by spirit and don't look with my eyes. Perception and understanding have come to a stop and spirit moves where it wants . . .
>
> 'A good cook changes his knife once a year – because he cuts. A mediocre cook changes his knife once a month – because he hacks. I've had this knife for nineteen years and I've cut up thousands of oxen with it, and yet the blade is as good and tough as if it had just come from the grindstone.'[9]

We also discipline ourselves through compassion, and often through the suffering that it takes to learn compassion. Compassion means, literally, 'feeling together with'. When I feel compassion I am in the deepest form of spontaneous response, but often this requires me to transcend rational ideas and prejudices and ego-level, stylized forms of relationship.

Dostoyevsky's great novel *Crime and Punishment* is about these themes. A poor young student, Raskolnikov, rejects all conventional morality. 'A man such as I,' he claims, 'is above the law.' To him, laws are mere outward forms imposed by others and he, as an intelligent and reasonable man – indeed a superior man – should be free to carve out his own morality. To prove this, he sets out to murder 'a useless old woman' and to show that he is above punishment. At the time he perceives his crime purely as a matter of theory, an act of intellect or ego.

Shortly afterwards Raskolnikov falls victim to terrible guilt and a deep fever. His guilt is not so much that he has killed the old woman, but that through his arrogance and wilfulness he has committed a deed that has damaged the divine within himself. He realizes he has broken an inner moral law and sinned against his own conscience. It is this he cannot live with.

Raskolnikov has never had much fellow feeling for anyone but his mother and sister; his fellow students reject him because of his superior attitude. After the murder, he feels he must break even with his family, and is now wholly isolated. At this point he meets the prostitute Sonya, a victim of all those social crimes and prejudices Raskolnikov has railed against. Downtrodden, ruined and ill, she nevertheless shows Raskolnikov the possibility of inner strength and moral courage against all adversity. Her strength is faith and Christian love, but the strength she gives Raskolnikov is through the compassion he feels for her.

Later, when Raskolnikov is convicted and sent away to penal servitude, he extends this attitude to his fellow prisoners, men whom he would earlier have described as 'members of the ant-heap'. Through compassion, Raskolnikov joins the human race and can now accept his own suffering. He serves out his duty to society for breaking its laws, but more importantly his love for Sonya and his fellow prisoners gives him a new lease on life through inner transformation. It is through this transformation that he learns humility.

Raskolnikov's original crime was possible only because he ignored the inner compass within himself. His SQ was blocked by the sheer force of his intellectual pride, which blinded him to his membership of humanity. From this position, his assumed moral superiority led to mere criminality. The compassion he eventually feels allows him to contact his own centre, to learn the lessons of his own conscience, and now to use his SQ to begin to rebuild his life and to join the world.

12. WHAT PERSONALITY
TYPE AM I?

The questionnaire that follows can give each of us some idea of our personality type (or types), and thus where we would find ourselves among the petals of the Lotus of the Self. The questions themselves are 'transparent', but there is no point in cheating. Nothing is at stake but gaining some personal insight.

The first seven questions for each personality type ask about occupational or leisure interests. They are solidly based on Holland's occupational tests, but don't include any questions about actual ability. The last five questions for each personality type harmonize with Cattell's work on motivation and Jung's on personality types as developed in the Myers-Briggs personality questionnaire. All these were described in Chapter 8. The actual questions asked here don't copy previous tests, and are intended only as a preliminary guide.

Answer all questions, using a separate sheet of paper for each set of twelve questions (a total of six sheets). For each question answer 'Y' (meaning 'yes, probably') or 'N' (meaning 'no, unlikely') – choose whichever is closer to the truth. When you have finished, add up the number of 'Y' answers on each sheet.

CONVENTIONAL PERSONALITY (JUNG'S EXTROVERTED PERCEPTION)

Which of the following five occupations or two leisure activities (or something similar to them) might interest or suit you, if you had the necessary skills?

- □ clerk
- □ receptionist
- □ library assistant
- □ accountant
- □ building inspector
- □ collecting (e.g. antiques, stamps, coins)
- □ card games (rummy, bridge)

Answer 'Y' or 'N' for each of the five following:

- □ I like to do tasks neatly and methodically
- □ My opinions and behaviour are usually middle-of-the-road
- □ My home and lifestyle are as practical and comfortable as I can make them
- □ I value the traditions of my groups (family, work, neighbourhood)
- □ I am more interested in actual, daily events than in artistic or philosophical discussions about them

SOCIAL PERSONALITY (JUNG'S EXTROVERTED FEELING)

Which of the following five occupations or two leisure activities (or something similar to them) might interest or suit you, if you had the necessary skills?

- [ ] nurse
- [ ] schoolteacher
- [ ] counsellor
- [ ] minister/priest/rabbi
- [ ] homemaker (partner/parent)
- [ ] sports (e.g. tennis, skiing)
- [ ] club membership

Answer 'Y' or 'N' for each of the five following:

- [ ] I enjoy talking to a wide range of people
- [ ] I am usually tactful about voicing my criticisms and disagreements
- [ ] I like to help people and to share experiences with them
- [ ] I enjoy cooperative situations
- [ ] Sometimes I find that I have expressed more warmth towards someone than I actually feel

INVESTIGATIVE PERSONALITY (JUNG'S INTROVERTED THINKING)

Which of the following five occupations or two leisure activities (or something similar to them) might interest or suit you, if you had the necessary skills?

- [ ] computer programmer
- [ ] laboratory technician
- [ ] translator
- [ ] doctor
- [ ] university teacher, researcher
- [ ] board games (e.g. Scrabble, chess)
- [ ] reading non-fiction

Answer 'Y' or 'N' for each of the five following:

☐ I make the effort to understand exactly what is being said to me

☐ I value intelligent discussion of issues

☐ If I can I reflect fully, however long it takes, before making an important decision

☐ I like to keep up with the latest developments in art, science, or my work and neighbourhood

☐ Sometimes I reject a new point of view at first, then later see that it may have some merit

ARTISTIC PERSONALITY
(JUNG'S INTROVERTED PERCEPTION)

Which of the following five occupations or two leisure activities (or something similar to them) might interest or suit you, if you had the necessary skills?

☐ writer
☐ designer
☐ actor/actress
☐ musician
☐ architect
☐ photography
☐ dancing

Answer 'Y' or 'N' for each of the five following:

☐ I often express myself on impulse

☐ People sometimes think I am a little controversial, or even shocking

☐ I am often interested in new ideas and neglected causes

☐ I admire originality in others

☐ I am more interested in the overall impression (beauty, meaning) than in the concrete details

REALISTIC PERSONALITY
(JUNG'S INTROVERTED FEELING)

Which of the following five occupations or two leisure activities (or something similar to them) might interest or suit you, if you had the necessary skills?

- ☐ cook
- ☐ carpenter
- ☐ optician
- ☐ engineer
- ☐ farmer
- ☐ home do-it-yourself improvements
- ☐ sailing or boating

Answer 'Y' or 'N' for each of the five following:

- ☐ On social occasions, I prefer to be with a few people whom I can really respect and trust
- ☐ I tend to hold firm to my opinions and plans, whatever others say
- ☐ I enjoy manual and physical activities, alone or as part of a team
- ☐ I don't make a promise unless I am sure I can keep it
- ☐ Other people sometimes think I am cold or indifferent, when actually I feel quite strongly about something

ENTERPRISING PERSONALITY
(JUNG'S EXTROVERTED THINKING)

Which of the following five occupations or two leisure activities (or something similar to them) might interest or suit you, if you had the necessary skills?

220

- □ sales representative
- □ travel agent
- □ manager or executive
- □ politician
- □ lawyer
- □ jackpot games (e.g. bingo, poker)
- □ travel

Answer 'Y' or 'N' for each of the five following:

- □ When I go out, I make the effort to be smartly dressed
- □ In a group, I enjoy being the centre of attention
- □ I like to take slight risks in work or leisure activities
- □ I enjoy competitive situations
- □ I sometimes get 'carried away' into commitments or actions I regret afterwards

On each personality type you will have scored between 0 and 12. This indicates the strength of your interest in that sector of life. An average adult will score 6 or more on perhaps three of the personality types. For instance, you might score highest (say 9) on the artistic type, but also score 7 on the enterprising type and 6 on the investigative type. These are the three petals on the Lotus of the Self which you most closely resemble, and indicate the paths of personal development that will come most easily to you. External circumstances, or a greater need for inner balance, may force you to develop yourself in other areas as well.

In Chapter 13 I shall outline six spiritual paths that an individual might follow in life to become more spiritually intelligent. At least three of these paths may be relevant, but at any given time one will most probably stand out.

Part V

CAN WE IMPROVE OUR SQ?

13. SIX PATHS TOWARDS GREATER SPIRITUAL INTELLIGENCE

> It is useless to waste your life on one path, especially if
> that path has no heart. Before you embark on a path, you
> ask the question: Does this path have a heart? If the
> answer is no, you will know it, and then you must choose
> another path. A path without heart is never enjoyable.
> You have to work hard even to take it. On the other
> hand, a path with heart is easy; it does not make you
> work at liking it.
>
> Carlos Castaneda, *The Teachings of Don Juan*

In the West we have believed strongly in the One Way, the
One Truth, the One God. We admire people who find their
path early in life and then stick to it; we mistrust doubt,
uncertainty and unsteadiness of purpose. By a 'path' I mean
finding my own deepest meaning and most profound integrity, acting from my deepest motivations and bringing this
action to bear upon my family, my community, my nation
and so on. My path is my journey through life, my relationships, my work, my goals, my dreams, and how I live these
things. To follow a path with spiritual intelligence, or a path
with heart, is to be deeply committed and dedicated.

A person may be fortunate enough to strike out early upon
a genuine life's path with heart – to become a doctor, say, or a

225

teacher. If so he is acting from his centre, from one of life's deepest motivations, and he is on a spiritually intelligent path. But all too often the pressure to commit early and then stick to it can lead people to ignore the wealth of paths that lie before them or, worse still, force them on to a path that lacks both spiritual intelligence and heart. A person may be forced on to a path by the expectations of parents or society, or seek it out for shallow motives such as personal recognition, personal power or great material gain. Some simply blunder on to a path because circumstances took them there, but then don't know how to get off. Yet others feel they have no path in life at all.

'Anders', the Swedish business executive whom I discussed in Chapter 2, is on such a path. From an early age he knew that he wanted to serve. Given his personality and talents he decided to serve through business, but he insists with passion that his life in business *be* a life of service, a life that he can share with his family and community with pride, a life that will leave the world a better place than he found it. This deep motivation centres him, indeed it comes from his own deepest centre. When we meet him, we meet a man whose personality exudes integrity. He inspires us.

To be aware that such a life is possible is the first step in raising SQ. To say that 'I want that sort of life' and to set about the difficult and often painful task of discovering where my own centre is, what my own really deepest motivations are, is the next step. To commit myself deeply to a path takes me further still. And to realize that there are many paths, and that in the course of my life walking along several, or to some extent even all, of them may be my greatest fulfilment – this may be the most profound realization yet of my spiritual intelligence.

We must understand that there are many paths – there is not just one way to be spiritually intelligent, nor even a best way. All are both valid and necessary. The world needs spiritually intelligent cooks, teachers, doctors, mechanics, parents, actors, therapists, businessmen and so on. Each of these paths requires its own variety of SQ, and each suits some personality types better than others. There is no job or profession that could not be more effective if done with raised SQ; there is no life that could not be more deeply fulfilling.

Nor is using and raising our SQ just one particular kind of activity. Rather, the SQ of an activity is measured by the depth, the nearness to the centre, of the motivation for that activity, whatever it happens to be. It might be praying or meditating, but it might also be cooking, working, making love or just drinking a glass of water, so long as the activity issues from a centred passion, from our life's deepest motivations and values.

SIX PATHS

The Lotus of the Self offers us a basic map of six personality types, each with its own associated deepest motivations, psychic energy and thus access to the centre. From this we can see a pattern of six distinctly different life paths leading to great spiritual intelligence – six spiritual paths that any one of us might follow in living a life with greater heart. But we also know from the way the Lotus of the Self is constructed that any one of us may be on more than one path at any one time.

The ego personality styles from which the outer ring of the lotus were constructed – the conventional type, the social type, the artistic type and so on – were taken from Holland's universally applied vocational guidance test (see Chapter 8), which illustrates how each individual is a combination of several ego styles. Each style is associated with one of the six spiritual paths, so most of us will find something relevant to ourselves and to raising our own SQ by looking at more than

227

one path, though we will probably find that we have one main path.

In the course of a lifetime an individual's main spiritual path frequently changes. It may do so gradually, or abruptly at the mid-life crisis of our forties or even a decade or so later. If this is a genuine energy shift, rather than just a traumatic episode, we are likely to remain on good terms with our previous path while adding other dimensions. Hinduism, for example, recognizes the classic life stages or paths of the child, the student, the householder and the holy man, each drawing on and being enriched by the others. All the world's great spiritual traditions, in fact, have recognized, at least tacitly, the need for a variety of spiritual paths or practices.

A classic way to get stuck in the use of our SQ is trying to solve the problems associated with one spiritual path by the methods appropriate to another. An artistic or realistic type (paths 4 and 5) cannot solve his problem of deep loneliness simply by joining some conventional tribe or group (path 1). An inarticulate, introverted investigative type (path 3) cannot become an outgoing public speaker simply by joining a committee (path 6). And not all marital problems (usually some combination of paths 4 and 5) can be solved by simple nurturing (path 2). We get stuck like this when we don't know any better alternatives. As the philosopher Ludwig Wittgenstein said, 'When all you have is a hammer, everything looks like a nail.' The purpose of outlining the six basic spiritual paths below is to offer some vision of a richer 'toolbox'. Some of the material will be familiar from Chapter 8, but is included here for completeness. 'Religious emphasis' refers to the key themes or concepts found in religious writings; 'practice' to practical activities such as praying or cooking.

PATH 1: THE PATH OF DUTY

Personality type	Conventional
Motivation	Gregariousness, belonging, security
Archetypes	Saturn, the tribe, participation mystique
Religious emphasis	Observance
Myth	The covenant between God and humanity
Practice	Doing one's duty
Chakra	Base, root (security, order)

Today I offer you the choice of life and good, or death and evil. If you obey the commandments of the Lord your God which I give you this day, by loving the Lord your God, by conforming to His ways and by keeping His commandments, statutes and laws, then you will live and increase, and the Lord your God will bless you in the land which you are entering to occupy. But if your heart turns away and you do not listen and you are led on to bow down to other gods and worship them, I tell you this day that you will perish . . . I summon heaven and earth to witness against you this day: I offer you the choice of life or death, blessing or curse. Choose life and then you and your descendants will live . . .

Deuteronomy 30: 15–20

This path is about belonging to, cooperating with, contributing to and being nurtured by the community. Security and stability depend upon our experiencing kinship with others and with our environment, usually from infancy. To that extent, following this path is important to us all. But for 10–15 per cent of Western adults it remains the primary concern.

The Old Testament quote above illustrates how this path is commonly understood in the Western consciousness. The central myth in its narrowest sense is that there is a pact between God and our tribe. We serve Him; He protects us. More broadly interpreted, the myth tells us that there is a

229

sacred covenant between God and humanity. But however it is perceived there are certain rules to be followed, duties to be performed, blessings to be received. The emphasis is always on fitting in, doing things in the acceptable way.

With all six spiritual paths discussed here, there is a spiritually dumb way to live it and the possibility of a journey towards greater spiritual intelligence. Growing towards higher SQ requires surfacing the motivations from which one is acting, and coming to act, if called for, from deeper and truer motivations – learning to act from the centre. Those who naturally walk the path of duty are at their best typically tidy, obedient, methodical and traditional. But if the path is followed in a spiritually dumb way it can lead to dogmatism, prejudice, small-mindedness, a dearth of imagination and a lack of drive.

The most spiritually dumb way to live this path is to act from the shadow motivation of narcissism. This is a motivation to withdraw entirely from the group and from relationships, to lose creative contact with one's environment and become completely wrapped up in oneself. Psychologists include in behaviour commonly associated with narcissism heavy smoking and drinking, lying in bed late, over-indulging in food and sex, and generally needing to indulge oneself while neglecting others and other concerns. The roots of narcissism are thought to lie in deep trauma – either pain and/ or neglect in infancy, or some deeply traumatic incident concerning relationships later in life. A person stuck in the narcissistic state can't make progress without addressing the original trauma or traumas through therapy or counselling.

Other ways of being spiritually dumb on the path of duty are to follow the group's rules and codes simply from fear, habit, boredom or just going along with the crowd, from motives of self-interest or guilt. The first step towards greater spiritual intelligence is to *want* to understand myself and to lead a more creative life. The next step is to surface the motives from which I have been acting and 'clear' them. I may have to go through a period of what Buddhists call 'revulsion', a sense of deep dissatisfaction with my original motives, or through a period of rebellion and become the Prodigal Son.

To walk the path of duty in a spiritually intelligent way I have to *want* to belong to my group, have to make an inner move of commitment to it, an actual choice to belong, and have to understand why. At the deepest level of all, I live belonging to my community and practising its daily routines as a sacred act. Such inner resolutions used to be articulated through initiation ceremonies, but in today's culture few of these remain. All these things require digging down to the roots of what makes my community what it is. What are its deepest values, its central myth, its 'totems'?

The central myth, we saw, of the path of duty is that my community has a covenant with God, or with some deep potentiality of the human spirit. Both the French Revolution and the American Declaration of Independence were based on a sacred belief in the Rights of Man, which itself rests on a deeper belief in the nature of humanity. The Roman Empire was fired by a passion for bringing the rule of law to the whole of humanity. The British Empire was based on a deep notion of bringing higher civilization, principles of justice and fairness and Christian values to 'benighted' peoples. A notion of 'manifest destiny', of being responsible for good against evil, still inspires American foreign policy, if not always wisely. Nazi Germany drew on Viking myths of Aryan superiority and Nordic values of strength and heroism in battle to build a new *Reich*. Even street gangs and football clubs have their myths and totems, their codes of honour and the uniforms, flags and insignia that symbolize these.

Recognizing what these are, and consciously swearing my loyalty and duty to them, takes me beyond the mere ego or

231

conformist level on the path of duty. It puts me in touch with that archetypal middle layer of the Lotus of the Self where I participate in something larger than my mere ego self, and swear allegiance to something I cannot always define in rational or logical terms. I *feel* loyalty to my group, I *serve* its interests, I *honour* its codes and rituals. I *love* it.

But there are obvious catches to stopping at this stage along the path of duty. The individual who participates in his or her community at this level may have made *personal* progress towards higher SQ, but in so doing may also be part of a larger movement that is itself *not* spiritually intelligent. The deepest and most sacred path of duty must take me beyond the mere confines of my own group, its myth and practices, to a place from which I can put the SQ of my finite group in perspective. The sacred aspect of the conventional life issues from the centre of the Lotus, from the centre and source of the self and of being itself, and thus the source of my group or community itself – indeed to the source of any group or community. My ultimate duty on the path of duty is to this source.

From this deeper and more spiritually intelligent perspective of the centre I see that my conventional personality's duty is to the holiness of the everyday, and that my ultimate community is the community of all sentient beings. From this level, I can see that my group is one of many valid groups, that its rules are one of many valid sets of rules, that my own customs and practices and daily habits reflect those of others. I escape prejudice and dogmatism, and I protect myself against blindly following my group into error or evil. If I tie my shoe laces from this perspective, cook a meal, make love, add up a customer's accounts, discipline my child, attend a community festival, play a game of golf, all from this deep perspective, then I am leading my life of duty in the most spiritually intelligent way possible. Every aspect of my apparently mundane, conventional life is in fact undertaken as a sacred act, every action that I undertake and every attitude that I hold dear is a celebration of how duty serves the centre and source of existence. It makes no difference what name I give it: at the source, all names of the holy are ultimately one. I reach it by following my deepest life's intention and by serving, with awareness and commitment, what I truly love and value.

PATH 2: THE PATH OF NURTURING

Personality type	Social
Motivation	Intimacy, parental
Archetypes:	Venus (Aphrodite), the Great Mother, earth
Religious emphasis	Love, compassion, *agape*
Myth	The Great Mother
Practice	Nurturing, protecting, healing
Chakra	Sacral (sex, empathy, nurturing)

Earth, divine goddess, Mother Nature, who dost generate all things and bringest forth ever anew the sun which thou hast given to the nations; Guardian of sky and sea and of all Gods and powers; through thy influence all nature is hushed and sinks to sleep. Again, when it pleases thee, thou sendest forth the glad daylight and nurturest life with thine eternal surety; and when the spirit of man passes, to thee it returns. Thou indeed art rightly named Great Mother of the Gods; Victory is thy divine name.

Twelfth-century Latin herbal text[1]

This path is about loving, nurturing, protecting and making fertile. It is the path of the goddess, whether she be the love goddess as in Venus (Aphrodite) or the mother goddess who gives birth and then cares for her young. She is also Mother Earth, who grounds us and gives us the bounty of her fertility. She is the eternal feminine in many of its aspects, though her inner archetype drives the deepest motivations of some men as well as those of many women. As we saw earlier, some 30 percent of the adult population are social types on the path of nurturing. They are found among parents, teachers, nurses, therapists, counsellors, social workers and saints. It is also the path of healing, associated with the healing properties of water and wholeness and with the cosmic force that the Chinese call Yin.

After humanity's transition from hunter-gathering to settled farm communities, the fertility of crops, domestic animals and human families became of prime concern. Myths of the Great Mother goddess arose in many regions and endured for thousands of years. Neolithic figurines of her with large breasts and full, ample hips date back to about 7000 BC. Mother goddess religions persisted widely until they became distorted or overthrown by more patriarchal emphases associated with the rise of cities, the frequency of war, the great Indo-European invasion and the spread of law. In Mesopotamia, this shift occurred around 3500 BC. The golden calf rejected by Moses' father god was a goddess fertility symbol.

The early mother goddesses and their associated religious cults were many-sided. The Sumerian goddess Inanna, for instance (c. 4000 BC), was mother, sexual being, political figure and patron deity of writing. Powerful and erotic hymns to her have survived, citing her influence on the crops, her tempestuous involvement with storms and rain, and the generative and healing powers of her womb and great breasts. Inanna's cult evolved into those of Ishtar (Babylon), Aphrodite (Greece) and Venus (Rome), all associated with the planet Venus, the brightest object in the sky except for the Sun and Moon.

In Eastern traditions the mother goddess has remained a strong force, both nurturing and sexual. The Hindu goddesses

Shakti and Kali look over creation and destruction. Kwan Yin is the powerful Chinese goddess of compassion. The Buddhist Tara, who was born from a tear of the Buddha of Compassion, carries unfortunate ones across the River of Suffering.

But as patriarchal forces began to dominate the West, the power and extent of the Great Mother goddesses were gradually reduced, leaving Venus only as a goddess of love and sexual desire, and the Virgin Mary as a mothering symbol. The late twentieth century saw a return of these goddesses to some extent in eco-feminism, some aspects of New Age movements and the kind of healing used in alternative health therapies. Many people believe these are the harbingers of a greater return.

As with the other paths, there is a range of spiritually dumb and spiritually intelligent ways to walk the path of nurturing. The most spiritually dumb or spiritually distorted is the shadow form, the opposite of love and nurturing, which is hate and revenge. Love can be patient and kind, but also tempestous, bitter and destructive. Those same qualities that can nurture can tear us to pieces, like the Greek anti-heroines who devour their own children. The snake-headed Medusa represents the mythological aspect of this dark side of woman.

Medusa was a beautiful and innocent priestess in the Temple of Athene, a goddess/maiden who possessed all the positive qualities of a young mother goddess. But then she was either seduced, or raped, by the sea god Poseidon. Athene, in fury and jealousy, turned Medusa into the hideous Gorgon, a hate-filled woman whose hair was a nest of writhing snakes and whose mere gaze could turn men to stone. Medusa has lived through the ages as the most powerful symbol both of woman wronged and of the destructive fury thus unleashed. Speaking of her own lost innocence at the hands of Poseidon's deceit and treachery, Medusa says:

We are made to love –
We women, and the injury which turns
The honey of our lives to gall, transforms
The angel to the fiend. For it is sweet
To know the dreadful sense of strength, and smite
And leave the tyrant dead with a glance; ay! sweet!
In that fierce lust of power, to slay the life
Which harmed not . . .[2]

Over the millennia the Medusa figure has undergone many transformations. In the original Greek myth, when Medusa is beheaded by the hero Perseus the winged horse Pegasus is born from her dead torso, and the blood dripping from her severed neck is found to have healing powers. Medusa herself, and thus the hatred she embodies, is often seen as two-sided – ugly and dangerous, of course, but also perhaps a source of fecundity and inspiration. She is the dark side of mothering and sexual woman, but as with the dark side of all our psychic energies she has a tremendous, potentially transformative power. Women, or men, who walk the shadow side of this path are 'at the edge'. Rage may destroy themselves or others, but it may turn to fierce and healing love.

Less dramatic is the mother or lover who suffocates, whose love cripples and imprisons its recipient rather than nurturing and liberating. She wants to possess the loved one, needs to be loved or needed more than she is able to love. The 'Jewish mother' of pre-PC ethnic jokes, with her chicken soup, her over-concern with bowel movements and her ambitions for 'my son the doctor', was this sort of figure.

Related to the nurturer who suffocates is the too-eager nurturer, the teacher who does not give the student space to work things out for himself, the parent who is afraid to let his child make his own mistakes and learn from them, the woman who wants to save her lover from his own weaknesses. These 'helpers' help too much. By not sufficiently trusting the resources and growing processes of those whom they wish to help their would-be nurture is mere coddling and can cause damage. The opposite extreme, of course, is failure to nurture at all, selfishness and neglect of others' needs.

And finally there is the spiritually dumb too narrow mother, helper or lover. The animal rights protestor who sends letter bombs to scientists, the anti-abortion campaigner who murders doctors, the fund-raiser for refugees who never contributes to his own community: all these people are stingy and narrow with love.

Such people are stuck at the ego level of love, lacking a wider perspective to include the genuine needs or being of the other. It does not take them beyond themselves, nor include them in something larger than themselves. For these reasons, it is not love issuing from the deepest motivation of this path, which is intimacy, nor from the deepest value of the path, which is nurturing.

To become more spiritually intelligent on the path of nurturing we must be more open to the person or people with whom we are in a caring relationship. We must learn to be receptive and to listen well with our true selves. We must be willing to be open, to be exposed, to take the risk of self-disclosure to others. We must, in short, be spontaneous.

Diana, Princess of Wales, had these qualities of deep listening and the courage to expose her own vulnerability. She made her whole self *there* for others. She was deeply spontaneous. She loved and needed to be loved – her wish was to be the Queen of Hearts. It was these qualities that caught the world's heart and imagination and made her a good example of someone more spiritually intelligent along the path of nurturing.

The Humanistic Psychotherapy of Carl Rogers, first developed in the 1930s but still popular today, is a good example of this level of nurturing. Rogers summed up its essential qualities in these words:

> How can I provide a relationship which this person may use for his own personal growth? No approach which relies upon knowledge, upon training, upon the acceptance of something that is *taught*, is of any use. The more that I can be genuine in the relationship, the more helpful it will be. It is only by providing the genuine reality which is in me, that the other person can successfully seek for the reality in him . . . The relationship is significant to the extent that I feel a continuing desire to understand . . . There is also a complete freedom from any type of moral or diagnostic evaluation.[3]

Rogers's vision is a secular version of St Paul's famous definition of love in the New Testament:

> And though I bestow all my goods to feed the poor, and though I give my body to be burned, and have not love, it profits me nothing.
> Loves suffers long, and is kind: love envies not; love vaunts not itself, is not puffed up.
> Doth not behave itself unseemly, seeks not her own, is not easily provoked, thinks no evil;
> Rejoices not in iniquity, but rejoices in the truth;
> Love bears all things, believes all things, hopes all things, endures all things.
> Love never fails.
>
> I Corinthians 13: 4–8

These, perhaps the greatest words ever written about love, point towards the most spiritually intelligent way to walk the path of love and nurturing. For it is not enough just to be emotionally intelligent about love. It is not enough to accept the other just as we find him or her, not enough just to meet the other's expressed needs, the other's given reality. Deep spirituality, the deeply spiritual centre of the self, is about potential; it is about what we and/or the other might become, or what we are despite what we express. Love that is very high in spiritual intelligence is transformative – it releases us into a higher expression of ourselves and allows the other to reach beyond himself.

Wise parenthood, of course, is about nurturing our children's potential. The spiritually intelligent parent does not simply impose his own values and expectations on his child. The spiritually intelligent parent offers a space, a nurturing soil, in which his child can grow beyond his parents and even beyond himself.

It is perhaps easy to love our children in this way. But it is also important to see and nurture the potential in those whom we don't necessarily find so sympathetic at first sight. The sex offenders I visited in prison seemed at first repulsive – their crimes were truly so. Yet if we can meet and love the humanity and the unlived potential of such broken people, we can hold up to them a mirror of the good that is inside them. We can let them feel the deeper self that is within us all, and in so doing transform both them and ourselves. We also help to transform the world. Mother Teresa walked the path of nurturing at this level.

PATH 3: THE PATH OF KNOWLEDGE

Personality type	Investigative
Motivation	Understanding, knowing, exploration
Archetypes	Mercury (Hermes), fire, air, Guide
Religious emphasis	Understanding, study
Myth	Plato's Cave
Practice	Study, experience
Chakra	Solar plexus (fiery heat and light)

For the Lord thy God is a consuming fire.

Deuteronomy 4:24

A quality of holiness, a quality of power,
A quality of fearfulness, a quality of sublimity
A quality of trembling, a quality of shaking,
Is the quality of the Garment of Zohorariel, YHWH,
    God of Israel,
Who comes crowned to the Throne of glory . . .
And of no creature are the eyes to behold it,
Not the eyes of flesh and blood, and not the eyes of His
    servants.
As for him who does behold it, or sees or glimpses it,
Whirling gyrations grip the balls of his eyes,
And the balls of his eyes send forth torches of fire,
And these enkindle him and these burn him . . .

The Zohar, thirteenth-century Jewish mystical text[4]

The path of knowledge ranges from understanding general
practical problems through the deepest philosophical quest
for truth to the spiritual quest for knowledge of God and all
His ways, and to ultimate union with Him through
knowing. Even John Lennon's question quoted earlier
('How can I go forward when I don't know which way
I'm facing?') shows that any directed activity in life requires
at least a rudimentary map of the territory and of our
purposes within it. This can occur on every scale, from
planning a social event through choice of a career or
partner to forming a deep perspective of the cosmos and
of our place within it.

This is a path beginning with simple curiosity and practical
need but one which, as passion deepens, takes us to the very
limit of what our understanding, and even our being, can
contain. The Hebrew God spoke to His people through a

pillar of fire. The deepest knowing takes us to the brink of being consumed by it.

In the early history of civilized people, knowledge and understanding were regarded as the special province of shamans or priests. Ordinary people took their advice or did what they were told. The idea that a wider range of people could make spiritual progress through knowledge and understanding entered the West via Orphism, a Greek religion that flourished around 800 BC. Orpheus believed that human beings are of mixed heavenly and earthly origin. Through 'enthusiastic' knowledge, seen as a kind of intoxicated passion, a person could be purified of his or her earthly make-up and acquire union with God. This might require many lifetimes, between which the soul of the dead one visited a well-spring in the House of Hades and chose to drink from the Well of Forgetfulness or the Well of Remembering. Drinking from the latter brought salvation because salvation requires knowing, and knowing requires remembering.

The Orphic enthusiast now possessed mystic knowledge available by no other means. The great Greek philosopher Pythagoras was a follower of Orphism, and he brought this notion of saving mystic knowledge into the Western tradition. Plato believed that this mystic knowledge gives us a deeper, truer perception of reality than is otherwise possible. It allows us to perceive the pure Forms of the Beautiful, the True, the Good and the One. He illustrates this with his famous Parable of the Cave.

In the parable, human beings dwell deep within a cave, their bodies chained in place and their necks fettered so they can only look forward at the wall of the cave. On the wall, they see shadows of artificial things projected there by passers-by. The cave dwellers take these shadows to be reality itself. But through mystical knowledge they slowly achieve liberation. They climb towards the mouth of the cave and their eyes are at first dazzled by the light. But then they learn to see in the light and they know reality as it truly is. They realize that in their ignorance they saw only the shadows of things. The aim of Plato's philosophy was to bring such realization.

The search for a truer reality beneath appearances has driven much of Christianity, Gnosticism, Renaissance magic and alchemy, modern science and the work of great modern thinkers like Freud and Marx. Both the Freudian unconscious and Marx's proletarian consciousness were examples of the veil of ignorance. The truth is not obvious at first but must be revealed through some special discipline, whether prayer or meditation, study, laboratory experiment, removing psychological defences (Freud) or social pressures (Marx). In the terms used by the philosopher of science Thomas Kuhn, true, really deeper understanding requires us to go through a 'paradigm shift' – to learn to see things in an entirely new way.

The path of knowledge is walked by those who are motivated by a love of learning and/or a deep need to understand, such as scholars, scientists and doctors. The worldwide medical emblem is the caduceus, a staff bearing two entwined serpents which was carried originally by Hermes (Mercury), messenger of the gods and guide of men. The third of the Hindu chakras, the solar plexus, is associated with understanding and also with fiery heat and light. This is understanding that is wider than mere logic or reason. At its deepest, it is the understanding of the soul, conveyed through the insights of literature, art, poetry, and great science, and felt as intense experience. I think of Archimedes jumping naked from his bath, running through the streets shouting, 'Eureka!' He had understood the flotation principle of physics.

Knowledge and understanding are passionate things which cause us to engage deeply with the world around or within us. The shadow form of this path is the man or woman who retreats from such engagement and would prefer not to understand. My mother used to tell me that I asked too many questions and that this would cause me nothing but suffering. 'Myself,' she said, 'I just "turn off the buttons".' Such people find it dangerous or painful to reflect on their experience, and thus become trapped on the surface of things or lost among the shadows on the wall of the cave.

Also in the shadow side of this path but very different from those who don't want to know is the legendary Faust. So badly does he wants the power that vast knowledge will give him that he is willing to sell his soul to the Devil in order to possess it. Some scientists who will pursue any morally dubious course of investigation in pursuit of the power or thrill of discovery for its own sake are cast in a Faustian mould.

Another spiritually dumb way to walk the path of knowledge is to be the cold or boring pedant who becomes preoccupied with some tiny piece of knowledge or isolated intellectual problem. Such people often have an intense passion about their work, but it is chained in service to the minuscule and cuts them off from a deeper understanding of wider life and true reality. George Eliot's Casaubon, from her novel *Middlemarch*, is the archetypal pedant, a narrow man with a thin and pointed nose who devotes his whole life to the pursuit of his 'great work' – a paltry collection of banal mediocrities without redeeming vision. Many academics are cut from Casaubon's cloth. The opposite is the wide, airy perspective of a bird or a man on a mountain top.

One of Newton's move negative legacies is the possibility of walking the path of knowledge in a spiritually dumb way. The Newtonian archetype, whether scientist, educator or management consultant, isolates knowledge and focuses on small areas of it. He isolates a knowledge of things from a wider knowledge of people, processes and life in general. He restricts himself to what can be quantified, mistrusting the emotions and relying heavily on logic and reason. He traps himself in his own Newtonian version of the cave and its shadows.

The natural progression towards higher SQ leads from reflection, through understanding, to wisdom. The way to solve any problem, practical or intellectual, in a spiritually intelligent way is to place it in a wider perspective from which it can be seen more clearly. The deepest perspective of all comes from the centre, from the ultimate meaning and value that drives the situation or problem. Gaining this perspective begins with a process of simple reflection – going over the day or the project, focusing on where there are difficulties, and thinking how these difficulties have arisen. Such reflection is a daily necessity of the spiritually intelligent life. The next step is to think of possible alternatives to the present situation and to reflect on the likely outcomes of pursuing any of these alternative paths. This leads to an understanding of how the situation can be improved, or indeed whether it can be improved at all.

It may be the case, for instance, that I have a serious illness. My first task would be to reflect on how I became ill, and then on the ways and means of cure, including consulting experts. But it may be that I have a fatal disease. Here, understanding would cause me to see my illness in the larger context of life and death, to see my life itself in the context of its finiteness. This would lead to still deeper reflection on how I want to spend the time left to me, and how I want to 'live' my death. This would lead inevitably to further reflection on what I truly value in life, on what the meaning of life has been for me, on what of myself I would hope to leave behind when I am gone, on what going means to me. If I am able, through this process of reflection, to gain a sufficiently large perspective on my impending death, I may acquire wisdom and, with it, peace.

All truly deep knowing is an engagement with the centre. Jesus said, 'You must die to the old in order to be born to the new.' New knowledge places what I have known in a different context, sometimes invalidating it. Deep knowledge transforms my very being and in doing so takes me through trial by fire, which may consume what I previously was. This is why the path of knowledge requires the discipline of reflection, prayer, meditation and study. There is a well-known story in the Jewish mystical tradition that illustrates this.

Rabbi Akiba and three other men enter the forest. But before they can get out of the forest one of the men dies, one becomes an apostate and the third goes mad. Only the rabbi emerges from the forest safely. The forest, here, is a symbol of mystical knowledge, the kind of knowledge that unites the knower with all that is most holy. The moral is that Rabbi Akiba, before setting out into the forest (the mystical path), had studied Jewish law and tradition for many years. He had prayed and disciplined both mind and soul, which enabled him to withstand the trial by fire of mystical knowledge. The other three men had hoped to take a spiritual short-cut.

PATH 4: THE PATH OF PERSONAL TRANSFORMATION

Personality type	Artistic
Motivation	Creativity, Eros, life instinct
Archetypes	Moon (Diana), Artemis, the cauldron, wise woman, the shadow
Religious emphasis	Wholeness, the quest, individuation (Jung), ritual
Myth	Journey to the Underworld, the Grail
Practice	Dream work, dialogue
Chakra	Heart (commitment)

Michael Robartes remembers forgotten beauty and, when his arms wrap her round, he presses in his arms the loveliness which has long faded from the world. Not this. Not at all. I desire to press in my arms the loveliness which has not yet come into the world . . .

. . . Mother is putting my new secondhand clothes in order. She prays now, she says, that I may learn in my own life and away from home and friends what the heart is and what it feels. Amen. So be it. Welcome, O life! I go to encounter for the millionth time the reality of experience and to forge in the smithy of my soul the uncreated conscience of my race.

James Joyce, *Portrait of the Artist as a Young Man*

'To press in my arms the loveliness which has not yet come into the world . . . to forge in the smithy of my soul the uncreated conscience of my race.' Joyce's vision of himself as a young man and a young artist captures the creative passion and transformative power that drive the artistic type. People who walk this path may bring into being hitherto unexpressed potential – feelings never before felt, visions never before seen, colours not yet imagined, thoughts not yet conceptualized and so on. They are what the poet Rilke calls 'the bees of the invisible'. Writers, artists, poets, musicians and their like constitute just 10–15 per cent of the population. But most of us, just by virtue of being human and in possession of any spiritual intelligence at all, walk this path to some extent.

The essence of the psychological and spiritual task facing those who walk the path of transformation is personal and transpersonal integration. That is, we must explore the heights and depths of ourselves and weld the disparate parts of our fragmented selves into an independent, whole person. To this extent, the path is crucial to us all. Its everyday challenges are a normal part of adolescence and a familiar aspect of middle age (the mid-life crisis), though they may return at any age. But for the artistic type *per se* the journey of personal integration, at its most spiritually intelligent, takes us necessarily into the realm of transpersonal integration – finding lost or fragmented aspects of our deepest selves at levels well beyond the ego and the existing culture, drawing buckets from the infinite well of the centre.

This path is the one most closely associated with the brain's 'God spot' activity, with those personalities who are open to mystical experiences, to more extreme emotions, with those who are 'eccentric', or different from the crowd, with those who often have to battle for (and frequently can lose) their sanity. We saw in Chapter 5 that 'God spot' activity, artistic ability, spiritual experience and mental imbalance are all highly correlated. For this reason, artists are often thought of as society's Wounded Healers (or shamans) – people who must make terrifying journeys into the unknown in an attempt to recapture lost parts of themselves. They may fail, but in the process of making their journey they bring back some treasure that heals the rest of us. These labour pains alone are the subject of much of the world's great literature. Dante, for instance, speaks of his own journey into the Dark Wood that made possible his later vision of Paradise:

> But at the far end of that valley of evil
>> Whose maze had sapped my heart with fear!
> I found myself before a little hill
>
> And lifted up my eyes. Its shoulders glowed
>> Already with the sweet rays of that planet
> Whose virtue leads men straight on every road,
>
> And the shining strengthened me against the fright
>> Whose agony had wracked the lake of my heart
> Through all the terrors of that piteous night.

Just as a swimmer, who with his last breath
    Flounders ashore from perilous seas, might turn
To memorize the wide water of his death –

So did I turn, my soul still fugitive
    From death's surviving image, to stare down
That pass that none had ever left alive.[5]

The obvious metaphor is that of a journey to the Underworld, into the realm of death or that of the Shadow: Demeter going to Hades to find her lost daughter Persephone who has been kidnapped by Pluto; Orpheus going down into the realm of the dead to recapture his lost Eurydice. Every night some of us make this journey when we wrestle with nightmares. Others do it through spells of madness or temporary breakdown. In each such journey there is a desperate sense of something being sought and of the necessity of sacrifice, perhaps permanent, in order to find it.

    The quest for the Holy Grail in Arthurian legend is another myth clearly associated with the path of transformation.[6] Here, the Land of the Fisher King (Pelles) is barren, the king is wounded, and only the finding of the Grail can bring healing. King Arthur's realm also needs healing. There are 150 Knights of the Round Table and each of them makes his own quest into the dark forest, but only three even *see* the Grail. In the Arthurian myth, it is Arthur's battle with his illegitimate son Mordred that threatens the kingdom. Arthur represents the forces of Light and Mordred those of Darkness (the Shadow). The Grail is the force that could heal the split, but the kingdom is destroyed by civil war. The modern myth of *Star Wars* has the same theme, but a more positive outcome: Luke Skywalker's saving of his father, Darth Vader, from the Dark Side frees the Empire from the shadow of destruction.

    Two distinct kinds of art can result from these quests or

journeys to the Underworld. If the healing that results is on a personal level, we get 'everyday' or personal art – a painting, say, a novel, a style of dress or a deep personal relationship that heals the artist. If the healing takes place on a transpersonal level, beyond the ego and beyond the existing culture, we get transpersonal or 'great' art, the art of a Bach or a Dante or a Dostoyevsky, which can heal a whole culture. The novelist E. M. Forster calls it 'prophetic art' because it prophesies the new – indeed it creates the new. Here, too, the art may take the form of or be inspired by a relationship that strikes the transpersonal level – Dante and Beatrice, Faust and Gretchen.

The motivating energy of the path is Eros, or Freud's Life Instinct. Eros is about the creative attraction of opposites and the order that can result. It is order out of chaos. In Greek mythology, first there was Chaos and then one of the earliest gods to be born was Eros, who could bring some order to the universe. The essence of any art is that it brings some order out of chaos. And the patron goddess of art is Diana, the Moon goddess, whose knowledge is knowledge of the Night, whose *light* is the light of the Night. To walk this path we must not fear the Dark, must not draw back from wrestling with the Shadow, must not be shy of the deep pain and the often life-threatening danger that entails. The artist often thrives because he or she is willing to look at aspects of the psyche or the culture or the species that others would reject.

There is a story about the twelfth-century magician and poet Milarepa, one of Tibet's greatest Buddhist teachers. Milarepa lived in remote mountain caves. One day he returned to his cave and found it inhabited by seven ferocious and threatening demons. He thought to himself, 'I could run away, or I could banish these demons.' He opts to banish the demons, and does so simply with six of them by using his traditional magic. But the seventh demon refuses to go away. Milarepa reasons, 'This demon is a creature of my own imagination and exists only through my own capacity to feel fear.' The story then continues with Milarepa offering the demon compassion and offering to share his cave with it. 'With friendliness and compassion, and without concern for his body, Milarepa placed his head in the mouth of the demon; but the demon could not eat him and so vanished like a rainbow.'[7]

In placing his head inside the jaws of the demon, Milarepa was willing to go to 'the edge'. We have already seen that all creativity happens at the edge of chaos, at the edge . . .

> between the known and the unknown
> between the knowable and the unknowable
> between meaning and meaninglessness
> between certainty and confusion
> between exilaration and depression
> between sanity and insanity
> between joy and despair
> between resistance and temptation
> between good and evil
> between Light and the Shadow
> between living and dying
> between security and terror
> between frenzy and control
> between ecstasy and nothingness
> between love and its loss
> between love and its absence
> between . . .

The list is endless

The risk of coming to the edge is that we may lose our head. The jaws of the demon may be too quick. But the risk of not coming to the edge is that we either live the shadow form of this path or walk it in a spiritually dumb way.

The shadow of creativity is destructiveness, or nihilism – Freud's Death Wish. Those who follow this path give themselves over with equal passion to self-destructive behaviour, and are driven to and seek out or create the ugly. This is creativity turned against itself: vandals on housing estates, perpetrators of senseless violence, 'artists' who exhibit the carcasses of rotting cows or jars of aborted foetuses. These are enemies of form, enemies of life itself, but they are passionate enemies. They are as driven in their quest for harm or ugliness as the positive artist is in his or her quest for balance or beauty.

Others who walk the path of transformation in spiritually dumb ways include aesthetes, people who produce sterile form divorced from vitality. Their passion is that of acquisition and display. Then there are those who impose arbitrary form without reference to organic growth or the original chaos itself. These people love straight lines and sharp corners and cannot bear anything to be out of place.

The opposite of order is chaos, and to have a spiritually dumb penchant for chaos often results in pure mess. The perpetrators are people who fear order or form, resist committed relationships, rebel for the sake of rebelling, fight 'the crowd' whatever it does. The saddest of them even fight order within themselves, arriving late for appointments, missing deadlines and suffering 'writer's block'.

Both of the spiritually dumb extremes described above result from unwillingess or inability to face conflict. Artistic people are particularly conflict-ridden: this can give them their motivation in the first place. They have the capacity to know and experience the extremes of light and darkness, or elation and despair. Fear or avoidance of these conflicts is a turning away from spiritual intelligence; willingness to face and attempt to resolve conflicts is a turning towards it. But borderline personalities can be too unstable to embark on this dangerous journey.

A willingness to remember and reflect on dreams, to engage

251

in creative dialogue with oneself or others, to place one's head in the jaws of the demon – these lead to greater spiritual intelligence. The more extreme the conflicts, the more exotic the fantasies and dreams, the more it helps to be anchored in some aspect of daily reality – a relationship, a family, a routine, a discipline. Jung credited his family and his busy practice of patients with keeping him moderately sane during his seven-year journey into near-madness.

The most spiritually intelligent of all journeys on this path is the journey to the centre. It is a journey of incredible terror requiring remarkable faith. And it requires a willingness that the ego might be sacrificed, that nothing of it might be left but the treasure that one finds and the healing that it might bring to others. This in turn requires overcoming that deepest of all conflicts, the fear of death.

PATH 5: THE PATH OF BROTHERHOOD

Personality type	Realistic
Motivation	Construction, citizenship
Archetypes	Mars (Ares), Gaia, Adam Kadmon, the Sword
Religious emphasis	Universal brotherhood, willing sacrifice, justice
Myth	World soul, Indra's net
Practice	Role reversals, building the dialogue 'container'
Chakra	Throat (struggle against secondary things)

The same stream of life that runs through my veins night and day runs through the world and dances in rhythmic measures.

It is the same life that shoots in joy through the dust of the earth in numberless blades of grass and breaks into tumultuous waves of leaves and flowers.

It is the same life that is rocked in the ocean-cradle of birth and death, in ebb and in flow.

I feel my limbs are made glorious by the touch of this world of life. And my pride is from the life-throb of ages dancing in my blood at this moment.

Is it beyond thee to be glad with the gladness of this rhythm? to be tossed and lost and broken in the whirl of this fearful joy?

All things rush on, they stop not, they look not behind, no power can hold them back, they rush on.

Keeping step with that restless, rapid music, seasons come dancing and pass away – Colours, tunes, and perfumes pour in endless cascades in the abounding joy that scatters and gives up and dies every moment.

Rabindranath Tagore[8]

'Mark Smith' is a highly skilled and very high-status engineer who is Vice President of Operations for his midwestern American company. He is in his early forties and has a large family of young children. Mark is a typical realistic type. He hasn't much to say. He shows little emotion and never discusses emotions. He is ambitious, competitive and wants all the best for his family. He takes great pride in his work, and feels strong loyalty to his colleagues at work. He has a keen sense of justice. At weekends he enjoys doing the family barbecue, repairing his truck and overhauling his boats.

Mark is different from the average realistic type only because events have forced him to walk a more spiritually intelligent version of his life's path. He has a fatal cancer that may kill him within two years. He shows little emotion about this, and doesn't like to talk about it, but the deep spiritual effects of his illness show through strongly in his personality. While his wife (a social type) sheds tears daily and combs every source of information for possible cures, Mark says he just wants to get on with life. 'I'm here now,' he says, 'and I just want to do the best that I can with that.' He exudes a calm strength that sustains his family and friends during the impending tragedy.

Despite the often unexciting and unexcitable exterior of realistic personality types (20 per cent of the population, mostly men), their path of brotherhood can be one of the most spiritually advanced paths to walk in life. Typically cut in what John Gray (*Men Are from Mars. Women Are from Venus*) would call the Martian mould – taciturn, practical, no-nonsense, uncomfortable with overt feelings – these people exemplify the ideals of the hero or the valiant warrior. Hemingway's heroes fit this mould. At their best, they would fight and even gladly die for what they see as justice. They love their group, their fellows, and their sense of brotherhood runs deep. Their fearlessness and lack of concern with death have deep philosophical and spiritual roots in the myths that inspire this path.

As long ago as the ancient Greek philosopher Plotinus the West had the myth of a universal soul, or world soul, of which individual souls are a part. In more recent times the philosophers Hegel and Schopenhauer spoke of the same reality. The Jewish mystics anthropomorphized the world soul into Adam Kadmon, the perfect man, of which we are all parts. The American writer Ralph Waldo Emerson called it 'that Unity, that Over-Soul, within which every man's particular being is contained and made one with another; that common heart of which all sincere conversation is the worship'.[9] Perhaps the most striking description of all comes from a Buddhist sutra: 'In the heaven of Indra there is said to be a network of pearls so arranged that if you look at one you see all the others reflected in it. In the same way, each object in the world is not merely itself but involves every other object, and in fact *is* every other object.'[10] Modern science presents the same holistic reality in the hologram, a laser-generated photograph in which the whole picture is contained within

254

each small part of any projected image. The very modern scientific myth of Gaia describes the earth and all who dwell on her as one living organism.

These myths take their adherents beyond a fear of death because they lead them into a realm of the soul that never dies, where the individual soul is and always will be a part of the greater, eternal world soul. According to the Yogic philosopher Sri Aurobindo, it is particularly those qualities of the soul that are developed on the path of brotherhood and the subsequent path of servant leadership that remain eternal. They are reincarnated as a deep, background 'mood' in the person that one becomes in the next life. The spiritual task of those who walk this path is to make contact with that deeper realm of all men and all being in which their ego selves are rooted. The spiritual discipline that makes this possible is a fearless and uncompromising pursuit of justice.

Those who walk path 2, the path of nurturing, often bear an unequal relationship to those whom they love and care for. There is a natural asymmetry in the relationship of a mother to her children: it is usually partisan, and it emphasizes bringing help and healing. Path 2 people also emphasize affection and empathy, and do their best to minimize any existing antipathy or conflict. Justice requires an ability to see and accept positive and negative emotions, the successes and failures of others. Justice requires a sense of the equality of all claims on me at some level, and a wise recognition that people are different and that conflicts are a real part of life. To walk this path I must put aside my own preferences, my own likely rewards, my own place in the pecking order of power.

The contemporary Harvard philosopher John Rawls described how to handle the demands of this path. According to Rawls, when I am called upon to make any decision about the distribution of rights or goods in my society, I must do so in total ignorance of my own place in the scenario I am planning.

I might be any one of society's protagonists, but I don't know which when I decide who gets what. In this way the principles of justice that I advocate are supposed to be free of personal bias. As an individual, my decisions might still be short-sighted or ill-informed, so ideally I will participate in a group, each of whom contributes a point of view. This is the philosophy that underlies ideal democracy, in which each person will consider the good of the whole, though today's politics is far from realizing the ideal. The original Athenian 'parliament', which operated as a dialogue group, was often more successful. Today, Quakers are also very often good at arriving at 'a sense of the meeting', as can be other small or intimate groups.

The shadow form of this path which emphasizes wholeness and spontaneity is self-loathing: the person who cannot believe in himself, the self-chosen outcast, the coward. To be spiritually dumb on this path is to live it at its most narrow. It means being interested only in my own unchallenging practical pursuits, making no effort to communicate or em-pathize with others, being emotionally lazy: 'Feelings are just too much trouble!' This is John Gray's Martian at his crude, tattooed worst, all day bent over the motor bike he is fixing, interested in nothing but machines and sport, valuing power for its own personal gain, competitive to the point of non-cooperation, hanging out with companions that are just like himself, emotionally stunted with his woman, stuck in the here and now.

The first step towards greater spiritual intelligence for the realistic type must be some sense of dissatisfaction with the way things are – a boredom with my own narrow interests, a loneliness from my lack of emotional contact, a frustration with my inability to articulate my thoughts and feelings. Next, I must have the the honesty to admit that these are failures of my own making. It is not just that I have not met the right person or the right group or found the magic interest. I must *want* to be different, must long to broaden myself and my interests, long to belong to a larger and more diverse group.

Like Mark Smith, many realistic types may get further along this path through challenge – going into battle, fighting for those one loves, fighting for a cause in which one believes, struggling to build a community, facing death.

This is ultimately a path of transpersonal service, rooted in the transpersonal reality of those parts of the soul that never die, those parts of the self that transcend the personal ego. When a man or woman of this type can centre himself at that level, the spiritual intelligence shines through. As Ralph Waldo Emerson expresses it,

> If he have not found his home in God, his manner, his forms of speech, the turn of his sentences, the build, shall I say, of all his opinions will involuntarily confess it, let him brave it out how he will. If he have found his centre, the Deity will shine through him, through all his disguises of ignorance, of ungenial temperament, of unfavourable circumstance. The tone of seeking is one, the tone of having is another.[11]

Justice is about seeing that everyone has his claim, brother-hood about the value of all men. Nothing puts us to this test more strongly than in confronting our feelings for our adversaries. Role reversal often leads to a deep respect not just for opinions different from my own, but also for the people who hold them. The camaraderie of soldiers from opposing sides who meet at still points in the fighting is well known. Respect for one's enemy takes me to that level of humanity and ideals where he and I hold something in common. It takes me to a level where I see we are both honest players in some larger evolutionary script, and I grow deeper to that level of soul that both unites all men and survives personal death.

PATH 6: THE PATH
OF SERVANT LEADERSHIP

Personality type	Enterprising
Motivation	Power, redemption, loyal service
Archetypes	Jupiter (Zeus), Great Father, Prophet
Religious emphasis	Surrender, union with God, priesthood
Myth	Exodus, the Crucifixion, the Bodhi tree
Practice	Self-knowledge, meditation, guru-yoga
Chakra	Brow (spirit, command)

Oh, this is the animal that never was.
They hadn't seen one; but just the same, they loved
its graceful movements, and the way it stood
Looking at them calmly, with clear eyes.

It had not *been*. But for them, it appeared
in all its purity. They left space enough.
And in the space hollowed out by their love
it stood up all at once and didn't need

existence. They nourished it, not with grain,
but with the mere possibility of its being.
And finally, this gave it so much power

that from its forehead a horn grew. One horn.
It drew near to a virgin, white, gleaming –
and was, inside the mirror and in her.

Rainer Maria Rilke
'The Unicorn'

All human groups – families, churches, corporations, tribes, nations – need leaders to provide focus, purpose, tactics and a sense of direction. To be an effective leader, a man or woman usually has the outgoing, self-confident manner of the enterprising personality type. He or she is at ease with power. A good leader must get on well with others in the group, must be, or at least appear to be, a person of integrity who can inspire the group with ideals, and must not be self-serving. A great leader serves something from beyond himself; a truly great one serves nothing less than 'God'. Ultimately, a leader creates or evokes in his followers the kind of meaning he himself is led by – superficial or deep, constructive or destructive.

The unicorn has always been a special symbol in Western culture, a beast conjured up by longing and the human capacity to dream. In Rilke's poem quoted above he is conjured up by love, and given a space to be by those who dare to believe in the possibility that he might exist. In the vision of quantum science, the whole of existence is a field of unicorns – a set of possibilities plucked out of the quantum vacuum's infinite sea of potentiality. Each of us is a servant of 'God' or the quantum vacuum, a servant of the manifold potentiality at the heart of existence.

Leaders who become aware of servanthood in this sense know that they serve more than family, community, business or nation, more even than 'vision and values' as these are normally understood. True servant leaders serve that deep longing in the human soul that conjures up unicorns. They make things happen that others have felt impossible, they create new ways for human beings to relate to one another, new ways for companies to serve society, new ways for society to *be*. The Buddha, Moses and Jesus were such leaders. In our own times we have had the good fortune to be served by Gandhi, Martin Luther King, Nelson Mandela and the Dalai Lama. Many others of lesser renown have served God and humanity through serving their own groups or companies. Ultimately, each of us has the capacity to be a servant leader.

The life of the servant leader improves the attitudes and

lifestyle – the conventions – of his tribe. In this way the service of path 6 feeds around into reinventing path 1, completing the cycle of the Lotus. There are many great myths of servant leadership – Buddha sitting under the Bodhi tree until he could bring enlightenment to all humanity, Moses leading his people out of captivity and bringing God's Law to the world, Christ dying on the cross so that all might know eternal life. Gandhi's role in bringing independence to India and a deeper spiritual vision to its people has acquired the role of modern myth.

Servant leadership is, in an important sense, the highest of the spiritual paths. Through the gifts endowed by their lives and personalities, these people have the opportunity to serve, heal and enlighten those whom they lead, but the path calls ultimately for great integrity (wholeness). The servant leader must be able to submit himself to the highest force imaginable. For enterprising personality types who naturally wield power and sway people, such surrender does not come easily. Its very possibility is an act of grace.

The central energy driving this personality type is power. The uses, misuses and abuses of power determine whether an individual will walk the path in a spiritually dumb or spiritually intelligent way. The path from dumbness to intelligence passes through all the snares and temptations of power.

The shadow form of servant leadership is the tyrant who twists power to serve his own or evil ends. Here is found the sadist, the person who derives pleasure from using his power to harm or humiliate others. A leader like Hitler does seem to serve a cause beyond himself – that is what gave him his charisma and made him so dangerous. But it is an evil cause that itself summons up the forces of the 'dark side' such as torture and death – destruction and limitation rather than the flowering of possibilities. Darth Vader from *Star Wars* is a mythical figure in this mould. The Cretan Minotaur who devours innocent youths deep in the crevices of his labyrinth was created by King Minos's lust for power.

The ordinarily spiritually dumb way to walk the path of leadership is to use my power in the service of myself, my own ends, my own gains. Corrupt politicians, petty tyrants and bullies serve power from the most shallow ego level of the self. They often become paranoid, expecting from others the disloyalty they themselves express.

Middling in spiritual intelligence is the leader who serves his group, community, business or nation from within their existing myths and traditions – the leader who safeguards existing possibilities. If, on the Lotus of the Self, we think of conventionality and art as two polar opposites in the way a personality type will use its energies and potential, these caretaker leaders lean towards the conventional. They do not deeply inspire or challenge those whom they lead, but they do reassure them. They serve the middle layer of the self, the group or collective that is within us all.

The most spiritually intelligent form of walking the path, we have seen, is servant leadership, which creates new visions and bring new possibilities into being. Katsuhiko Yazaki is one such leader alive today. Yazaki is a Japanese businessman in his early fifties. He owns a global mail-order company named Felissimo with offices in Japan, Europe and North America. He tells his own story in his 1994 book, *The Path to Liang Zhi* ('The Path to True, Inner Self-Knowledge').

As a very young man, Yazaki inherited a 'storeless business' from his father. Goods were sold door to door, by word of mouth, through the network. Over the years, he built this up to a successful mail-order business that left him very wealthy. By his mid-forties he had everything he thought he wanted: success, wealth, esteem in the community, a happy family. But something was missing. Some friends showed him a book about Zen and told him of a Master Kido Inoue who taught it.

261

Yazaki went to Master Inoue's monastery for a week of meditation. He found it difficult, at times painful, but liberating. 'One moment,' he says, 'I felt as if I had found peace, another moment I felt like a prisoner of my delusions. I was astonished at the realization of what I had been calling "me". This was the first time I realized how many delusions were within myself. It was also the first time I realized how many delusions I had that were causing ups and downs in my daily life. Until this point, I had never confronted realities about myself so directly.'

Yazaki emerged from his monastery cell after a week 'to see the beauty of the world for the first time'. He realized that he had been living his life in shadow and that the world itself was being damaged by human shadows. 'Humans,' he wote, 'by separating the world from the self, nature from humanity, and the self from others, trap themselves in delusions to protect the ego. They inevitably enter a frightening scenario of hypocrisy and self-righteousness.'

After these insights Yazaki rededicated his business life. He wanted to use his company to do something for the earth's environment and for future generations. At that point he renamed his company Felissimo, which relates to the Spanish and Italian words for 'happy', because his vision of the proper role of business became to increase the sum of human happiness. He formed his new concept of the 'ultra store', a store that can 'gather value over a wide area' by transcending the limits of geographical space and present time. He felt he could help his customers to realize images of their future selves and to imagine more fulfilling future lifestyles by marketing his goods globally, thus expanding service and awareness at a more universal level. He attended the Rio Earth Summit Conference and dedicated himself and much of his money to saving the earth's environment. He started a foundation to study the needs of future generations and to back educational projects.

'I believe,' he says, 'that these international activities all flowed from what I learned in Master Inoue's monastery.' Service at this level is serving God.

The nineteenth-century Vedanta philosopher Vivekananda said, 'This universe is simply a gymnasium in which the soul is taking exercise.' Vivekenanda was one of those who inspired Mahatma Gandhi's view of 'trusteeship', his own vision of servant leadership. Speaking of trusteeship in economic affairs, Gandhi said that when an individual obtains more than his proportionate share of the world's wealth he should become a trustee of that portion for God's people. The same can be said of power and influence. As Jesus said, 'Not my will, Lord, but thine.' Those simple words define completely the spiritually intelligent way to walk the path of leadership.

SEVEN PRACTICAL STEPS TO BETTER SQ

Seven Steps to Greater Spiritual Intelligence
- Become aware of where I am now
- Feel strongly that I want to change
- Reflect on what my own centre is and on what are my deepest motivations
- Discover and dissolve obstacles
- Explore many possibilities to go forward
- Commit myself to a path
- Remain aware there are many paths

Each of the six spiritual paths towards greater SQ has a progression from spiritually dumb to spiritually intelligent. The work to be done is specific to each path. The path of nurturing, for instance, requires us to grow from selfish, jealous or absent love to unselfish, nurturing love; the path of duty requires me to get from being a mere follower of the crowd to someone who celebrates the holiness in the every-day. But for all their differences, the progressions share a set of seven steps which I want to summarize here.

Step 1: You must become aware of where you are now. For example, what is your present situation? What are its consequences and repercussions? Are you harming yourself or others? This step requires cultivating self-awareness, which in turn requires cultivating the habit of reflecting on your experience. Many of us don't. We just live from day to day, activity to activity and so on. Higher SQ means getting to the deepness of things, thinking about things, assessing yourself and your behaviour from time to time. Daily is best. This can be done through a few moments of quiet time set aside, daily meditation, work with a counsellor or therapist, or just going over each day before you fall asleep at night.

Step 2: If your reflections lead you to feel that you, your behaviour, your relationships, your life, your job performance could be better, you have to *want* to change, to make an inner commitment to change. This will involve thinking honestly about what the change will cost you in terms of energy and sacrifice. Are you prepared to cut down your drinking or smoking? To devote more attention to listening to yourself and others? To undertake a daily discipline like reading or exercise or caring for an animal?

Step 3: A still deeper level of reflection is now required. You must get to know yourself, where your own centre is and what your deepest life motivations are. If you were going to die next week, what would you like to be able to say you had accomplished or contributed in life? If you were given another year, what would you do with it?

Step 4: What are the obstacles that stand in your way? What has stopped you living out of your centre before? Anger? Greed? Guilt? Fear? Simple laziness? Ignorance? Self-indulgence? Now make a list of what has been holding you back, and develop an understanding of how you can remove these obstacles. It may be a simple act of awareness or decisiveness, or a culminating sense of what the Buddhists call 'revulsion' – simply feeling sick of yourself. But equally it may be a long, slow process for which you need a 'guide' – a therapist, good friend or spiritual adviser. This step is often bypassed but is crucial and needs recurrent attention.

Step 5: What practices or disciplines should you adopt? What path should you follow? What commitments would be worth making? At this stage, you need to become aware of the various possibilities for moving forward. Devote some mental and spiritual work to exploring several of these possibilities, let them run in your imagination, find out what their practical requirements are and decide how feasible each of these is for you.

Step 6: Now you must commit yourself to a path in life and work towards the centre while walking it. Again, reflect daily on whether you are doing your best for yourself and others, whether you are getting the most out of the situation, whether you are feeling peace or satisfaction with the way things are going, whether there is *meaning* for you here. Living a path towards the centre means turning your everyday thoughts and activities into ongoing sacrament, surfacing the natural sacredness that is in every meaningful situation.

Step 7: And finally, while you walk your own chosen path with grace, always remain aware that there are other paths. Honour those who walk them, and that in yourself which at some future time might need to take another path.

ALL PATHS LEAD
TO AND FROM THE CENTRE

In the breakthrough, where I stand free of my own will and of the will of God and of all his works and of God himself, there I am above all creatures and am neither God nor creature. Rather, I am what I was and what I shall remain now and forever. Then I receive an impulse [awareness] which shall bring me above all the angels. In this impulse I receive wealth so vast that God cannot be enough for me in all that makes him God, and with all his divine works. For in this breakthrough I discover that I and God are one. There I am what I was, and I grow neither smaller nor bigger, for I am an immovable cause that moves all things.

Meister Eckhart, medieval German mystic[12]

It is true of all the spiritual paths that when I walk them with spiritual intelligence I do so in contact with the deepest centre of the self. From that centre 'I am an immovable cause that moves all things' because I and all my actions initiate from the centre of existence itself. They are *nothing but* some of the infinite potentialities of this centre expressing themselves. This is a place beyond ego and beyond all specific forms through which my own tradition expresses itself – beyond all known symbols, beyond anything that can be expressed in words. In the language of Meister Eckhart, I and God are one. In the language of another image I have used often in this book, I am a wave on the sea and I realize that I and the sea are one. The fifteenth-century Indian poet Kabir uses this image to ask,

I have been thinking of the difference
between water
and the waves on it. Rising,
water's still water, falling back,
it is water, will you give me a hint
how to tell them apart?

Because someone has made up the word
'wave', do I have to distinguish it
from water?

There is a Secret One inside us;
the planets in all the galaxies
pass through his hands like beads.

That is a string of beads one should look at
with luminous eyes.[13]

The mystics of every great tradition have spoken of this place within the self. It is the pure light, the fire, that shines or burns within us, the source of all that soul brings into the world. Spoken of in such terms, the centre sounds awe-inspiring, attractive and holy – but perhaps too abstract for many of us to grasp. Yet each of us lives it and experiences it when we live our daily lives in a spiritually intelligent way. It is the feeling of holiness in everyday objects and events, the sense of the sacred in an act of loving, the almost unbearable ecstasy we feel when understanding something deeply for the first time, the sense of elation when we bring something new into the world, the sense of deep satisfaction when we see justice done, the deep sense of peace when we know that that which we serve serves God.

All six of the spiritual paths lead to the centre, to an experience that could be called 'enlightenment'. But when lived in the most spiritually intelligent way possible, all paths also lead *from* the centre, back to the world. The Buddha went through many years of search and suffering to achieve enlightenment, but when he had done so he did not allow himself simply to disappear into Nirvana. Rather, the Buddha returned to the world so that all might become enlightened. An ordinary person high in SQ does not just seek the bliss of knowing the centre, but responds to it spontaneously and then takes responsibility for bringing back to share with the world the light he has seen, the energy he has gained, the integrity he has experienced. He becomes an enlightened parent, an enlightened teacher, an enlightened cook, an enlightened lover and so on.

There is a spiral of existence, to and from the centre on each path outlined by the Lotus of the Self, and also round each petal of the lotus. None of us is really complete, really whole, really enlightened, until we have to some extent walked *all* of the six spiritual paths – until we have found a creative way to live convention, known how to love deeply and without selfishness, known how to understand, found something we can create, served our fellows, and known the servant leadership that serves God.

There is also a spiral of existence that leads from one life to the next, from making that last return to the centre that is called death and then being reborn again. As a young teenager, I built a Wilson cloud chamber. It is a scientific instrument in which one can see the tracks of atoms in a cloudy vapour. In the cloud chamber, I could see charged atomic particles suddenly emerge out of the nothingness of the vapour: they would travel for a few inches and then disappear back into the vapour – only to emerge in another place at another time. Quantum field theory tells us that we are like those charged particles. We are 'excitations of energy' on the quantum vacuum that emerge from nothingness, travel for a while in this world, and then merge back into the vacuum from which we came – only to re-emerge as another pattern of energy at another time. Death is a journey through life: it is a path at the centre of every path, an essential part of the spiral of existence.

Speaking of his experience of oneness with the centre, where he becomes 'an unmovable cause that moves all things', Meister Eckhart calls this his condition of being 'unborn': 'Therefore also I am unborn, and following the way of my unborn [unmanifest] being I can never die. Following the way of my unborn being I have always been, I am now, and shall eternally remain.'[14]

The man searches for the ox (his true self).

He discovers the ox's footprints (he understands the teaching about life and self).

The man perceives the ox (he has repeated experiences of unity with the source of existence).

He catches the ox, but realizes that if he wants the ox to submit he must train him.

270

The man tames the ox (he trains his own mind).

He rides the ox home (he brings his experience of unity with the source into daily life).

The ox disappears because the man learns that any specific manifestation of reality, including the path he has been following, is impermanent and can be transcended.

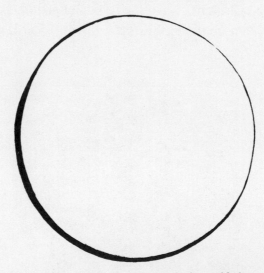

Everything disappears: both the ox and the self that perceived the ox are transcended.
Whip, rope, person, and ox — all merge in No-Thing.
This heaven is so vast no message can stain it,
How many snowflakes exist in a raging fire?
Here are footprints of the patriarchs.

The man begins to perceive the cosmic forces of creation and destruction from a standpoint beyond these, but he cannot yet relate easily on everyday levels. He is 'the fool on the hill', a little overshadowed by his own vision.

The man, now a master, is back in the marketplace. 'I search for nothing, I live an ordinary life, but everything I look upon becomes enlightened.'

273

When we live our own or to some extent all of the spiritual paths to and from the centre, the high SQ or enlightenment that we achieve has about it the incredible grace of the everyday. In Zen Buddhism there is a saying, 'Before I was enlightened, I hewed wood and drew water. After enlightenment, I hewed wood and drew water.' This is not saying that enlightenment does not bring progress and transformation, but rather that real transformation is to bring us back to the place from which we started, only now we live it fully alive and aware.

In *A Manual of Zen Buddhism*, D. T. Suzuki reproduces some fifteenth-century versions of ten original twelfth-century Chinese drawings, with accompanying short poems, that illustrate what I mean by the spiral of existence, and the Zen understanding of enlightenment.[15] They use the allegory of a man herding an ox.

In 'Little Gidding', from his *Four Quartets*, the poet T. S. Eliot expresses the same spiral of existence and the meaning of the ox-herding pictures:

> We shall not cease from exploration
> And the end of all our exploring
> Will be to arrive where we started
> And to know the place for the first time.
> Through the unknown, remembered gate
> When the last of earth left to discover
> Is that which was the beginning;
> At the source of the longest river
> The voice of the hidden waterfall
> And the children in the apple-tree
> Not known, because not looked for
> But heard, half-heard, in the stillness
> Between two waves of the sea.
> Quick now, here, now, always –

A condition of complete simplicity
(Costing not less than everything)
And all shall be well and
All manner of thing shall be well
When the tongues of flame are in-folded
Into the crowned knot of fire
And the fire and the rose are one.

All paths lead to and from the centre. Following them is a quest, but at a certain point realizing them is an act of surrender. Even the craving to become enlightened eventually disappears.

14. ASSESSING MY SQ

Unlike IQ, which is linear, logical and rational, spiritual intelligence cannot be quantified. The questions that follow are simply an exercise in reflection. They have been organized into seven sections, one for each personality type or petal of the lotus, and a seventh that reveals how close you have got to the energies of the centre. It is assumed that you will have completed the questionnaire on personality types in Chapter 13. As we saw there, each of us usually consists of a mixture of qualities belonging to at least three personality types. Similarly, in this questionnaire at least three of the spiritual paths will be relevant to each of us. Nevertheless, it is still best to do no more in a single day than the questions associated with one path, giving yourself time to reflect in between.

There are four groups of questions for each spiritual path or personality type. These relate to:

☐ a general survey of your relevant experience
☐ common obstacles to progress
☐ some possible themes for further progress
☐ some transpersonal, or more conventionally spiritual, aspects of any given path

Needless to say, though these questions will give you a lot to think about they only scratch the surface of what can be a lifetime's journey.

PATH 1: DUTY

1. What groups have you been glad to belong to in your life? Family? Friends? Work? Neighbourhood? Nation? Ethnic group? None?

2. Which of these groups (if any) have you become estranged from? Why? Are you left with any bad feelings? Disagreements? Traumatic incidents? Guilt? Do you still feel bound by any of the group's rules or customs? If so why?

3. Is there any group to which you would like to belong more fully? Is this practical?

4. What is your moral code now? What is its source? How far do you follow it? Have you thought of a change that might improve one of your groups for everyone (or nearly everyone) concerned? Have you done anything about it? Have you made any important resolution in the past year and kept to it?

PATH 2: NURTURING

1. Are there now (or have there been in the past) any people to whom you would happily give more than you receive? Are there any people (now or in the past) from whom you happily receive more than you give?

2. Are there any people whom you are currently neglecting, harming or bearing a grudge against? Why? Have you made any positive or negative decisions about this?

3. Are there any people (now or in the past) whom you want or wanted to help but cannot? How do you feel about that? Can you have close friends if they don't need your help

277

or advice? Can you, in intimate relationships, be open and honest about difficult topics?

4. Do people find you easy to talk to? Do you sometimes help someone in need who approaches you, even though they are outside your social circle?

PATH 3: UNDERSTANDING

1. Do you take an active interest in the lifestyles of those around you? Family? Work? Neighbourhood? Current affairs? Have you recently read or discussed anything to do with psychology, philosophy, ethics or similar subjects?

2. If you feel bogged down in a problem do you usually put it aside, or do you try another approach? Do you have any unmade decisions, confusion about some subject, or long-term practical problems? What would have to happen for you to make progress on any of these?

3. Can you usually see some value in both sides of an argument? If so, what happens? Can you progress beyond this point? Do people often surprise you, or is your intuition about them correct more often than not?

4. Are you intellectually seeking something? Try to define what, exactly, you would like to understand better. What might help with this? What hinders you? How important is this to you? Can you accept your present lack of under-standing without giving up?

PATH 4: PERSONAL TRANSFORMATION

1. 'We never possess anything unless we possess it first with passion.' How far is this true in your life relationships, causes, art, vocation etc.)? Are there ways of feeling that you try to avoid?

2. Recall a person, dream, daydream or story that filled you with a passionate or romantic longing, but which did not reach a completely happy conclusion. Was there something missing or incomplete about your life at the time? Did you try to realize your dream? If so, what happened? Did you give up out of pain, humiliation or cynicism? If not, what held you back – morals, justified prudence, timidity, or all three? Find a way to express some part of this emotion or theme now, perhaps through poetry, writing, dancing, listening to music or talking to someone you trust. (Talent, here, is less important than being authentic.) In any given emotional situation, do you usually see many possible styles of expressing your feelings?

3. Can you see that your emotions and longings are cut from the same cloth as those of writers, artists or musicians whom you respect? Take one such work of art that moves you. Find out something about its creator and compare his or her life with yours. Do you see that even pain can become a contribution to others, if placed in context and transformed?

4. Take any example of personal behaviour that moves you deeply. What are its pros and cons? Now try to find a complementary or counter-balancing example of behaviour. See if the two can have a satisfying dialogue. Are there any examples of rebels or rogues with whom you identify or feel sympathy? What can you learn about yourself from that?

PATH 5: BROTHERHOOD

1. Ideally, would you like to be able to have a conversation with anybody? Pick any meeting with others that has interested you. Can you imagine yourself reversing roles with any or all of the others there? Do you take an active interest in local or citizenship affairs?

2. Are there some people with whom you can't feel at ease? Why? What is your emotion? (Boredom? Fear? Anger? Competitiveness? Contempt? Regret? Something else?) Do you think that you would behave differently from these people if you were given their background and situation?

3. Is justice important to you? For everyone, or just for a few groups that are close to your heart? If you are only concerned with justice for some groups, what have you got in common with them?

4. Are you disturbed or embarrassed by the subject of death? Do you believe in any kind of life after death? Heaven? Reincarnation? The survival of your ideas or your family? Have you ever had an experience of love for, and unity with, all beings? Have you ever felt that you could lay down your life for certain people or causes?

PATH 6: SERVANT LEADERSHIP

1. Have you been accepted as the leader of any group? How did that make you feel? Have you ever had visions of or longings for the way an ideal group or society could live? Did you do anything about it, however small? Have you abandoned it? Why? Can you make further progress with your vision? Does it need refining?

2. Have you 'inherited' some of your views of society and/or your role in it? That is, have you adopted, without reflection, ideas and views from earlier in your life? Have you accepted what parents, friends, work associates or a spouse partner wanted you to do? Have you made hasty decisions when confused or stressed? How much of this have you outgrown? Does any modified form of such inherited purposes still interest you?

3. Can you always find, despite the difficulties, the deep energy needed to deal with an emergency? If your deep vision

is challenged, do you give up? Become assertive because you 'know best'? Debate the issue democratically?

4. Are you willing to stand up and be counted for what you most value, even if that has no immediate chance of being accepted by others? Have you ever had an experience of something holy, sacred, a source of intelligent energy from beyond yourself? Have you tried to express it in some way, to some degree? Can you imagine practical structures that might express it?

THE CENTRE

1. Have you ever felt yourself to be in the presence of a powerful spiritual force that goes beyond your everyday self? If so, did it include a sense of love for or unity with all things? Did it include a sense of an intelligent and sacred source of energy from beyond yourself? Was the experience beyond time, space and form – an indescribable void of which you were yet consciously aware? Have any of these experiences remained important to you?

2. Do you often have nightmares? Do you sometimes feel that all your luck, good and bad, is caused by hidden forces? Do you find it difficult to feel close to anyone? Do you often feel that life is pointless? Do you really dislike being alone? (These are all negative forms of spiritual energy that must be overcome if you are to raise your SQ.)

3. If, after long discussion, you still disagreed with your associates on a point of principle, what would you do? Imagine several different situations and their possible outcomes.

4. Do you have moments not just of pleasure but of deep contentment? What are you usually doing at the time? Do these moments inspire you or give you strength at other times? If you were to die tonight, would you feel that your life has in some way been worthwhile? How?

15. BEING SPIRITUALLY INTELLIGENT IN A SPIRITUALLY DUMB CULTURE

An American businessman was standing on the jetty of a Mexican coastal village when a small boat with just one fisherman docked. Inside the boat were several large yellowfin tuna. The American complimented the Mexican on the quality of his fish and asked how long it had taken to catch them.

The Mexican replied, 'Only a little while.'

The American then inquired why he didn't stay out longer and catch more fish.

The Mexican said he had enough to support his family's immediate needs.

The American then asked, 'But what do you do with the rest of your time?'

The Mexican said, 'I sleep late, fish a little, play with my children, take siesta with my wife, Maria, stroll into the village each evening where I sip wine and play guitar with my *amigos*. I have a full and busy life, *Señor*.'

The American scoffed, 'I am a Harvard MBA and could help you. You should spend more time fishing and with the proceeds buy a bigger boat. With the proceeds from the bigger boat you could buy several boats. Eventually you would have a fleet of fishing boats. Instead of selling your catch to a middleman you would sell directly to the processor, eventually opening your own cannery. You would control the product, processing and distribution. You would need to leave this small coastal fishing village and move to Mexico City, then Los Angeles and eventually New York, where you would run your expanding enterprise.'

The Mexican fisherman asked, 'But *Señor*, how long would this all take?'

To which the American replied, 'Fifteen to twenty years.'

'But what then, *Señor*?'

The American laughed and said that was the best part. 'When the time is right you would sell your company stock to the public and become very rich. You would make millions.'

'Millions, *Señor*? Then what?'

The American said, 'Then you would retire. Move to a small coastal fishing village where you would sleep late, fish a little, play with your kids, take siesta with your wife, stroll to the village in the evenings where you could sip wine and play your guitar with your *amigos*.'

We can easily see that the American businessman in this story is spiritually dumb, while the Mexican fisherman is spiritually intelligent. Why? The fisherman has an intelligent sense of his own deep life's purposes, his own deepest motivations. He has evolved a lifestyle that meets his own and his family's needs, he takes time for the things that matter to him, he is at peace, he is centred. The American business-man, on the other hand, is a child of his own spiritually dumb culture. He is driven, he has to achieve for the sake of achievement, he is out of touch with those things in life that deeply motivate someone like the fisherman, he has absorbed goals that make no sense just because he learned them at Harvard. The fisherman will most likely live a long life and die at peace. The businessman is set for a coronary at fifty-five and will die feeling he never achieved his goals.

KNOWING OUR DEEPEST MOTIVES

Our motives – some people call them our life's intentions or life's purposes – are a deep kind of psychic energy. They move potentialities from the centre of the self towards the surface or ego layer. It is through our motives that we act in and on the world. Some of our motives are conscious. I know that I want to take good care of my children, I know that I want to write books, I know that I want to make enough money to support the lifestyle I want, and so on. Some of these motives have an unconscious layer buried within our personal unconscious or within the shared unconscious of our race. We have seen that deep motives of gregariousness, intimacy, exploration, construction, self-assertion and creativity drive most of us at the unconscious level. The motive of intimacy or parenthood underlies my wanting to take good care of my children, the motive of creativity drives my wish to write books, there is a certain amount of self-assertion in the lifestyle I have chosen, and so on. But deeper still are the very primary motives of my self's centre – a motive for meaning, a motive for wholeness or integrity, a motive to undergo development and transformation during the course of my life.

In a spiritually dumb culture our motives became distorted. The social and economic pressures that surround us urge us to mistake wants for needs. And they urge us to want *more* than we need, to want constantly and insatiably. Our culture's measures of success make us want more possessions, more money, more power, more 'fish'. The fact that so many of us in the West are overweight is one of the commonest spiritual illnesses brought about by distorted motivation. We eat to fill an emptiness that will not go away.

One way to be more spiritually intelligent about personal motivation is to look for the reality behind any surface desire. Usually, when we follow the pattern of programmed response that our culture encourages, we go straight from wanting it to buying it or doing it. Little encourages us to stop and reflect, to ask ourselves, 'What deeper need lies behind this desire? Will fulfilling it really satisfy this deeper need?' Spiritual intelligence calls upon us to reflect more deeply on what we think we want, to put the want into a deeper, wider framework of our deepest motivations and life's purposes.

The short-circuitry of our motivations encouraged by our spiritually dumb culture does not stop at material possessions. It often invades our career choices, our relationships and our leisure activities. When people feel empty they may go to a wild disco or take drugs. When they feel inadequate they chase after the most sexually attractive person available. But this kind of reaction is unlikely to satisfy a deep need for meaning, personal integrity and development. To satisfy my motivations and needs at this level, I have to learn to know *myself* at a deep level.

A HIGH DEGREE OF SELF-AWARENESS

Self-awareness is one of the highest criteria of high spiritual intelligence but one of the lowest priorities of our spiritually dumb culture. From the moment we begin school we are trained to look outward rather than inward, to focus on facts and practical problems in the external world, to be goal-oriented. Virtually nothing in Western education encourages us to reflect on ourselves, on our inner lives and motives. We are not encouraged to let our imaginations run. With the near death of any generally accepted public religion, little encourages us to reflect on what we believe or what we value. Many of us are even uncomfortable with 'empty' time, or with silence. We fill our time with constant activity, if only watching the television, and we fill our silence with noise.

Developing greater self-awareness is a high priority for

raising SQ. The first step, obviously, is simply to become aware of the problem, to become aware of how little I know about 'me'. Then I must commit myself to some simple daily practices that will improve my communication with myself. These might include,

□ meditation, which can be learned from many easily available sources

□ reading a poem, or a couple of pages from a book that means something to me, and reflecting why

□ going for a 'walk in the woods' – taking my mind off busy, goal-oriented activity by some kind of 'time out' that leaves me space to think

□ really listening to a piece of music and examining the mental and emotional associations that result

□ really noticing some scene or event from the day and going over it later, looking for the more subtle nuances and associations

□ keeping a diary in which I recall not only the events of the day, but how I responded to them and why

□ keeping a diary of dreams and reflecting on them

□ at the end of each day, going over it. What were the things that struck or affected me most? What did I enjoy about the day? What do I regret? How could the day have been different? How could I have felt or behaved differently, and what effect would that have had?

A very central part of self-awareness involves learning where the boundaries of my comfort zone are. This is another way of asking: where is my edge? What is that place on the edge of my personal or work relationships or activities where I have to stretch myself, where I am challenged? My edge is my growing point, the place from which I can transform myself.

Our spiritually dumb culture seldom forces us to face our personal edge, but cocoons us with ready distractions and easy options. What would be the more difficult option in this case? I must learn to ask myself questions like: What would I learn or achieve if I took that more difficult option? Is it a matter of greater discipline, more personal self-sacrifice, less selfishness, more commitment? What stops me making the effort?

BEING RESPONSIVE TO THE DEEP SELF

And finally there is the deep self that lives within each of us, anchored in the cosmos as a whole and originating with the human need to live meaning, vision and value. High SQ requires us to serve that deep self, too, with awareness.

It is not always possible to see the deep self in myself, to sense what really deeply motivates me, to know what I deeply most value. Our spiritually dumb culture does not encourage or nourish this depth of personal insight, and has few myths or deep, collective values that nourish the associative, middle layer of the self. The modern collective unconscious resonates to the beat of consumer advertising, and to the sex and violence of immediate gratification. Very few of us are nourished by a living spiritual vision that places our lives in that deeper and wider context within which the centre of the self is anchored.

Nevertheless the deep self is there within us. Known or unknown, nourished or left to starve, it is there as what makes us most ourselves. It breaks through occasionally in rare moments of love or intimacy, of joy or wonder, even sometimes in moments of our greatest sorrow or when we are confronted with our worst fear. Even when we can't sense it in ourselves, reflection on the qualities or actions of others, in reality or fiction, can make us aware of human potential and teach us something about our own deep selves.

287

A CAPACITY TO USE
AND TRANSCEND DIFFICULTIES

Our spiritually dumb culture is a victim culture. My unhappy childhood distorted my motivations and personality early in life. Germs invade my body and I get ill. I get bullied at work.

The first step towards spiritual intelligence in this context is to take back responsibility for my life. I must use the deep spontaneity which is the gift of my native SQ to respond honestly and freshly to my environment and to the situation that I am in now. And I must take responsibility for my role in it. I may find myself in a painful or unpleasant situation, but only I can influence how I respond to it. Only I can set my attitude towards the things that happen to me. Only I can assign a meaning to what happens to me. I may have an incurable disease, but I decide how to respond to that. Only I can die for me.

In *Man's Search for Meaning*, Viktor Frankl points out that our capacity to use and transcend our pain is one of the great freedoms available to each one of us. As an inmate of the Auschwitz concentration camp he knew the worst suffering possible, but he chose his own reaction and transcended his suffering to find a meaning for his life. We can view pain, suffering or hardship as threatening or incapacitating, but equally we can view them as challenges and even as opportunities. At its most extreme, this is true even of my impending death. I can 'die well', at peace with life and myself, or I can die in bitter agony. I can blame my company for my meaningless work, or I can change the company from within or change my job. If neither is possible, I can still control my attitude to the work, influence my relationships at work. We are all inspired by the incredible stories of handicapped people who write novels with their toes, cancer victims who run marathons for cancer research, bereaved parents who set up memorial funds for their

288

lost children. How much easier is it for most of us to be small heroes simply by taking responsibility for our daily lives and transcending our ordinary obstacles?

STANDING AGAINST THE CROWD

Our culture is a crowd culture. The media encourage us all to think the same thoughts and have the same opinions. Mass production encourages us to narrow our range of tastes, whilst mass advertising does its best to ensure what those narrow tastes are. Similarly, it is also a fad culture: if giving up smoking is in, we all stub out the cigarettes. Our intellectuals entertain the same trendy thoughts, our management consultants all sell the same 'transformation' package, our spiritual seekers all turn to the same crystals and potions. We no longer know how to think for ourselves.

One of the main criteria for high spiritual intelligence is being what psychologists call 'field-independent'. That means being able to stand against the crowd, to hold an unpopular opinion if that is what I deeply believe. But here again we come to the necessity for self-awareness, and the deep awareness that I have a personal centre. If I exist merely from the ego layer of myself, I am merely a set of individualized coping mechanisms that I have evolved in response to my experience, a mask. So in a negative way I am still dependent upon the reactions and opinions of others. And if I live from the associative, middle layer of myself, I am a part of the group.

High SQ requires us to have a functioning ego and a healthy participation in the group, but both must be rooted in the deep centre of ourselves. From this centred perspective, from what we might call the perspective of 'deep subversiveness', I stand out, but now I can contribute something – my perspective. I know who *I* am, and what *I* believe. This is not egoism but true individuality, and it often requires great courage.

The young son of a Chilean biologist, Umberto Maturana, became unhappy at school because he felt his teachers were making it impossible for him to learn. They wanted to teach him what they knew, rather than drawing out what he needed to learn. As a result Maturana wrote 'The Student's Prayer', of which this translation is an abridged version. It perfectly expresses the spiritually intelligent individual's response to the conforming pressures of parents, teachers, bosses or the crowd.

> Don't impose on me what you know,
>   I want to explore the unknown
>   and be the source of my own discoveries.
> Let the known be my liberation, not my slavery.
>
> The world of your truth can be my limitation;
>   your wisdom my negation.
>   Don't instruct me; let's walk together.
> Let my richness begin where yours ends.
>
> Show me so that I can stand
>   on your shoulders.
> Reveal yourself so that I can be
>   something different.
>
> You believe that every human being
>   can love and create.
>   I understand, then, your fear
> when I ask you to live according to your wisdom.
>
> You will not know who I am
>   by listening to yourself.
>   Don't instruct me; let me be.
> Your failure is that I be identical to you.[1]

RELUCTANCE TO CAUSE HARM

Our culture is atomistic. It separates me from you, it separates 'us' from those who are different, it isolates human beings from one another, from other living creatures and from nature in general. Freud declared that love and intimacy are impossible: we can never love our neighbour as we love ourselves.

Spiritual intelligence requires us to become aware of our deep selves, of our personal centre, which is rooted in the centre of existence itself, in the quantum vacuum. According to quantum field theory, we have seen, each of us is an excitation of energy, a pattern or wave on the 'pond' of the vacuum. We cannot draw a boundary between the waves and the pond, nor can we draw any hard and fast boundary between ourselves and other 'waves'. I am inside you and inside every creature and inside every speck of stardust, and each of these is inside me. And all of us are individual forms that contain the same centre. A person high in SQ knows that when he harms others he harms himself. When I pollute the atmosphere with my garbage or my anger, I pollute my own lungs or psyche. When I selfishly or unnecessarily cause suffering to others, that suffering comes back as a pain in my own being, as something that distorts me, makes me 'ugly'. When I isolate myself from others, I isolate myself from that sea of energy and potential that is my own centre. High SQ requires me to use my deep spontaneity to respond to all others and to all existence, and to take responsibility for my role in caring for these things. When I cause unnecessary harm I abdicate this responsibility, which is the deepest purpose and meaning of my life.

BEING SPIRITUALLY
INTELLIGENT ABOUT RELIGION

We saw at the very beginning of this book that high SQ has no necessary connection with religion. A very religious person may be spiritually dumb; a hard-and-fast atheist may be spiritually intelligent. And yet the challenge of achieving high spiritual intelligence is in no way anti-religion. Most of us need some 'religious' framework as a guide for living our lives: the thoughts of great teachers, the deeds of saints, the behavioural cues of an ethical code. Most of us thrive on holding some very deep, basic beliefs. A great many of us would be lost without them. Indeed, the existence of a 'God spot' in the neurological make-up of our brains indicates that the capacity for some form of religious experience and/or belief confers an evolutionary advantage on our species. It plugs us into meaning and value in an accessible way, causes us to strive, gives us a sense of purpose, a sense of context.

So what is the difference between spiritually dumb and spiritually intelligent religion? It is certainly not a difference *between* religions, for there are spiritually dumb and spiritually intelligent versions of every religion on the planet. The difference lies in my attitude, in the quality of my questioning and my searching, in the depth and breadth of my beliefs, in the deep source of my beliefs.

SQ originates, as we know, in the deep centre of the self, the part grounded in all the infinite potentiality of the quantum vacuum. In nature, the vacuum is capable of every form; it suffuses every form. Thus any religious system that is in touch with the centre contains its own version of that whole truth that is contained in the quantum vacuum. Any religious form rooted in the centre is a valid expression or form for the centre. That is the most and the best that any one of us or any one set of beliefs, any one tradition can be – a valid expression, a valid form for the centre. I may find that Christianity is the form that best speaks to me, but if I am a spiritually intelligent Christian what I love about my religion is that it does express the ultimate, deepest sea of potentiality in the universe – I know that it is one beautiful form that God can take. But as the Jewish mystics remind us, God has 'ten' faces (in other words 'many' faces), and the true mystic is the one who knows as many of those faces as possible so as best to know the God who is behind every face.

As a spiritually intelligent Christian, Muslim, Buddhist or whatever, I love and respect my tradition – but I love it because it is one of the many forms expressing the potentiality of the centre. I have a deep and abiding respect for other traditions and other forms, and may even imagine myself capable of living some of those forms. As the thirteenth-century Sufi mystic Ibn al'Arabi expressed it:

> My heart has become capable of every form: it is a pasture
>   for gazelles and a convent for Christian monks,
> And a temple for idols and the pilgrim's Ka'ba and the
>   tables of the Torah and the book of the Koran.
> I follow the religion of Love: whatever way Love's
>   camels take, that is my religion and my faith.[2]

BEING SPIRITUALLY INTELLIGENT ABOUT DEATH

Perhaps the most spiritually dumb aspect of modern culture is our inability to deal with death. We are embarrassed by it, even terrified of it, and so we deny it. Most Western countries have few meaningful rituals for death. Virtually none has a larger perspective within which death can be seen as a natural part of life's processes. Sensitive doctors like Ireland's Michael Kearney have shown that most of the physical pain we feel in the course of dying really arises from our fear in the face of a process we don't understand. Patients who overcome this feel pain much less and need far fewer drugs to treat it.[3]

Our fear of death arises from a lack of perspective, an inability to put death within a larger framework. But this is not simply a failure to understand death. It is a still deeper failure to understand and appreciate life, a deeper failure to put life into a larger perspective of meaning and value.

The Interlude on p. 115 of this book told the story of our origins and cycles of development. We are part of a long history of constant creation and destruction, of matter and consciousness arising out of the quantum vacuum, traversing space and time for a brief while, and then returning to the vacuum. We are the brief forms that infinite potentiality takes before it borrows us back to create other forms.

One evening last year while I was meditating, I became aware with the deepest certainty and sense of peace that I carry my death always with me. My death is a constant companion of my life, a constant, further state of my present existence. Death is not an 'after', not an 'ending', but rather it is a state of ongoing existence, a further level of my being. In the terms that a quantum field theorist would use, my present living form is a state of excited energy, whereas death is that deeper state of still energy that I carry within me and into which I will one day be reabsorbed. Physicists tell us that all energy is conserved. The amount of energy in the universe never changes, and the energy that I now am, the energy that is concretized in my present living body, will exist forever. The process of living and dying simply means that this borrowed energy that I am will one day take on some other form. My deep *being*, that deeper sea of potentiality on which my present life is but a wave, has no beginning and no ending.

Life and death, then, are all part of a cyclic process of energy arising out of the quantum vacuum, briefly taking on a form and then dissolving back into the vacuum again. On and on, forever, so long as universes are born and die. The seasonal and yearly cycles of nature on earth replay the same drama, as indeed do the individual molecules in our bodies as they come and go through the more persistent pattern of energy that is us. Death is simply a necessary and natural part of the constant transformation of the energy that is life, which we see constantly (and without fear) in the changing seasons. Rilke knew about this when he wrote about 'death, familiar and ours', in the ninth of his Duino Elegies.

Earth: is it not *this*, your desire? Invisibly . . .
within ourselves . . . to establish your being?
Is not your dream one day to stand here
invisible? Earth! No longer visible!
And if not transformation, what have you set me as a
    mission?
Earth, World that is dearest, I shall; oh, believe it!
Seasons of Spring are no longer needed,
every one of them richer than blood could endure,
to win me and keep me your own . . .
yours from the first: unnamed but already indentured.
You were never mistaken; Death, familiar and ours,
is your gift, was your sacred invention.
See, I am living! What lives me? Nor childhood, nor
    future
diminish. Surpassing all number,
sheer *being* leaps in my heart.[4]

A spiritually intelligent understanding of death is able to see this whole larger context of being of which death is but one state of the continuing process.

REMEMBERING THE QUESTIONS

We come now to the end of this book. For me it has been a long and at times painful journey, for the demands of spiritual intelligence are not easy.

High SQ requires us to be deeply honest with ourselves, deeply aware of ourselves. It requires us to face choices and to realize that sometimes the right choices are difficult ones. High SQ demands the most intense personal integrity. It demands that we become aware of and live out of that deep centre of ourselves that transcends all the fragments into which our lives have shattered. It demands that we re-collect ourselves, including those parts of ourselves that it has been painful or difficult to own. But most of all, high SQ demands that we stand open to experience, that we recapture our ability to see life and others afresh as through the eyes of a child. It demands that we cease to seek refuge in what we know and constantly explore and learn from what we do not know. It demands that we live the questions rather than the answers. I will end by quoting Rilke once again:

> I want to beg you as much as I can to be patient
> Toward all that's unsolved in your heart,
> And to learn to love the questions themselves,
> Like locked rooms.
> Or like books that are written in a foreign tongue.
>
> Do not seek the answers that cannot be given to you,
> Because you would not be able to live them,
> And the point is to live everything.
>
> Live the questions now,
> Perhaps you will then, gradually,
> Without noticing it,
> Live along some distant day
> Into the answer.[5]

APPENDIX

Many systems of psychological classification correlate well with the Lotus of the Self. The chart below summarizes those systems which I know correlate at least 75 per cent with the lotus. Some systems of classification have been omitted because they have no useful correlation (the seven colours of the rainbow, or the seven heavens), and others because they are not widely known.

Some very brief notes may help to guide further research with the fifteen systems represented:
1. See Chapter 6–8 of this book.
2. See Chapter 6 of this book, also Briggs Myers and Myers, Chapter 8.
3. See Chapter 7.
4. Some such scheme is common in various forms of psychotherapy. White (1993) correlates a similar scheme with the chakras.
5. See Tripp (1970) or Chevalier and Gheerbart (1996), also Chapter 7 of this book
6. See Chevalier and Gheerbart (1996).
7. See Samuels (1985) or Chevalier and Gheerbart (1996).
8. Myss (1997) correlates the chakras with the sacraments in this fashion.

Lotus Correlates

	CONVENTIONAL	SOCIAL	INVESTIGATIVE	ARTISTIC	REALISTIC	ENTERPRISING	–
A. EGOIC, WESTERN							
1. OCCUPATIONS (Holland)	CONVENTIONAL	SOCIAL	INVESTIGATIVE	ARTISTIC	REALISTIC	ENTERPRISING	–
2. PERSONALITY TYPES (Jung)	Extroverted Perception	Extroverted Feeling	Introverted Thinking	Introverted Perception	Introverted Feeling	Extroverted Thinking	(Transcendent Function)
3. MOTIVES (Cattell)	Gregariousness	Parental	Exploration	'Sex' (Creativity)	Construction	Self-Assertion	Religious
4. STAGES OF LIFE	Infancy (0–1½ years)	Early Childhood (1½–6)	Latency (6–11)	Adolescence (11–18)	Early (18–35)	Maturity (35–70)	Any Age
B. ARCHETYPAL							
5. PLANETS Roman / Greek	SATURN / Cronos	VENUS / Aphrodite	MERCURY / Hermes	MOON (Diana) / Artemis, Hecate	MARS / Ares	JUPITER / Zeus	SUN / Apollo
6. ELEMENTS etc.	Underworld	Earth	Air	Upper World	Fire	Water	(Plenum/Vacuum)
7. GENERAL (Jung, etc.)	TRIBE/Participation Mystique	EARTH MOTHER	GUIDE/Child/Trickster	SHADOW/Hero Eros/Maiden	WORLD-SOUL Agape/Gaia	GREAT FATHER Logos/Redemption	SELF Ens
C. RELIGIOUS							
8. SACRAMENTS (Christian)	BAPTISM	COMMUNION	PENITENCE	MARRIAGE	CONFIRMATION	ORDINATION	EXTREME FUNCTION
9. CHAKRAS (Hindu)	I Root, Base	II Sacral	III Solar Plexus	IV Heart	V Throat	VI Brow	VII Crown
10. KABBALAH (Jewish)	Malkuth	Netzach	Hod	Yesod	Geburah	Chesed	Tiphareth
11. BARDOS (Tibetan Buddhism)	Dharma vs Craving	Sangha vs Hatred	Buddha vs Ignorance	Wrathful Deities vs Shadow	Peaceful Deities vs Death	Tutelary Buddha vs Pride	(Primary Clear Light)
12. LEVELS (K. Wilber)	3. Magic	4. Mythic	5. Rational	6. Vision-Logic	7. Psychic	8. Subtle	9. Causal
D. INWARDS MOVEMENT							
13. PATHS	DUTY	NURTURING	UNDERSTANDING	PERSONAL TRANSFORMATION	BROTHERHOOD	SERVANT LEADERSHIP	(NIRVANA)
14. RESPONSES	KINSHIP vs Estrangement	COOPERATION vs Opposition	EXPLORATION vs Retreat	CELEBRATION vs Mourning	WHOLENESS vs Inadequacy	LOYALTY vs Betrayal	EQUANIMITY vs Disturbance
15. THERAPY (Content)	Traumas, Guilt	Antagonisms, Projections	Practical Problems, Defences	Games/Splits	'Past-Life' Incidents	Basic Purposes	–

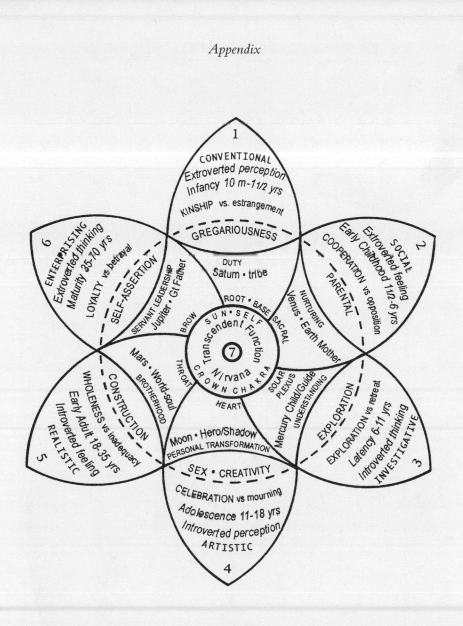

The Lotus of the Self.

9. See Chapter 7. Also White (1993), Campbell (1974), Myss (1997) and Feuerstein (1996).

10. For the Western mystical or esoteric approach to this Jewish system, see Knight (1972). He also correlates part of the Tree of Life with the seven planets, almost as shown (only Saturn has moved). For the orthodox view, see Scholem (1963).

11. See Evans–Wentz (1960), also Campbell (1974), who correlates the bardos with the chakras in roughly this way. I have correlated 1, 2 and 3 with the Three Jewels vs the Three Poisons (see any introduction to Buddhism).

12. See Wilber (1995). Seven of his ten levels correlate, in order, with the inner parts of the petals and the centre, but his arrangement is more hierarchical.

13. See Chapter 13.

14. See Chapter 9 of this book, also Guest and Marshall (1997) for a related pattern.

15. To discuss these attributions adequately would take several chapters.

BIBLIOGRAPHY

Ahern, Geoffry, *Spiritual/Religious Experience in Modern Society*, Alastair Hardy Foundation, Oxford: 1990.

Allport, Gordon, *The Individual and His Religion*, Macmillan, New York: 1950.

Banquet, P. P., 'Spectral Analysis of the EEG in Meditation', *Electroencephalography and Clinical Neurophysiology*, *35*, pp.143–151: 1973.

Batchelor, Stephen, ed., *The Jewel in the Lotus*, Wisdom Publications, London: 1987.

Benson, H., *The Relaxation Response*, William Morrow, New York: 1975.

Blakemore, Colin and Greenfield, Susan, *Mindwaves*, Basil Blackwell, Oxford: 1987.

Bly, Robert, trans., *The Kabir Book*, Beacon Press, Boston: 1971.

Boden, Margaret G., *Computer Models of Mind*, Cambridge University Press, New York: 1988.

Bohm, David, *Quantum Theory*, Constable, London: 1951.

Bressler, S. L. and Freeman, W. J., *Electroencephalography and Clinical Neurophysiology*, Vol. 50, pp.19–24, 1980.

Briggs Myers, Isabel with Myers, Peter B., *Gifts Differing*, Davies-Black Publishing, Palo Alto, CA: 1995.

Brod, J. H., 'Creativity and Schizotypy', in Gordon Claridge, ed., *Schizotypy*, Oxford University Press, Oxford and New York: 1997.

Caird, D., 'Religiosity and Personality: Are Mystics Introverted, Neurotic or Psychotic?', *British Journal of Social Psychology*, *26*, 345–346: 1987.

Campbell, Joseph, *The Mythic Image*, Princeton University Press, Princeton: 1974.

Campbell, Joseph with Moyers, Bill, *The Power of Myth*, Doubleday, New York: 1988.

Carse, James, *Finite and Infinite Games*, Ballantine Books, New York: 1986.

Castaneda, Carlos, *The Teachings of Don Juan*, Penguin, London: 1970.

Cattell, R. B., *Personality and Motivation Structure and Measurement*, World Book Company, New York: 1957.

Chalmers, David J., 'Moving Forward On the Problem of Consciousness', *Journal of Consciousness Studies*, Vol.4, No.1, 1997.

Chevalier, Jean and Gheerbrant, Alain, eds, *The Dictionary of Symbols*, Penguin Books, London: 1996.

Claridge, Gordon, ed. *Schizotypy*, Oxford University Press: Oxford and New York: 1997.

Coles, Robert, *The Spiritual Life of Children*, Houghton Mifflin, Boston: 1990.

Cook, C. M. and Persinger, M. A., 'Experimental Induction of a "Sensed Presence" in Normal Subjects and an Exceptional Subject', *Perceptual and Motor Skills*, *85* (2), pp.683–93: October 1985.

Coughlan, C. D. and Dodd, J. D., *The Ideas of Particle Physics*, 2nd edition, Cambridge University Press, Cambridge and New York: 1991.

Crick, Francis, *The Astonishing Hypothesis*, Simon and Schuster, London, New York, etc.: 1994.

Damasio, Antonio R., *Descartes' Error*, Papermac (Macmillan), London: 1996.

Dante, A., *The Divine Comedy: The Inferno and Paradiso*, trans. J. Ciardi, Mentor Books, New York: 1954.

De Hennezel, Marie, *Intimate Death*, Warner Books, London: 1997.

Deacon, Terrance, *The Symbolic Species*, Allen Lane The Penguin Press, London: 1997.

Del Guidice, E., Preparata, G. and Vitiello, G., 'Water as a Free Electric Dipole Laser', *Physical Review Letters*, *61*, pp.1085–8: 1988.

Dennett, D. C., *Consciousness Explained*, Little Brown, Boston: 1991.

Descartes, René, *Meditations*, Bobbs-Merrill, New York: 1960.

Desmedt, J. E. and Tomberg, C., *Neuroscience Letters*, Vol.168, pp.126–9, 1994.

Dostoyevsky, Fyodor, *Crime and Punishment*, Penguin Books, London: 1998.

Douglas, R. and Martin, K., 'Neocortex', in G. M. Shepherd (ed.) *The Synaptic Organization of the Brain*, 4th edition, Oxford University Press, Oxford and New York: 1998.

Edelman, Gerald, *Bright Air, Brilliant Fire*, Allen Lane The Penguin Press, New York and London: 1992.

Eliot, T. S., *Four Quartets*, Faber, London: 1994.

Emerson, Ralph Waldo, 'The Over-Soul', in *Selected Essays*, Penguin Classics, London: 1985.

Evans-Wentz, W. Y. ed., *The Tibetan Book of the Dead*, Oxford University Press, Oxford: 1960.

Feuerstein, G., *The Shambala Guide to Yoga*, Shambala Press, Boston and London: 1996.

Frankl, Viktor E., *Man's Search for Meaning*, Pocket Books, Washington Square Press, New York, London, etc.: 1985.

Freud, Sigmund, *The Ego and the Id*, standard edition, *Collected Works*, Vol.19, Hogarth Press, London: 1923.

Gardner, Howard, *Multiple Intelligences*, HarperCollins (Basic Books): New York, 1993.

Ghose, G. M. and Freeman, R. D., *Journal of Neurophysiology*, Vol.58, pp.1558–1574, 1992.

Goddard, D., *A Buddhist Bible*, Book Faith India, Delhi: 1999.

Goleman, Daniel, *Emotional Intelligence*, Bantam Books: New York, London, etc.: 1996.

Gottfriedson, G. D. and Holland, J. L., *Dictionary of Holland Occupational Codes*, 3rd edition, Psychological Assessment Resources Inc., Florida: 1996.

Graves, Robert, *The White Goddess*, Faber, London: 1961.

Gray, C. M. and Singer, W., 'Stimulus Dependent Neuronal Oscillations in the Cat Visual Cortex Area', *Neuroscience [Suppl]* 22:1301P, 1987.

Gray, C. M., and Singer, W., 'Stimulus-Specific Neuronal Oscillations in Orientation Columns of Cat Visual Cortex', *Proceedings of the National Academy of Sciences of the United States of America*, 86:1698–702, 1989.

Gray, John, *Men Are from Mars, Women Are from Venus*, HarperCollins, London: 1992.

Green, Michael, 'A Resonance Model Gives the Response to Membrane Potential for an Ion Channel', *Journal of Theoretical Biology*, Vol.193, pp.475–483, 1998.

Greenleaf, Robert, *Servant Leadership: A Journey into the Nature of Legitimate Power and Greatness*, Paulist Press, New York: 1977.

Grof, Christina and Grof, Stanislav, *The Stormy Search for the Self*, Thorsons, London: 1991.

Guest, Hazel and Marshall, I. N., 'The Scale of Responses: Emotions and Mood in Context', *International Journal of Psychotherapy*, *2* (2), pp.149–169: 1997.

Guyton, A. C., *Structure and Function of the Nervous System*, W. B. Saunders, Philadelphia, London and Toronto: 1972.

Haldane, J. B. S., 'Quantum Mechanics as a Basis for Philosophy', *Philosophy of Science*, *1*, pp.78–98: 1934.

Hameroff, S. and Penrose, R., 'Conscious Events as Orchestrated Time-Space Selections', *Journal of Consciousness Studies*, Vol.3 (1), pp.36–53, 1996.

Happold, F. C., *Mysticism*, Penguin, London: 1963.

Hardy, Alastair, *The Spiritual Nature of Man*, Oxford University Press, Oxford: 1979.

Hari, Riitta and Salmelin, Riitta, 'Human Cortical Oscillations: A Neuromagnetic View Through the Skull', *Trends in Neuroscience (TINS)*, Vol.20, No.1, pp.44–49, 1997.

Harvey, Andrew, *The Essential Mystics*, Castle Books, New Jersey: 1996.

Heschel, Abraham, *God in Search of Man*, Farrar, Straus and Giroux, New York: 1955.

Hillman, James, *The Soul's Code*, Random House, New York: 1996.

Hobsbawm, Eric, *The Age of Extremes*, Michael Joseph, London: 1994.

Hogen, Y., *On the Open Way*, Jiko Oasis Books, Liskeard, Cornwall: 1993.

Holland, J. L., *Making Vocational Choices*, 3rd edition, Psychological Assessment Resources, Inc., Florida: 1997.

Houston, Jean, *A Passion for the Possible*, Thorsons, London: 1998.

Huxley, Julian, *Religion Without Revelation*, New American Library, New York: 1957.

Inchausti, Robert, *Thomas Merton's American Prophecy*, State University of New York Press, Albany: 1998.

Jackson, Michael, 'A Study of the Relationship Between Spiritual and Psychotic Experience', unpublished D. Phil. thesis, Oxford University, 1991.

Jackson, Michael, 'Benign Schizotypy? The Case of Spiritual Experience', in Gordon Claridge, ed., *Schizotypy*, Oxford University Press, Oxford: 1997.

BIBLIOGRAPHY

James, William, *The Varieties of Religious Experience*, The Modern Library, New York: 1929.

Jamison, Kay Redfield, *Touched with Fire*, The Free Press, New York: 1993.

Jarrett, Keith, *The Eyes of the Heart*, ECM Records, 78118–21150–2/4.

Jobst, Kim A., Shostak, Daniel and Whitehouse, Peter J., 'Diseases of Meaning: Manifestations of Health and Metaphor', *Journal of Alternative and Complementary Medicine*, 1999.

Saint John of the Cross, *Collected Works*, Trans. Kavanaugh K. and Rodriguez O., ICS Publications, Washington DC: 1991.

Joyce, James, *A Portrait of the Artist as a Young Man*, Viking Press, New York: 1916 (1963).

Jung, C. G., *Psychological Types*, *Collected Works*, Vol. 6, Routledge, London, etc: 1921.

Jung, C. G., 'On the Nature of the Psyche', in *Collected Works*, Vol.8, Routledge & Kegan Paul, London: 1954.

Jung, C. G., 'Psychotherapists or the Clergy' (1932), *Collected Works*, Vol.11, Routledge & Kegan Paul, London: 1954.

Jung, C. G. *Memories, Dreams, Reflections*, Collins and Routledge & Kegan Paul, London: 1963.

Kaku, Michio, *Hyperspace*, Oxford University Press, Oxford and New York: 1994.

Kandel, E. R. and Hawkins, R. D., 'The Biological Basis of Learning and Individuality', *Scientific American*: September 1992.

Kearney, Michael, *Mortally Wounded*, Touchstone Books, New York: 1996. Also published in Dublin.Mereier Press (Marino): 1966.

Kearney, Michael, 'Working with Soul Pain in Palliative Care', unpublished.

Kleinbard, David, *The Beginning of Terror: A Psychological Study of Rainer Maria Rilke's Life and Work*, New York University Press: New York, 1993.

Knight, G., *A Practical Guide to Qabalistic Symbolism*, 2 vols, Helios, UK: 1972.

Kuffler, S. W. and Nicholls, J. G., *From Neuron to Brain*, Sinauer, Mass.: 1976.

Kuhn, Thomas, *The Structure of Scientific Revolutions*, University of Chicago Press, Chicago: 1962.

Laing, R. D., *The Divided Self*, Penguin, London: 1959 (1990).

Laing, R. D., *The Politics of Experience and The Bird of Paradise*, Penguin, London: 1967.

Lawrence, D. H., *Collected Poems*, Penguin, New York: 1993.

Llinas, Rodolfo and Ribary, Urs, 'Coherent 40-Hz Oscillation Characterizes Dream State in Humans', *Proceedings of the National Academy of Science, USA*, Vol.90, pp.2078–2081: March 1993.

Locke, John, *An Essay Concerning Human Understanding*, Oxford Clarendon Press, Oxford: 1947.

Losada, Marcial, translation and abridgement of Umberto Maturana's 'The Student's Prayer', unpublished.

McClelland, J. L. and Rumelhart, D. E., *Parallel Distributed Processing*, Vol.2, MIT Press, London and Cambridge, Mass.: 1986.

Marshall, I. N., 'Consciousness and Bose-Einstein Condensates', *New Ideas in Psychology*, Vol.7, no.1, pp.73–83, 1989.

Marshall, I. N., 'Some Phenomenological Implications of a Quantum Model of Consciousness', *Minds and Machines*, 5, pp.609–620: 1995.

Bibliography

Marshall, I. N., 'Three Kinds of Thinking', in *Towards a Scientific Basis for Consciousness*, eds S. R. Hameroff, A. W. Kaszniak and A. C. Scott, MIT Press, Cambridge, Mass. and London: 1996.

Martin, P. W., *Experiment in Depth*, Routledge & Kegan Paul, London and Boston: 1955 (1976).

Matthews, John, *The Arthurian Tradition*, Element Books, Shaftesbury, UK: 1989.

May, Rollo, *Love and Will*, W. W. Norton, New York: 1969.

Merton, Thomas, *The Asian Journal*, New Directions, New York: 1968 (1975).

Minsky, Marvin, *Computation*, Prentice-Hall, London: 1972.

Myss, Caroline, *Anatomy of the Spirit*, Bantam Books, New York: 1997.

Nietzsche, F. *Thus Spoke Zarathustra*, Trans. R. J. Hollingdale, Penguin Books, England: 1961.

Olivier, Richard, *Shadow of the Stone Heart: A Search for Manhood*, Pan Books, London: 1995.

Pagels, Elaine, *The Gnostic Gospels*, Random House, New York: 1979.

Pare, Denis and Llinas, Rodolfo, 'Conscious and Pre-Conscious Processes As Seen From the Standpoint of Sleep-Waking Cycle Neurophysiology', *Neuropsychologia*, Vol.33, No.9, pp.1155–1168, 1995.

Persinger, M. A., 'Feelings of Past Lives as Expected Perturbations Within the Neurocognitive Processes That Generate the Sense of Self: Contributions from Limbic Lability and Vectorial Hemisphericity', *Perceptual and Motor Skills*, 83 (3 Pt. 2), pp.1107–21: December 1996.

Popper, K. R. and Eccles, J. C., *The Self and its Brain*, Springer-Verlag, Berlin: 1977.

Post, Felix, 'Creativity and Psychopathology. A Study of 291 World-Famous Men', *British Journal of Psychiatry*, 165, 22–34.

Pratt, Annis, *Dancing with Goddesses*, Indiana University Press: Bloomington and Indianapolis, 1994.

Ramachandran, V. S. and Blakeslee, Sandra, *Phantoms in the Brain*, Fourth Estate, London: 1998.

Reps, Paul, *Zen Flesh, Zen Bones*, Penguin, London: 1971.

Ribary, V., Llinas, R. et al. 'Magnetic Field Tomography of Coherent Thalamocortical 40-Hz Oscillations in Humans', *Proceedings of the National Academy of Science, USA*, 88, 11037–11041: 1991.

Richardson, A. J., 'Dyslexia and Schizotypy', in Gordon Claridge, ed., *Schizotypy*, Oxford University Press, Oxford: 1997.

Rilke, Rainer Maria, *Duino Elegies*, trans. Stephen Cohn, Carcanet Press, Manchester, UK: 1989.

Rilke, Rainer Maria, *Rilke on Love and Other Difficulties*, Translated by J. J. L. Mood, W. W. Norton & Co, New York and London: 1975.

Rilke, Rainer Maria, *Sonnets to Orpheus*, trans. C. F. MacIntyre, University of California Press, Berkeley and Los Angeles: 1961.

Rilke, Rainer Maria, *Letters to a Young Poet*, trans. Stephen Mitchell, Vintage Books, New York: 1986.

Rinpoche, Sogyal, *The Tibetan Book of Living and Dying*, Rider, London and San Francisco: 1992.

BIBLIOGRAPHY

Rogers, Carl, *On Becoming a Person*, Constable, London: 1961.

Rumelhart, D. E. and McLelland, J. L., eds, *Parallel Distributed Processing*, 2 vols, MIT Press, Cambridge, Mass.: 1986.

Russell, Bertrand, *The Analysis of Matter*, Kegan Paul, London: 1927.

Samuels, A., *Jung and the Post-Jungians*, Routledge & Kegan Paul, London and Boston: 1985.

Scholem, Gershom, ed., *The Zohar*, Schocken Books, New York: 1963.

Seymour, J. and Norwood, D., 'A Game for Life', *New Scientist*, 139: 23–6, 1993.

Singer, W. and Gray, C. M., 'Visual Feature Integration and the Temporal Correlation Hypothesis', *Annual Reviews of Neuroscience*, 18, pp.555–586: 1995.

Singer, W. 'Striving for Coherence', *Nature*, Vol.397, pp.391–393: 4 February 1999.

Skarda, C. A. and Freeman, W. J., 'How Brains Make Chaos in Order to Make Sense of the World', *Behavioural and Brain Sciences*, 10 (2), pp.161–173: 1987.

Suzuki, D. T., *Manual of Zen Buddhism*, Rider, London: 1950 (1983).

Tagore, Rabindranath, *Gitanjali*, Macmillan, London: 1912 (1992).

Tarnas, Richard, *The Passion of the Western Mind*, Pimlico, London: 1996.

Tilley, D. R. and Tilley, J., *Superfluidity and Superconductivity*, Adam Hilger Ltd, Bristol and Boston: 1986.

Tolkien, J. R. R., *The Lord of the Rings*, Unwin Paperbacks: London, 1978.

Treisman, Ann, 'Features and Objects in Visual Processing', *Scientific American*, vol. 255, no.5: November 1986.

Tripp, E., *Dictionary of Classical Mythology*, HarperCollins, London: 1998.

Tucci, Giuseppe, *The Theory and Practice of the Mandala*, Rider, London: 1961.

Walsch, Neale Donald, *Conversations with God*, Hodder and Stoughton, London: 1995

White, R., *Working with Your Chakras*, Piatkus, London: 1993.

Wilber, Ken, ed., *The Holographic Paradigm and other Paradoxes*, New Science Library, Boulder, USA: 1982.

Wilber, Ken, *Eye to Eye*, Anchor Books, New York: 1983.

Wilber, Ken, *Sex, Ecology and Spirituality*, Shambala, Boston and London: 1995.

Wright, Peggy Ann, 'The Interconnectivity of Mind, Brain, and Behavior in Altered States of Consciousness: Focus on Shamanism', *Alternative Therapies*, 1, No.3, pp.50–55: July 1995.

Yazaki, Katsuhiko, *The Path to Liang Zhi*, Future Generations Alliance Foundation, Kyoto, Japan: 1994.

Yeats, William Butler, *Selected Poems and Two Plays*, ed. M. L. Rosenthal, Collier Books, New York: 1962.

Zohar, Danah, *The Quantum Self*, Bloomsbury, London and William Morrow, New York: 1990.

Zohar, Danah and Marshall, I. N., *The Quantum Society*, Bloomsbury, London and William Morrow, New York: 1994.

NOTES

PROLOGUE

1. Quoted in Jean Houston, *A Passion for the Possible*.

CHAPTER 1

1. Daniel Goleman, *Emotional Intelligence*.
2. See Terrance Deacon, *The Symbolic Species*.
3. See James Carse, *Finite and Infinite Games*.
4. T. S. Eliot, *Four Quartets*.
5. Quoted in Andrew Harvey, *The Essential Mystics*, pp.155–6.
6. Abraham Heschel, *God in Search of Man*.
7. Quoted in Richard Olivier, *Shadow of the Stone Heart*, pp.33–4.

CHAPTER 2

1. See K. A. Jobst et al., 'Diseases of Meaning: Manifestations of Health and Metaphor'.
2. D. H. Lawrence, *Collected Poems*.

CHAPTER 3

1. Title, and much contents, taken from I. N. Marshall, 'Three Kinds of Thinking'.
2. Gerald Edelman, *Bright Air, Brilliant Fire*.
3. This is standard information in any neurology textbook. See, e.g., A. C. Guyton, *Structure and Function of the Nervous System*.

4. See, e.g., M. G. Boden, *Computer Models of Mind*, or Marvin Minsky, *Computation*.
5. James Carse, *Finite and Infinite Games*.
6. D. E. Rumelhart and J. L. McLelland, eds, *Parallel Distributed Processing*.
7. *Ibid*.
8. E. R. Kandel and R. D. Hawkins, 'The Biological Basis of Learning and Individuality'.
9. J. Seymour and D. Norwood, 'A Game for Life'.
10. Ann Treisman, 'Features and Objects in Visual Processing'.
11. Antonio Damasio, *Descartes' Error*, pp.34–51.
12. See C. M. Gray and W. Singer, 'Stimulus-Specific Neuronal Oscillations in Orientation Columns of Cat Visual Cortex'; W. Singer and C. M. Gray, 'Visual Feature Integration and the Temporal Correlation Hypothesis'; W. Singer, 'Striving for Coherence'.
13. A very good reference is H. Benson, *The Relaxation Response*. Also J. P. Banquet, 'Spectral Analysis of the EEG in Meditation'.
14. Ken Wilber, *Eye to Eye*.
15. Sogyal Rinpoche, *The Tibetan Book of Living and Dying*, p.40.

CHAPTER 4

1. Denis Pare and Rodolfo Llinas, 'Conscious and Pre-Conscious Processes As Seen From the Standpoint of Sleep-Waking Cycle Neurophysiology'.
2. John Locke, *An Essay Concerning Human Understanding*, II.2.
3. Francis Crick, *The Astonishing Hypothesis*, p.3.
4. Michael Jackson, 'Benign Schizotypy? The Case of Spiritual Experience'.
5. Francis Crick, *The Astonishing Hypothesis*, p.246.
6. For illustrations, and the description of MEG technology, see Riitta Hari and Riita Salmelin, 'Human Cortical Oscillations: A Neuromagnetic View Through the Skull'.
7. Rodolfo Llinas, ' "Mindness" As a Functional State of the Brain,' in Colin Blakemore and Susan Greenfield, eds, *Mindwaves*, p.339.
8. There is also a French team which has published interesting work on the binding problem, 40 Hz oscillations and consciousness. See J. E. Desmedt and C. Tomberg, *Neuroscience Letters*, 1994.
9. G. M. Ghose and R. D. Freeman, *Journal of Neurophysiology*.
10. S. L. Bressler and W. J. Freeman, *Electroencephalography and Clinical Neurophysiology*.
11. Rodolfo Llinas and Urs Ribary, 'Coherent 40-Hz Oscillation Characterizes Dream State in Humans'.
12. Denis Pare and Rodolfo Llinas, 'Conscious and Pre-Conscious Processes As Seen From the Standpoint of Sleep-Waking Cycle Neurophysiology'.
13. *Ibid*, p.1155.
14. David J. Chalmers, 'Moving Forward On the Problem of Consciousness'.
15. René Descartes, *Meditations*.
16. In a *Scientific American* article published a few years ago, Crick does say

outright that we may have to understand consciousness through meaning. But as David Chalmers points out, there is meaning and meaning. A reductionist like Crick means by 'meaning' simply, 'certain correlations with the environment and certain effects on later processing' (Chalmers), whereas many of us think that 'meaning' refers to loftier things as well.

17. David J. Chalmers, 'Moving Forward On the Problem of Consciousness'.
18. Julian Huxley, *Religion Without Revelation*.
19. C. G. Jung, 'On the Nature of the Psyche'.
20. I. N. Marshall, 'Some Phenomenological Implications of a Quantum Model of Consciousness'.
21. This argument for there being such a quantum basis to consciousness in the brain was first proposed by Ian Marshall in 'Consciousness and Bose-Einstein Condensates'.
22. J. B. S. Haldane, 'Quantum Mechanics as a Basis for Philosophy'.
23. David Bohm, *Quantum Theory*.
24. E. del Guidice et al, 'Water as a Free Electric Dipole Laser'.
25. S. Hameroff and R. Penrose, 'Conscious Events as Orchestrated Time-Space Selections'.
26. I. N. Marshall, 'Consciousness and Bose-Einstein Condensates'.
27. Danah Zohar, *The Quantum Self*.
28. Danah Zohar and I. N. Marshall, *The Quantum Society*.
29. Michael Green, 'A Resonance Model Gives the Response to Membrane Potential for an Ion Channel'.
30. R. Douglas and K. Martin, 'Neocortex'.
31. D. R. Tilley and J. Tilley, *Superfluidity and Superconductivity*.
32. G. D. Coughlan and J. G. Dodd, *The Ideas of Particles Physics*.

CHAPTER 5

1. Reported in V. S. Ramachandran and Sandra Blakeslee, *Phantoms in the Brain*, p.175.
2. Ibid.
3. M. A. Persinger, 'Feelings of Past Lives as Expected Perturbations Within the Neurocognitive Processes That Generate the Sense of Self: Contributions from Limbic Lability and Vectorial Hemisphericity'.
4. C. M. Cook and M. A. Persinger, 'Experimental Induction of a "Sensed Presence" in Normal Subjects and an Exceptional Subject'.
5. Peggy Ann Wright, 'The Interconnectivity of Mind, Brain, and Behavior in Altered States of Consciousness: Focus on Shamanism'.
6. Reported in London *Sunday Times*, 2 November 1997. Also in Chapter 9 of V. S. Ramachandran and Sandra Blakeslee, *Phantoms in the Brain*.
7. M. A. Persinger, see note 1.
8. William James, *The Varieties of Religious Experience*, pp.17–19.
9. F. C. Happold, *Mysticism*, pp.134–5.
10. William James, *The Varieties of Religious Experience*.

11. Rainer Maria Rilke, 'Experience', in *Briefe aus den Jahren 1914–1921*, 227. Translated and published as Appendix 3 in J. B. Leishman and Stephen Spender translation of *Duino Elegies*.
12. Michael Jackson, 'Benign Schizotypy? The Case of Spiritual Experience'.
13. Geoffry Ahern, 'Spiritual/Religious Experience in Modern Society'. This study is also reported extensively in Michael Jackson, 'Benign Schizotypy? The Case of Spiritual Experience'.
14. All reported in Michael Jackson, 'Benign Schizotypy? The Case of Spiritual Experience', p.238 in Gordon Claridge, ed., *Schizotypy*.
15. *Ibid*, p.239.
16. Michael Jackson, 'A Study of the Relationship Between Spiritual and Psychotic Experience'.
17. Michael Jackson, 'Benign Schizotypy? The case of Spiritual Experience', in Gordon Claridge, ed., *Schizotypy*, p.236.
18. *Ibid*, p.237.
19. *Ibid*. p.242.
20. D. Caird, 'Religiosity and Personality: Are Mystics Introverted, Neurotic or Psychotic?'
21. William James, *The Varieties of Religious Experience*.
22. E. Underhill, quoted in Michael Jackson, 'Benign Schizotypy? The Case of Spiritual Experience'.
23. Gordon Claridge, ed., *Schizotypy*, p.31.
24. Quoted in David Kleinbard, *The Beginning of Terror*, p.227.
25. Quoted in Gordon Claridge, ed., *Schizotypy*.
26. A. J. Richardson, 'Dyslexia and Schizotypy', in Gordon Claridge, ed., *Schizotypy*.
27. Felix Post, 'Creativity and Psychopathology'.
28. Kay Redfield Jamison, *Touched with Fire*.
29. *Ibid*, Appendix B.
30. C. G. Jung, *Memories, Dreams, Reflections*, p.184.
31. Quoted in David Kleinbard, *The Beginning of Terror*, p.2.
32. J. H. Brod, 'Creativity and Schizotypy', in Gordon Claridge, ed., *Schizotypy*.
33. Michael Jackson, in Gordon Claridge, ed., *Schizotypy*, p.240–1.
34. *Ibid*, p.241.

CHAPTER 6

1. Jean Chevalier and Alain Gheerbrant, eds, *The Dictionary of Symbols*, 'The Lotus'.
2. Holland's percentages as quoted in this chapter relate only to white Americans. Global, cross-national and cross-cultural figures have not been worked out, though the percentages of the various types would be expected to vary considerably from one nation or one culture to the next.

CHAPTER 7

1. R. B. Cattell, *Personality and Motivation Structure and Measurement*, Part IV.
2. Joseph Campbell, *The Mythic Image*, p.341.
3. Caroline Myss, *Anatomy of the Spirit*.

CHAPTER 8

1. Giuseppe Tucci, *Mandala*, pp.14–15.
2. Quoted in Joseph Campbell, *The Mythic Image*, p.280.
3. Giuseppe Tucci, *Mandala*, p.78.
4. St. John of the Cross, *The Living Flame of Love*, Stanza I.
5. Quoted in Robert Inchausti, *Thomas Merton's American Prophecy*, p.76.
6. *Ibid*, p.91.
7. P. W. Martin, *Experiment in Depth*, pp.175–6.
8. Y. Hogen, *On the Open Way*, p.27.
9. Quoted in F. C. Happold, *Mysticism*, p.28.
10. A. Samuels, *Jung and the Post-Jungians*, p.91.
11. *Ibid*, p.89.
12. Sri Ramakrishna, quoted in Joseph Campbell, *The Mythic Image*, p.381.
13. Dante, *Paradiso*, XXXIII, 94–6.
14. 'Surangama Sutra', D. Goddard (Ed.) *The Buddhist Bible*, p.217.
15. Thomas Merton, *The Asian Journal*, p.82.

CHAPTER 9

1. C. G. Jung, 'Psychotherapists or the Clergy', *Collected Works*, Vol.11, para 497.
2. Michael Kearney, 'Working with Soul Pain in Palliative Care', p.2. See also his *Mortally Wounded* for more of his thoughts on the nature and consequences of soul pain.
3. Viktor Frankl, *Man's Search for Meaning*, p.28.
4. Abraham Heschel, *God in Search of Man*, p.6.

CHAPTER 10

1. Quoted in F. C. Happold, *Mysticism*, p.73.
2. James Hillman, *The Soul's Code*, p.6.
3. Abraham Heschel, *God in Search of Man*.
4. Christina Grof and Stanislav Grof, *The Stormy Search for the Self*.
5. See, e.g., Robert Coles, *The Spiritual Life of Children*.
6. Joseph Campbell, *The Power of Myth*, p.110.
7. Viktor Frankl, *Man's Search for Meaning*, p.138.

8. Marie de Hennezel, *Intimate Death*, pp.xi and xii.
9. J. R. R. Tolkien, *The Lord of the Rings*, p.48.

CHAPTER 11

1. Eric Hobsbawm, *The Age of Extremes*.
2. Rainer Maria Rilke, *Letters to a Young Poet*.
3. Sogyal Rinpoche, *The Tibetan Book of Living and Dying*.
4. Richard Tarnas, *The Passion of the Western Mind*.
5. Both quoted in Abraham Heschel, *God in Search of Man*, p.148.
6. Keith Jarrett, *The Eyes of the Heart*.
7. R. D. Laing, *The Politics of Experience and The Bird of Paradise*, p.118.
8. Quoted in Elaine Pagels, *The Gnostic Gospels*, p.74.
9. Quoted in Andrew Harvey, *The Essential Mystics*, pp.27–8.

CHAPTER 13

1. Quoted in Robert Graves, *The White Goddess*, Ch.4.
2. L. Morris's *Epic of Hades* (1879), quoted in Annis Pratt, *Dancing with Goddesses*, p.16.
3. Carl Rogers, *On Becoming a Person*, Ch.2.
4. Translated by Gershom Scholem.
5. *Inferno, Canto* I.
6. John Matthews, *The Arthurian Tradition*.
7. Stephen Batchelor, ed., *The Jewel in the Lotus*, 'Red Rock Agate Mansion', p.121.
8. Rabindranath Tagore, *Gitanjali*, verses 69–70.
9. Ralph Waldo Emerson, 'The Over-Soul', p.206.
10. Quoted in Ken Wilber, *The Holographic Paradigm and Other Paradoxes*, p.25.
11. Ralph Waldo Emerson, 'The Over-Soul', p.218.
12. Quoted in Ken Wilber, *Sex, Ecology and Spirituality*, p.302.
13. Robert Bly, trans., *The Kabir Book*, No. 22.
14. Quoted in Ken Wilber, *Sex, Ecology and Spirituality*, p.302.
15. Another version of these pictures is offered in Paul Reps, *Zen Flesh, Zen Bones*. The present version is by Ilaira Bouratinos.

CHAPTER 15

1. 'Caring' by Marcial Losada, inspired by Umberto Maturana's 'The Student's Prayer'. Not previously published.
2. Ibn al'Arabi, *The Tarjuman Al-Ashwaq*, Book XI.
3. Michael Kearney, *Mortally Wounded*.
4. Rainer Maria Rilke, *Duino Elegies*, Ninth Elegy.
5. Rainer Maria Rilke, 'Live the Questions Now', from *Love and Other Difficulties*.

INDEX

313

323